To Glyn

with love

Gibbo

The Land Registration Act 2002: A Practical Guide

AUSTRALIA
Law Book Co.
Sydney

CANADA and USA
Carswell
Toronto

HONG KONG
Sweet & Maxwell Asia

NEW ZEALAND
Brookers
Wellington

SINGAPORE and MALAYSIA
Sweet & Maxwell Asia
Singapore and Kuala Lumpur

The Land Registration Act 2002: A Practical Guide

by

Ian Clarke, LL.B. (Hons), MCIArb

Barrister of Lincoln's Inn

London
Sweet & Maxwell
2002

Published in 2002 by Sweet & Maxwell Limited,
100 Avenue Road,
Swiss Cottage,
London NW3 3PF
(http://www.sweetandmaxwell.co.uk)
Set by LBJ Typesetting Ltd of Kingsclere
Printed and bound in Great Britain by
Ashford Colour Press, Gosport, Hampshire

British Library Cataloguing in Publication Data

ISBN 0421 786906

Preface

The Land Registration Act 2002 is the largest single piece of law reform that the Law Commission has undertaken.[1] It has one purpose: to put in place the necessary legal framework which will enable registered conveyancing to be dealt with electronically. This involves changes not only to the substantive law but the manner in which the conveyancing process is undertaken and perceived. "The [Act] will bring about an unprecedented conveyancing revolution within a comparatively short time. It will also make other profound changes to the substantive law that governs registered land. These changes, taken together, are likely to be even more far-reaching than the great reforms of property law that were made by the 1925 property legislation."[2]

Whilst that last statement may be arguable, there can be no doubt that the Act will give rise to a conveyancing revolution which will prove challenging and demanding. Those who must assimilate the provisions of the Act and the new Land Registration Rules (which have, as yet, to be published) will find themselves in new and relatively uncharted territory. This introduction to the Land Registration Act 2002 aims, so far as the statutory material is currently available, to provide a guide both to the policy that underlies the Act and the detail of its contents. Many of the concepts that are embodied in the Act reflect those derived from the Land Registration Act 1925 and accordingly, wherever possible, references have been included to the appropriate text dealing with the provisions of that earlier Act in *Ruoff & Roper* on the Law and Practice of

---

[1] Land Registration for the Twenty-First Century, A Conveyancing Revolution (2001), Law Com No. 271, para 1.1.

[2] *ibid.*

Registered Conveyancing.[3] Assistance will continue to be derived from those principles and the case-law under the old legislation although since the Act is not a consolidating statute, care should be taken in this regard. I have tried to avoid the simple repetition of the text of the Act in narrative form by way of annotation; such an approach is seldom illuminating. Instead, I have endeavoured to identify the principal changes wrought by the Act and to explain the Act's provisions by annotations and cross-references in order to familiarise the reader with the Act's provisions.

The Bill received Royal Assent on February 26, 2002. At the time of writing no provisions of this Act have been brought into force and no rules under the Act have been made. It is thought that the Act will be brought into force in stages, perhaps beginning in October 2003. Draft rules will, for the purposes of consultation, be available during the Summer of 2002. The drafts are well advanced.

I am grateful to the staff at Sweet & Maxwell for undertaking the task of keeping track of the changes to the Bill during its passage through Parliament.

Ian Clarke
LINCOLN'S INN
May 2002

[3] *Ruoff and Roper: Registered Conveyancing*, published by Sweet and Maxwell.

Contents

Part 4—Notices and Restrictions

Notices

Restrictions

Part 5—Charges

Relative priority

Powers as chargee

Realisation of security

Miscellaneous

Part 6—Registration: General

Part 7—Special Cases

Part 8—Electronic Conveyancing

Part 9—Adverse Possession

Part 10—Land Registry

List of Abbreviations

LPA 1925	Law of Property Act 1925 (15–16 Geo. 5, c. 20), as amended.
SLA 1925	Settled Land Act 1925 (15–16 Geo. 5, c. 18), as amended.
LRA 1925	Land Registration Act 1925 (15–16 Geo. 5, c. 21), as amended.
LRR 1925	Land Registration Rules 1925 (S.I. 1925 No. 1093), as amended.
"the Act"	Land Registration Act 2002
Ruoff & Roper	Ruoff & Roper on the Law and Practice of Registered Conveyancing (1991) (looseleaf).
Law Com No. 271	Land Registration for the Twenty-First Century, A Conveyancing Revolution (2001), Law Com No. 271.

PART I

AN OUTLINE OF THE ACT

Chapter 1

The Objectives of the Act

The Land Registration Act 2002 aims to bring about an electronic system of conveyancing and to put in place the legal and regulatory framework to enable that to occur as soon as practicable. **1.001**

> "The fundamental objective of the [Act] is that, under the system of electronic dealing with land that it seeks to create, the register should be a complete and accurate reflection of the state of the title of the land at any given time, so that it is possible to investigate title to land on line, with the absolute minimum of additional enquiries and inspections."[1]

As a consequence of this objective, the Act makes a number of alterations to the law, which are considered in outline in the following chapters. The Act will also require a change in attitude. The widely-held perception that it is unreasonable to expect people to register their rights over land is challenged and largely abrogated. Such a perception is inconsistent with the objective of the Act to ensure that the register is as inclusive as possible and is a legacy of the concept in unregistered conveyancing of possession being of prime importance. Under the Act it is the register and the register alone which will confer title on an individual and thus it is, insofar as is possible, to the register that a person must have regard. **1.002**

Accordingly, the main changes brought about by the Act may be summarised as follows:

1. It increases substantially the circumstances which give rise to the requirement for compulsory registration.

---

[1] *Land Registration for the Twenty-First Century, A Conveyancing Revolution* (2001) Law Com No. 271 para. 1.5, p. 2.

2. It bestows upon the registered proprietor unfettered powers of disposition[2], subject to any entry on the register to the contrary.
3. It significantly reduces in number and extent the range of overriding interests which can affect either the first registered proprietor or a registered disponee and further, provides for a number of those that are preserved to cease after 10 years from the coming into force of Schedules 1–3.
4. Under the Act it is possible for land vested in Her Majesty in right of Crown to be registered as demesne land thus enabling substantial amounts of land to be registered for the first time.
5. It introduces the statutory provisions necessary for a system of electronic conveyancing and for the regulation of such a system which, it is envisaged, will be introduced over a number of years.
6. It fundamentally changes the law in relation to adverse possession by making provision for the acquisition of title to be more difficult. It requires notices to be served on the registered proprietor by the adverse possessor and for a procedure to be adopted whereby (depending on the steps takes) the adverse possessor's claim is adjudicated upon and either permitted or refused. In the former case, the register is altered to reflect the extinguishment of title. This system thus requires notice and reflects the policy of the Act namely that the basis of title to registered land is the fact of registration and not possession. These changes materially assist the registered proprietor and it is envisaged that they strike a fairer balance between the land owner and the squatter than does the present law.[3]
7. The Act brings into being the Office of the Adjudicator to Her Majesty's Land Registry in order to determine disputes concerning registered land.

These matters and the other aspects of the Act are considered in more detail in the following chapters.

---

[2] See section 23, *infra*.

[3] Law Com No. 271, para. 1, 13, p. 5.

Chapter 2

The Principal Features of the Act

In this chapter the principal changes effected by the Act are considered in outline. This consideration does not aim to replicate the detail contained in the text of the Act or the annotations to that text since to do so would result in a mere duplication of the contents of Part II of this Guide. This chapter aims to highlight the changes that the Act has brought about. **2.001**

Scope of Title Registration[1]

The Act makes provision about the registration of title in relation to the matters set out in section 2, namely: **2.002**

"(a) unregistered legal estates which are interests of any of the following kinds:

  (i) an estate in land,
  (ii) a rentcharge,
  (iii) a franchise,
  (iv) a profit à prendre in gross, and
  (v) any other interest or charge which subsists for the benefit of, or is a charge on, an interest to the title to which is registered; and

(b) interests capable of subsisting at law which are created by a disposition of an interest the title to which is registered."

For the first time, it enables the registration of profits à prendre in gross and franchises with their own title provided they are held for an interest equivalent to a fee **2.003**

[1] Section 2, *infra*.

simple or under a lease of which there is still seven years or more to run.[2] This is a reflection of the fact that such rights are, in themselves, often very valuable and are frequently bought and sold. At present such rights can only be noted in the register and it is considered that they should be registered separately in order to facilitate their transmission and reflect their status.

First Registration

Voluntary registration[3]

2.004 In accordance with the objective of the Act, voluntary first registration will be encouraged. It is envisaged that the fees payable upon such a registration will be less than those that will be payable in the event that the registration is compulsory. The events which permit voluntary first registration are less demanding than those which prevail under the Land Registration Act 1925 (as amended). Any person may apply to the Registrar to be registered as the proprietor of an unregistered legal estate to which section 3 applies[4] provided the estate is vested in him or he is entitled to require the estate to be vested in him.[5] There are, of course, a number of qualifications to this. Leases granted for a term of which less than seven years remain unexpired cannot be voluntarily registered[6]; nor can a person apply to be registered if his entitlement arises by reason of a contract to buy the land in question. In such a circumstance, registration is compulsory.

Compulsory registration

2.005 Section 4(1) sets out the circumstances in which the registration of an unregistered estate becomes compulsory. In outline, these circumstances are the transfer of a

---

[2] See section 3, *infra*.

[3] *ibid.*

[4] *i.e.* an estate in land; a rentcharge, a franchise or a *profit à prendre* in gross: section 3(1).

[5] Section 3(2).

[6] Unless the right to possession under the lease is discontinuous: section 3(4).

qualifying estate[7]; the grant out of a qualifying estate in land of a term of years absolute with more than seven years to run from the date of grant for valuable or other consideration or by way of a gift or in pursuance of an order of the Court; the grant out of a qualifying estate in land of a term of years absolute to take effect in possession after the end of the period of three months beginning with the date of the grant or the creation of a protected first legal mortgage of a qualifying estate.[8]

The reduction of the period required for a term of years absolute to trigger compulsory registration from 21 to seven years[9] reflects the objective of the Act to secure the speedy first registration of all unregistered titles and the fact that it appears that, at present, most business leases (which are the most frequently encountered form of commercial dealing with land) are granted for periods of less than 21 years and, under the Land Registration Act, 1925 are thus not compelled to be registered.[10] Coupled with the broad definition of transfer in section 4(1) and the triggering event of the creation of a protected first legal mortgage over a qualifying estate, it can be seen that the obligations to register an unregistered estate will arise with much greater frequency. Significantly, section 5 of the Act allows the Lord Chancellor, by order, to amend section 4 in relation to the events which give rise to compulsory first registration. One can anticipate that the events which compel registration will become less and less substantial. **2.006**

---

[7] A qualifying estate being an unregistered legal estate which is either a freehold estate in land or a leasehold estate in land held for a term which, at the time of the transfer, grant or creation, has more than seven years to run: section 4(2).

[8] In addition the transfer of an unregistered legal estate in land in circumstances which section 171A of the Housing Act 1985 applies (on the grant of a lease in such circumstances) on the grant of a lease in pursuance of Part 5 of that Act trigger, compulsory registration.

[9] And that lesser period is capable of alteration further: section 118.

[10] BPS/IPG, Annual Lease Review 2000, page 6 notes that "Considerably shorter terms are evident in new lease agreements with almost three-quarters of new leases . . . now lasting just 15 years": Law Com No. 271, para. 2.6, n. 12, p. 11.

Demesne Land[11]

2.007 Historically, only *estates* in land have been capable of registration.[12] Such a requirement clearly excludes from the system of registration the substantial amount of land within England and Wales held in the name of the Crown in demesne in its capacity as Sovereign or lord paramount. Sections 79 to 81 of the Act enable the Crown, for the first time, to register demesne land and thus facilitate the objective under the Act of ensuring that all land within England and Wales is contained in the register.

Submarine Land

2.008 Land covered by water within the county boundaries has always been registrable; however, section 130 of the Act extends the scope of registrable land to the territorial limits of England and Wales and thus permits the registration of land outside the county boundaries. This extension was prompted by the Crown Estate which is anxious to have that right in order to register the sea-bed and thus prevent encroachment by adverse possessors who might construct pipelines on other works on the sea bed.

PPP Leases in London[13]

2.009 Notwithstanding that these may otherwise be registrable, they are excluded from registration by the provisions of section 90(1) and (2). This exclusion is founded upon the sheer complexity of mapping and otherwise defining such sub-terranian land. In the event that the political climate allows such a lease to be granted, the inclusion of PPP leases within Schedules 1 and 3 as overriding interests both on first registration and on a registered disposition will provide the necessary protection.

---

[11] Sections 79–81.

[12] *i.e.* those held from the Crown as lord paramount, see also LRA 1925, s. 2.

[13] Defined in section 90(6). In summary, they would be such leases as may be granted in relation to any public-private partnership relating to transport in London and to the Underground.

Summary

Apart from instances where title to unregistered land is voluntarily registered in accordance with section 2, registration will only be compelled upon a disposition which triggers compulsory registration in accordance with section 3. *Mandatory registration in the absence of any disposition or dealing with the land is not a feature of the Act.* It was excluded because of the strain it was likely to place on the resources of both the conveyancing profession and the Land Registry. However, the Law Commission's clear recommendation is that the ways in which all remaining land with unregistered title in England and Wales might be brought onto the register should be re-examined five years after the Act is brought into force.[14] Such mandatory registration in the absence of any triggering disposition may yet come to pass. **2.010**

Cautions against First Registration[15]

Only cautions against first registration survive the alterations brought about by the Act; in all other regards (subject to the transitional provisions imposed by Schedule 12) cautions are abolished. As under the Land Registration Act 1925, a caution against first registration provides the mechanism by which a person, having some estate or interest in the land affected, may be notified of any application for first registration. In circumstances where the estate can be registered, a caution against first registration cannot be placed by an individual in relation to his own estate: such a caution is not a substitution for first registration.[16] **2.011**

Powers of Disposition[17]

The Act makes provision for the power of the registered proprietor *in relation to disponees* to be unfettered save otherwise where noted in the register. Such a provision is **2.012**

---

[14] Law Com No. 271, para. 2.13, pp. 12–13.

[15] See sections 15–22, *infra*.

[16] Although this prohibition will not come into force until two years after section 15 is brought into force: Schedule 12, para. 14.

[17] See sections 23–26, *infra*.

necessary in order to facilitate and ease the on-line investigation of title and the conveyancing process. A registered proprietor with limited powers of disposal (*e.g.* a charitable trust or other trust or a local authority) must have that limitation recorded in the register so that any prospective disponee may be immediately alerted to and take steps to comply with it. In the absence of any such registration, the disponee need not be concerned.

The bestowal on a registered proprietor of unfettered powers of disposition subject to any entry in the register is without prejudice to any rights or liabilities that may accrue as against him by reason of an unauthorised disposal. The protection afforded by section 26[18] only operates to prevent the title of the disponee being questioned and does not affect the lawfulness (or otherwise) of the proprietor's disposition or any liability he may have by reason of the disposition.

Registrable Dispositions[19]

2.013 The Act comprehensively lists the transactions that are registrable dispositions, *i.e.* being those dispositions which, when transferred or created, are required to be completed by registration. Schedule 2[20] further sets out with precision the registration requirements in relation to each registrable disposition.

Priorities[21]

2.014 The basic rule contained in section 28[22] is that the priority of an interest is determined with reference to the date of its creation, whether or not it is protected in the register. However, that basic rule is subject to a number of extensive and important exceptions. Where a registrable disposition is registered, it takes priority over any interest that affected the estate immediately prior to the disposition but was not protected in the register at the time of its

---

[18] See para. A26.1–C26.1, *infra.*

[19] See section 27, *infra.*

[20] See para. SC2, *infra.*

[21] See sections 28–31, *infra.*

[22] See para. A28.1 *et seq.*, *infra.*

registration. Therefore, unless certain exceptions apply,[23] an interest which is unregistered will lose priority to an interest which is subsequently noted in the register. Again, such a provision is consistent with the objectives of the Act. If the register is to be as inclusive as possible, there must be both an incentive to enter interests in the register and a protection for those who have done so. Rights of pre-emption, equities arising by estoppel and mere equities are all treated as proprietary interests from the time of their creation for the purposes of the Act.[24]

Notices and Restrictions[25]

Cautions against dealings and inhibitions are, prospectively abolished subject to the transitional provisions of Schedule 12. Thus the only method of protecting an interest in registered land after the implementation of the Act will be by the entry of a notice or a restriction (or both) as appropriate. **2.015**

A *notice* is the appropriate entry in the register to protect encumbrances on land that are intended to bind third parties, such as the burdens of a lease or an easement or a restrictive covenant. By way of further example, an individual who claims a proprietary right in an estate and who is not in actual occupation and thus does not have an overriding interest, would enter a notice in the register.

A *restriction* regulates the circumstances in which a disposition of a registered estate or charge may be the subject of an entry in the register. It will thus be used in circumstances where the sale proceeds are payable to trustees in order to require payment to two or more trustees so that a good discharge can be given to the purchaser; it would also be appropriate in circumstances where, for example, the consent of a third party[26] was appropriate in order to authorise a sale. As noted above,[27]

---

[23] For example, the interest is an overriding interest under Schedule 1 or 3.

[24] Sections 115 and 116, *infra*.

[25] Sections 32–47, *infra*.

[26] Such as the Charity Commission.

[27] Powers of Disposition, para. 2.012, *supra*.

a vendor with limited powers of disposition should have those limited powers recorded by way of a restriction.

Both a notice and a restriction can be entered without the consent of the registered proprietor. On the entry of a notice or a restriction in this manner, the Registrar will give notice to the registered proprietor who can then apply for the cancellation of the notice or object to the restriction in question.[28] Pursuant to section 77, a duty is imposed (the breach of which sounds in damages) on a person to act reasonably in exercising the right to apply for the entry of a notice or a restriction.

Charges[29]

2.016 Section 49(1) alters the method by which a subsequent chargee can give notice to a prior chargee of the subsequent charge and thereby preclude the prior chargee from making any further advances on the security of the prior charge. This change reflects the current practice amongst lenders of not relying on the Registrar to serve notice as the Land Registration Act 1925 currently envisages.[30] Further, section 49(4) permits a new method of making further advances on the security of a prior charge in circumstances where the prior charge is stated to be for an agreed maximum amount and the advances made and all associated costs and interest due does not exceed that maximum.

Section 50 imposes an obligation on the Registrar to give registered chargees notice of the creation of any overriding statutory charges.[31]

Overriding Interests[32]

2.017 The scope of those interests which are overriding interests under the Land Registration Act 1925 is extensive. They include easements (whether or not they have been expressly granted or reserved), the rights of persons in actual

---

[28] See Sections 73 and 108, *infra*.

[29] See sections 48–57, *infra*.

[30] LRA, s. 30 (1); see para. C49.1.2, *infra*.

[31] See paras A50.1–C50.1, *infra*.

[32] See sections 11, 12, Sch. 1 (First Registration); sections 29, 30, Sch. 3 (Registered Dispositions).

occupation, leases granted for 21 years or less as well as some obscure and unusual interests that can, by their nature, have a highly adverse impact on the registered proprietor. The Law Commission therefore considered that overriding interests present a very significant impediment to one of the main objectives of the Act, namely that the register should be as complete a record of title as it can be, so that title to land can be investigated almost entirely on-line.[33]

The Act aims to restrict the scope of overriding interests as far as is possible. "The guiding principle on which it proceeds is that interests should be overriding only where it is unreasonable to expect them to be protected in the register".[34] As a result of this principle, the Act defines the categories of overriding interests more narrowly and, in a large number of instances, excludes those which were formerly overriding interests under the Land Registration Act 1925 from its ambit entirely. Furthermore, certain classes of overriding interests fall to be phased out after the period 10 years following upon the coming into force of Schedules 1 and 3.[35] In the meantime they can be protected by entries in the register without charge. In addition, any express creation of an interest that would otherwise be overriding will (since the Act will require simultaneous creation and registration of such an interest after the advent of electronic conveyancing) begin to appear in the register in any event. Thus the existence of such interests will be apparent from the register.

Overriding interests after 10 years

The likely extent of overriding interests that will be binding on a registered disponee of registered land 10 years or more after the Act is brought into force are as follows: **2.018**

1. Leases granted for three years or less.[36]

---

[33] Law Com No. 271, para. 2.24, pp. 16–17.

[34] *ibid.*, para. 2.25, p. 17.

[35] See section 117, *infra*. The Law Commission is satisfied that this is compliant with the Human Rights Act 1998: Law Com No. 271, para. 8.89, p. 177.

[36] It being envisaged that the current specified term of seven years will be reduced pursuant to section 118(1) to three years. See also section 33(b)(i).

2. The interests of persons in actual occupation where the actual occupation is apparent and the interest is a beneficial interest under a trust or arose informally, such as an equity arising by estoppel.
3. Legal easements and *profits à prendre* that have arisen by implied grant or reservation or by prescription.
4. Customary and public rights.
5. Local land charges.
6. Certain mineral rights.[37]

Special Cases[38]

Demesne Land

2.019 This is the only special case of significance and has been mentioned above.[39] The policy behind the registration of demesne land is self-evident. Substantial inroads would otherwise have been made into the principle of an inclusion in the register in circumstances where a substantial landowner was unable to register land by reason of the doctrine of feudal tenure. The Act enables the Crown to register its demesne land and makes provision for the Crown to lodge cautions against the first registration of land held in demesne.[40]

Moreover, the Act makes provision to ensure that in circumstances where land escheats to the Crown, it remains in the register until the land is disposed of or pursuant to an order of the Court.

The provisions relating to the Crown both in relation to demesne land and land that has escheated apply with some modifications to the Duchies of Cornwall and Lancaster.

The Law Commission concluded with the observation that it could not immediately see any good reason for the

---

[37] Law Com No. 271, para. 2.27, p. 17.

[38] See Part 7, sections 79–90, *infra*.

[39] See para. 2.007, *supra*.

[40] Sections 79 and 81.

retention of the remaining aspects of feudalism in England and Wales and noted that the Scottish Parliament had recently abolished the admittedly more pervasive feudal system that applied in Scotland.[41]

Alteration Rectification and Indemnity[42]

Whilst the provisions relating to the alteration and rectification of the register are re-cast, they remain substantially unaltered. Similarly the indemnity provided by the Registrar is re-worded but without substantial change. **2.020**

Electronic Conveyancing

Given the prominence of this aspect to the overall scheme of the Act, it is dealt with in Chapter 3. **2.021**

Adverse Possession

Given the prominence of this aspect to the overall scheme of the Act, it is dealt with in Chapter 4. **2.022**

The Adjudicator[43]

The Act creates the position of the Adjudicator to Her Majesty's Land Registry. His role will be to determine references made to him by the Registrar and certain appeals in relation to network access agreements when electronic conveyancing is in place.[44] The appointment of the Adjudicator is by the Lord Chancellor and he will be independent of HM Land Registry. The Adjudicator is subject to the supervision of the Council of Tribunals. **2.023**

The Process and Mechanics of Registration

One of the matters raised in the consultation process giving rise to the Law Commission's report was the somewhat arbitrary distinction between that which was **2.024**

---

[41] See Law Com No. 271, para. 2.37, p. 20; Feudal Tenure etc (Scotland) Act 2000.

[42] See section 103 and Sch. 8.

[43] Sections 107–114.

[44] Sections 73 and 108.

contained in the Land Registration Act 1925 and that which was contained in the Land Registration Rules 1925; many matters of fundamental importance to the process of land registration appeared only in the Land Registration Rules, which addresses the issues of principle, leaving the details and mechanics to be provided by the rules. Draft rules are expected to be published shortly.

The three principal changes made by the Act concerning the process and mechanics of registration are as follows:

1. The Registrar has power to record in the register the fact that a right to determine a registered estate has become exercisable.[45]
2. The registrar has power to disclose information about the history of a title to those who have reason to so enquire.[46]
3. Charge Certificates are abolished by virtue of the fact that the Act makes no provision for them.The role of the land certificate is considerably reduced.[47]

Transitional provisions

2.025 Schedule 12 makes extensive provision for the transition from the scheme under the Land Registration Act 1925 to the scheme under the Act. Clearly these provisions are important and are dealt with elsewhere.[48] The manner and speed with which the Act is brought into force is at present uncertain and, as indicated, the rules that fall to be made under the Act (and which will deal with the detail of many of the changes it implements) have yet to be published. Thus the full scope and complexity of the transitional period is, at present, uncertain. The practical considerations of implementing electronic conveyancing and the fact that it is envisaged that both a paper-based and electronic system of conveyancing will co-exist for a time should ensure that the implementation of the Act's

---

[45] Section 64, *infra*.

[46] Section 69, *infra*.

[47] See Schedule 10, para. 4, *infra*.

[48] See SC12.1 *et seq.*, *infra*.

primary objective will occur gradually and with sufficient period for adjustment. However, it will be a process that will be conducted remorselessly and one not capable of being ignored. The envisaged benefits of electronic conveyancing (speed and costs savings) will not materialise if the old and new systems co-exist indefinitely. Thus this transitional state of affairs will only last for as short a period as possible.

Chapter 3

Electronic Conveyancing

Introduction

Making provision for the transition from a paper-based system of conveyancing to one that is entirely electronic is the most important single feature of the Act.[1] This transition is not only inevitable in the light of the continuing development of information technology but is also the logical culmination of an ongoing process at HM Land Registry whereby the register itself has been progressively computerised.[2] Indeed 40 years ago "the register" meant "the whole collection of records kept at HM Land Registry which [took] the physical form of a "vast card index" relating to an equally vast number of individual properties[3]": Direct access to the computerised register has been in place since 1995 and is operated as "Land Registry Direct".[4] Certain matters are capable of electronic notification directly to HM Land Registry and thus the era of electronic conveyancing has tentatively begun.[5] An application to register dealings with registered land can also be lodged electronically.[6] It is inevitable that this trend will continue. It is envisaged that electronic conveyancing will only employ well-established computer technology and it will be capable of operation from the personal computers that most practitioners already have. It is suggested that **3.001**

[1] Law Com No. 271, para. 2.41, p. 21.

[2] See *Ruoff & Roper*, paras 1–11.

[3] See *Wolstenholme & Cherry*, Conveyancing Statutes, Vol. 6, p. 5, citing *Curtis and Ruoff*, Registered Conveyancing (2nd ed., 1965) p. 14.

[4] See *Ruoff & Roper*, paras F–11, F–12.

[5] *e.g.* notification of the discharge of a registered charge may be made electronically (LRR 1925, r. 151A).

[6] Land Registration Rules 2001, S.I. 2001 No. 619.

the move to electronic conveyancing therefore will not require any great capital outlay by practitioners.[7]

Paper-based Conveyancing Practice in relation to Registered Land

3.002 Most transactions involve the execution of a contract for the sale or disposition of an interest in registered land followed by a transfer giving effect to that disposition. The disponee habitually protects his position by making a priority search against the registered title under the Land Registration (Official Searches) Rules 1993. Once executed, the transfer (which should be in the prescribed form) is submitted to HM Land Registry for registration.

The execution of the transfer only operates in equity and does not transfer the legal estate until an entry is made in the register. Thus, a disposition creates an interest in registered land prior to its registration. Depending on the varying administrative pressures at the respective land registry at which registration must occur, a considerable period of time can pass between the execution of the transfer (and thus the creation of the equitable interest) and its entry in the register at HM Land Registry. This gap, the so-called "registration gap" has been a source of problems.[8] On registration, the entry in the register takes effect from the date on which, under the rules, the application for registration is deemed to have been delivered to the Land Registry.[9] The "registration gap" can be artificially increased by any mistakes or deficiencies in the paperwork accompanying the application for registration. About 50 per cent of applications are defective in some way or another, although fewer mistakes occur with the new-style land registry forms, which are likely to be the model for electronic instruments.[10]

---

[7] Law Com No. 271, para. 2.41, p. 21.

[8] See *Abbey National Building Society v. Cann* [1991] 1 A.C. 56; *Brown & Root Technology Limited v. Sun Alliance & London Assurance Co.* [2001] Ch. 733.

[9] LRR 1925, r. 83.

[10] Law Com No. 271, para. 2.45, n. 94, p. 22.

Clearly, therefore, the existing system, although time-honoured, is cumbersome and slow and possibly more expensive. It also carries with it the disadvantage of the "registration gap" which means that at certain times, the register may (at best) be out-of-depth.

Against this background and the existence of information technology that would obviate the need to continue to use this system, the change to electronic conveyancing is an obvious step and development.

Electronic Conveyancing: an Hypothetical Transaction

It is envisaged that, subject to the rules (which have, as yet, to be made or indeed even published in draft form) a system of electronic conveyancing would operate in the following manner. First a system of secure electronic communications must be in place and the relevant conveyancers must have access to that system. Under the Act this is envisaged in accordance with a network access agreement. Such an agreement would permit access by authorised professionals to the electronic communications network through which transactions would take place. **3.003**

Chain management: It is via this system that not only will the necessary conveyancing and registration steps will be facilitated but it is envisaged that it will be employed to co-ordinate managed chains of transactions, particularly in relation to domestic conveyancing. It is envisaged that somebody (whether or not at HM Land Registry) will be made responsible for managing chain sales in order to facilitate them and iron out any difficulties or delays that occur at any given stage. This would operate as follows: when a party instructs a solicitor to act on his behalf in the purchase of a property which comprises part of a chain, that solicitor will be required to notify "the chain manager" of the fact of that instruction. Moreover, the solicitor will be required to notify the chain manager of the completion of various pre-contractual stages to the transaction, such as the completion of any investigations as to title, the carrying out of local authority searches, the making of a mortgage offer, etc. The chain manager will then be able to maintain an overview of how the chain is progressing and identifying any persons in the chain who are delaying the process. The state a the chain will be made available to all those in it via secure intranet link. Whilst it is not envisaged that the chain manager will have any powers of coercion or compulsion, it is hoped that his over-arching role will enable him to encourage any recalcitrant parties to complete any steps that remain to be performed. The Law Commission considers that this power to manage chains is an important feature of the proposals and policy of the Act since chains are a major cause of disquiet in the conveyancing process, particularly in relation to domestic conveyancing. It is hoped that the chain manager will be able to alleviate the frustrations that are suffered by so many involved in the sale and purchase of domestic property and to prevent chains from collapsing.[11]

Contract: When the terms of the contract have been agreed, it will be sent prior to its execution to HM Land Registry where it will be checked electronically against the title details in order to identify any deficiencies or errors that it may contain. In the event that these are identified, it is envisaged that they will be rectified prior to the conclusion of the contract.

The conclusion of the contract will be in electronic form and it will be signed electronically by the contracting parties or their agents. It is envisaged that once concluded, the contract will be required to be protected in the register by the entry of a notice against the title contracted to be transferred. This will occur simultaneously with the making of the contract and will confer priority protection on the purchaser.[12]

Completion: The process for completing the transfer will be similar. The draft transfer and any charge will be prepared in electronic form and agreed between the parties and submitted to HM Land Registry. A similar checking process will be undertaken and a "notional register" will then be prepared at HM Land Registration in consultation with the parties to indicate the form that the register will take when the transaction is completed. Completion, when it occurs, will necessarily entail the simultaneous occurrence of the following events:

---

[11] Law Com No. 271, para. 2.52, pp. 24–25.

[12] See Section 72(6)(a)(ii), *infra*.

1. The execution of the transfer and any charges in electronic form and their transmission to the registry where they will be stored;
2. The registration of the dispositions in the register so that it conforms with the notional register previously agreed with the Registry;
3. The appropriate and automatic movement of funds and payment of stamp duty and Registry fees.[13]

Abolition of the Registration Gap

The method of electronic conveyancing clearly abolishes the registration gap since there will be a requirement for the transfer and the registration thereof to take place simultaneously and, pursuant to section 93(2) of the Act, no disposition can, in such circumstances, take effect unless it is electronically communicated to the Registrar and the relevant registration requirements are met. **3.004**

Compulsory Use of Electronic Conveyancing

Section 93 of the Act permits the imposition of a compulsory system of electronic conveyancing. It is envisaged that such a power will not be exercised lightly. Undoubtedly those that enter into a network access agreement with HM Land Registry will be required to conduct electronic conveyancing in accordance with the network transaction rules.[14] However, the Act draws a distinction between compelling compliance with the network transaction rules in relation to those who have network access agreements and compelling compliance generally and thus making electronic conveyancing compulsory. It is envisaged that the move from a paper-based system to an all-electronic system of conveyancing will take some years and the two systems will necessarily co-exist during the period of transition. However, the Law Commission recommends that the period of transition needs to be kept to a minimum for two principal reasons. First, it will be very difficult both for practitioners and for HM Land Registry **3.005**

---

[13] Law Com No. 271, para. 2.55, p. 25–26.

[14] See Schedule 5, paras 2 and 5, *infra*.

to operate the distinct systems side by side. Secondly, if electronic conveyancing is to achieve its true potential and deliver the savings and benefits that it promises, it must be the only system. A chain of domestic transactions will only move at the speed of the slowest link. One paper-based conveyancing link in a chain which is otherwise electronic will have the effect of slowing the entire chain down to the speed of the paper-based conveyancer and will not be subject to the scrutiny and controls that electronic conveyancers are subject to. Accordingly, the Law Commission envisages that there must be a residual power to require transactions to be conducted in electronic form. It is hoped that the eventual exercise of the power will be merely a formality because solicitors and licensed conveyancers will have chosen to conduct conveyancing electronically in view of the advantages that it offers to them and to their clients.[15] Whether this optimism is replicated in practice remains to be seen.

Finance

3.006 Consideration is being given towards the creation of a system of banking arrangements that would complement electronic conveyancing. A variant on the CREST system that applies to share dealings has been considered and HM Land Registry has also been considering the possibility of an escrow bank. However, in the absence of a definite model for electronic conveyancing the detailed consideration of the establishment of a scheme for the transfer of funds which would facilitate the electronic conveyancing of property has not been progressed. One must anticipate that upon the implementation of the Act, this will be remedied.

Stamp Duty will be extended to cover dispositions made in electronic form.

Electronic Conveyancing and First Registration

3.007 It is not envisaged that electronic conveyancing will have a significant impact on applications for first registration since, on whatever basis they are made, the Registrar will

---

[15] Law Com No. 271, para. 2.61, p. 28.

have to investigate title to the estate in question in order to satisfy himself as to the nature of the title with which it should be registered.

Do-it-yourself Conveyancing

Electronic conveyancing will not compel those who wish to conduct their own conveyancing transactions to use a solicitor or licensed conveyancer. Such persons account for less than 1 per cent of all registered transactions. Once a system of electronic conveyancing is in place, the Registrar will be obliged to provide assistance for those who wish to undertake their own conveyancing transaction and will act at their direction but will not be authorised to provide any advice.[16] **3.008**

Rules

The detail of the implementation of any system of electronic conveyancing will depend upon the terms of such rules as may be made under the Act and, in particular, under Schedule 5. No rules have, as yet, been made. Draft rules will be published for consultation and it is understood that these are well advanced. **3.009**

[16] Schedule 5, para. 7

Chapter 4

Adverse Possession

Disapplication of Periods of Limitation

Under section 96 of the Act, the provisions of the Limitation Act 1980 whereby title to land is extinguished by virtue of a person's adverse possession are, in relation to a registered estate in land or a registered rentcharge, disapplied in relation to actions for the recovery of land (except in the favour of a chargee)[1] and actions for redemption. The scheme implemented by that section and Schedule 6 of the Act means that once it is fully implemented, the obtaining of title by adverse possession from a reasonably careful registered proprietor is, save in one limited circumstance, effectively impossible. **4.001**

This disapplication only relates to *estates in land or rentcharges, title to which is registered*. Thus, the provisions of the Limitation Act 1980 will continue to apply at least in the following circumstances:

1. Where the land is not registered. Thus for example where, in relation to a lease granted for a term of 21 years or less prior to the coming into force of the Act (and which is therefore an overriding interest) there has been adverse possession. Clearly this category will diminish as time passes and will be extinct 21 years or more after the coming into force of the Act. Leases which are overriding interests created after coming into force of the Act cannot be barred by the provisions of the Limitation Act 1980 since they will be for a period of seven years or less.
2. Since licensees and tenants at will cannot be registered as proprietors of an estate in land, their right

[1] See section 96(1).

to obtain possession as against an adverse possessor will depend upon the provisions of the Limitation Act 1980.

3. A landlord's right of re-entry will continue to be subject to the Limitation Act 1980 and will be statute-barred after the expiry of a period of 12 years from the date upon which the right to re-enter arose (presuming that no waiver has occurred in the meantime). Since a right to re-enter is not an estate in land, it cannot be subject to the disapplication imposed by section 96.
4. Where an adverse possessor ("AP1") has obtained title to land by reason of a period of adverse possession of 12 years or more and he is dispossessed by a second adverse possessor ("AP2"), AP2 must rely upon the provisions of the Limitation Act 1980 in order to obtain title because the title of AP1 will not have been registered and thus will be outside the provisions of section 95(1).
5. Chargees—see below.

Chargees

4.002 The exception contained in section 96(1) ensures that the Limitation Act 1980 remains applicable to the right of the chargee to recover possession or to foreclose where a chargor is in possession. The basis for this is straightforward. A chargee has two remedies first his personal remedies against the chargor for monies due under the charge and secondly his remedies against the property by way of security for that liability. By retaining the application of the Limitation Act 1980 in relation to the rights of the chargee, the Act is subjecting the chargee's personal rights against the chargor and his rights as against the security to the same consistent system of limitation.

Mortgagees in Possession

4.003 The Act effects a change in the law in relation to mortgagees in possession. Under section 16 of the Limitation Act 1980, once a mortgagee has been in possession of land for 12 years or more, the mortgagor loses his right to redeem the mortgage and the mortgagee thus becomes the owner of the land. This provision is disapplied by section 95(2) and thus a mortgagee in possession who wishes to obtain the extinguishment of the mortgagor's registered title must comply with the provisions of the Act.

The reasons behind this change can be summarised as follows:

1. First, a mortgagee who exercises his power to take possession should not be treated as if he were in adverse possession since he is taking possession pursuant to the terms of his mortgage and his possession is plainly not adverse. A mortgagee is either a tenant under a long lease in the case of a mortgage by demise or sub-demise[2] or he has the same rights as if he were such a tenant in the case of a charge by way of legal mortgage.[3] A tenant can never adversely possess against his landlord while the lease subsists and accordingly possession by a mortgagee of the mortgaged property cannot be termed adverse.
2. The genesis of section 16 derives from the Real Property Limitation Act 1832, s.28. The practice then for mortgages to be made by an outright transfer of the mortgagor's legal estate to the mortgagee with a proviso for reconvenaynce on redemption has long since ceased, as is recognised by the provisions of the Law of Property Act 1925. This change and the others specified in the Law Commission's report[4] compelled the disapplication of section 16 in relation to mortgagees in possession.

An Overview of the New Scheme of Acquisition of Title by Adverse Possession under the Act

On completion of 10 years' adverse possession[5] an adverse possessor will be able to apply to be registered as the proprietor of the estate in question. Upon receipt of that **4.004**

---

[2] Pursuant to LPA, ss. 85–86.

[3] LPA 1925, s. 87.

[4] Law Com No. 271, para. 14.17, p. 309.

[5] Or in the circumstances specified in Schedule 6, para. 1(2) of the Act, *infra*.

notice, the Registrar will notify the registered proprietor of the property (together with the additional persons specified in paragraph 2 (1) of Schedule 6[6]) of that application. In the event that the persons notified fail to object to the registration of the applicant with title to the registered land, the applicant will be registered as proprietor and will take the estate free of any registered charge affecting the estate immediately before his registration although that registration will not affect the priority of any other interest affecting the estate. Whilst rules may be made concerning the form, content and service of notices under the Act,[7] the current practice (and one that will continue) is to give notice to the registered proprietor at the address entered on the register. Thus the importance of maintaining up-to-date addresses in the register[8] cannot be underestimated. This requirement is too frequently overlooked.[9]

However, if any of the individuals given notice of the application object, then, unless the adverse possessor can satisfy the Registrar that one of the conditions in paragraph 5 of Schedule 6 is met,[10] his application will fail. These conditions are stringent and do not (with the exception of the third condition contained in paragraph 5(4) of the Schedule) enable a squatter simply to obtain registration and thus title to the registered estate by virtue of the duration of his adverse possession. This third condition would enable the applicant to obtain registration of a registered estate in circumstances where (a) the land in question is adjacent to land belonging to the applicant; (b) the exact line of the boundary has not been fixed definitively pursuant to section 60; (c) the 10-year adverse possession period is satisfied and the applicant reasonably believes that the land to which the application relates belonged to him during that period and (d) the estate to which the application relates has been registered for more than one year prior to the date of application. This

---

[6] See paras SC6.1 *et seq.*, *infra*.

[7] Sch. 10, para. 5. No rules have, as yet, been made.

[8] Currently up to three addresses can be entered in the register: LRR 1925, r. 315.

[9] *Ruoff & Roper*, para. 3–10.

[10] See paras SC6.1.2 *et seq.*, *infra*.

scenario is most likely to be satisfied in the following circumstances. Two registered properties, Blackacre and Whiteacre are adjacent to each other and divided by a fence. If it should transpire that the fence is some distance inside Blackacre leaving a strip apparently within Whiteacre's cutilage but registered as part of Blackacre and the owner of Whiteacre has for at least 10 years prior to the date of his application to the Registrar been in adverse possession of that strip of land, then provided he reasonably believes that land belongs to him (such belief being manifested, perhaps, by the proprietor of Blackacre having tended and maintained it as part of his garden) then provided Whiteacre has been registered for more than one year prior to the date of the application, the proprietor of Whiteacre may be able to satisfy the third condition and thus obtain title to the strip of land in question.

So, on an application after 10 years' adverse possession in accordance with the Act, the applicant's request will either be granted (either by reason of the absence of any objection or by reason of his satisfaction of any of the three conditions in paragraph 5 to Schedule 6) or it will be rejected by reason of the registered proprietor's or some other person's objection to the application and the applicant's failure to satisfy any of those conditions.

However, that rejection is not the end of the matter. The applicant may, if his initial application is rejected, make a further application to be registered as the proprietor of the estate if he continues in adverse possession from the date of the first application until the last day of the period of two years beginning with the date of its rejection. Subject to the next paragraph, if he makes such an application, he is *without more* entitled to be registered as the proprietor of the land in question.

To this there are a number of exceptions. First, the restriction on applications contained in paragraph 8 of Schedule 6 applies.[11] Secondly, an application may not be made in circumstances where the applicant is a defendant in proceedings which involve asserting a right to possession of the land; or judgment for possession of the land has been given against him in the last two years; or he has been evicted from the land pursuant to a judgment for possession.

---

[11] See paras S6.1.3 *et seq.*, *infra.*

Absent any such feature, inertia by the registered proprietor following upon a successful objection to the adverse possessor's first application will result in the automatic extinguishment of the registered proprietor's title in the event that a second application is made after the requisite period.

Apportionment and Discharge of Charges

4.005 Paragraph 10 of Schedule 6[12] provides that where a registered estate continues to be subject to a charge notwithstanding the registration of an adverse possessor as proprietor and the charge affects property other than the estate, the adverse possessor may require the chargee to apportion the amount secured by the charge at that time between the estate and the other property on the basis of their respective values. Having apportioned the charge, the adverse possessor is entitled to redeem it in accordance with the provisions of paragraph 10.

Rules

4.006 Whilst paragraph 15 of Schedule 6 envisages that rules may be made governing the procedure to be followed pursuant to an application under Schedule 6, none have (as yet) been made.

---

[12] See para. S6.1.6 *et seq.*, *infra.*

PART II

LAND REGISTRATION ACT, 2002

Land Registration Act 2002

2002 CHAPTER 9

Part 1

Preliminary

1 Register of title

(1) There is to continue to be a register of title kept by the registrar. **A1.1**

(2) Rules may make provision about how the register is to be kept and may, in particular, make provision about—

(a) the information to be included in the register,
(b) the form in which information included in the register is to be kept, and
(c) the arrangement of that information.

Subsection (1): "Register" means the register of title, except in the context of cautions against first registration: section 132(1). **C1.1**
"Registrar" means the Chief Land Registrar (section 132(1)) who remains the head of Her Majesty's Land Registry: section 98.

Subsection (2): Currently the register comprises three parts: the Property Register, the Proprietorship Register and the Charges Register: LRR 1925, r. 3. Clearly the Act envisages that this may change. The Lord Chancellor may, by statutory instrument, make land registration rules with the advice and assistance of the Rule Committee (section 127(1), (2)). Schedule 10, paragraph 4 expressly permits rules about the form and content of a certificate of registration of title. No rules have, as yet, been made. **C1.1.1**

2 Scope of title registration

This Act makes provision about the registration of title to— **A2.1**

(a) unregistered legal estates which are interests of any of the following kinds—

(i) an estate in land,

(ii) a rentcharge,
(iii) a franchise,
(iv) a profit à prendre in gross, and
(v) any other interest or charge which subsists for the benefit of, or is a charge on, an interest the title to which is registered; and

(b) interests capable of subsisting at law which are created by a disposition of an interest the title to which is registered.

C2.1 This section describes the interests for which the Act makes provision concerning their registration.

C2.1.1 Subsection 2(a): Specifies the unregistered estates which are capable of registration. "*An estate in land*" means an estate in fee simple absolute in possession or a terms of years absolute (LPA 1925, s. 1(1)[1]). "Land" includes buildings and other structures; land covered by water (either internal waters of the United Kingdom or those adjacent to it if specified for this purpose by order: section 130) or mines and minerals, whether held with the surface or note: section 132(1).

A rentcharge in possession which issues out of or is charged on land being either perpetual or for a term of years absolute is a legal interest: LPA 1925, s. 1(2)(b). Such interests cannot be created after August 21, 1977, and most will be abolished in 2037: Rentcharges Act 1977.

A franchise is a royal privilege or a right bestowed by virtue of the Crown's perogative: *e.g.* the right to tolls or to hold markets and fairs. Clearly such rights can be valuable. Under the LRA 1925 such a right was denied its own separate registration and could only be protected on the register by a notice of caution if the encumbered land itself was registered. This is no longer the case.

A *profit à prendre* in gross does not exist for the benefit of other land and can be sold or leased. Examples of such profits are fishing and shooting rights. Like franchises, they can be valuable and had the same limited scope for entry on the register under the LRA 1925. This has been remedied.

C2.1.2 Subsection 2(b) relates to registrable dispositions. The only interests or charges in or over land which are capable of subsisting or of being conveyed or created at law are specified in LPA 1925, s. 1(2).

---

[1] See App.1, *infra*.

PART 2

FIRST REGISTRATION OF TITLE

CHAPTER 1

FIRST REGISTRATION[2]

Voluntary registration

3 When title may be registered

(1) This section applies to any unregistered legal estate which is an interest of any of the following kinds— **A3.1**
- (a) an estate in land,
- (b) a rentcharge,
- (c) a franchise, and
- (d) a profit à prendre in gross.

(2) Subject to the following provisions, a person may apply to the registrar to be registered as the proprietor of an unregistered legal estate to which this section applies if—
- (a) the estate is vested in him, or
- (b) he is entitled to require the estate to be vested in him.

(3) Subject to subsection (4), an application under subsection (2) in respect of a leasehold estate may only be made if the estate was granted for a term of which more than seven years are unexpired.

(4) In the case of an estate in land, subsection (3) does not apply if the right to possession under the lease is discontinuous.

(5) A person may not make an application under subsection (2)(a) in respect of a leasehold estate vested in him as a mortgagee where there is a subsisting right of redemption.

---

[2] This chapter makes provision for when title can (s. 3) and must (s. 4) be registered. It specifies who must register the estate (s. 6) and the consequences of non-compliance (s. 7, 8). The title with which registration can be concluded are provided for (ss 9–13).

(6) A person may not make an application under subsection (2)(b) if his entitlement is as a person who has contracted to buy under a contract.

(7) If a person holds in the same right both—

(a) a lease in possession, and
(b) a lease to take effect in possession on, or within a month of, the end of the lease in possession,

then, to the extent that they relate to the same land, they are to be treated for the purposes of this section as creating one continuous term.

C3.1 This section makes provision for voluntary registration. Given the policy behind the Act, one must expect that voluntary registration will be encouraged. The fee incentives for voluntary registration brought by the Land Registration Act 1997 can be expected to continue.

C3.1.1 Subsection (1): See notes to section 2 (a), *supra*.

C3.1.2 Subsection (2): A person in whom any of the interests specified in subsection (1) are vested or who is entitled to have the same vested in him may apply for voluntary registration.[3] That right is subject to a number of limitations set out in the following subsections:—

C3.1.3 Subsection (3): Subject to subsection (4), a leasehold estate is only capable of registration if the term granted exceeds seven years. The exception provided for in subsection (4) is for discontinuous leases. These are rare (sometimes used for time share arrangements) and are registrable whatever their duration. Subsection (7) provides that where a person enjoys a lease in possession and a lease that takes effect in possession at the end of the lease in possession (or within a month thereof), the terms granted by the lease in possession and the lease that takes effect at its end are to be aggregated and treated as one continuous term for the purposes of calculating the seven year period. Section 118(1) allows the seven year period to be changed by order. A PPP lease is excluded from these provisions: s. 90(1).

C3.1.4 Subsection (5): Where there is a subsisting right of redemption, a mortgagee by demise or sub-demise (see LPA 1925, ss. 85 and 86) cannot apply to be registered. This accords with the position under the

---

[3] That application can be the subject of an objection: s. 73 (1) and may be referred to the Adjudicator under s. 108.

Land Registration Act 1925. Such a mortgagee will (or should) be protected by an entry in the register against the land charged.

Subsection (6): This precludes the voluntary registration of an interest under an estate contract, which must be registered. **C3.1.5**

Compulsory registration

4 When title must be registered

(1) The requirement of registration applies on the occurrence of any of the following events— **A4.1**

(a) the transfer of a qualifying estate—

(i) for valuable or other consideration, by way of gift or in pursuance of an order of any court, or

(ii) by means of an assent (including a vesting assent);

(b) the transfer of an unregistered legal estate in land in circumstances where section 171A of the Housing Act 1985 (c. 68) applies (disposal by landlord which leads to a person no longer being a secure tenant);

(c) the grant out of a qualifying estate of an estate in land—

(i) for a term of years absolute of more than seven years from the date of the grant, and

(ii) for valuable or other consideration, by way of gift or in pursuance of an order of any court;

(d) the grant out of a qualifying estate of an estate in land for a term of years absolute to take effect in possession after the end of the period of three months beginning with the date of the grant;

(e) the grant of a lease in pursuance of Part 5 of the Housing Act 1985 (the right to buy) out of an unregistered legal estate in land;

(f) the grant of a lease out of an unregistered legal estate in land in such circumstances as are mentioned in paragraph (b);

(g) the creation of a protected first legal mortgage of a qualifying estate.

(2) For the purposes of subsection (1), a qualifying estate is an unregistered legal estate which is—

(a) a freehold estate in land, or
(b) a leasehold estate in land for a term which, at the time of the transfer, grant or creation, has more than seven years to run.

(3) In subsection (1)(a), the reference to transfer does not include transfer by operation of law.

(4) Subsection (1)(a) does not apply to—

(a) the assignment of a mortgage term, or
(b) the assignment or surrender of a lease to the owner of the immediate reversion where the term is to merge in that reversion.

(5) Subsection (1)(c) does not apply to the grant of an estate to a person as a mortgagee.

(6) For the purposes of subsection (1)(a) and (c), if the estate transferred or granted has a negative value, it is to be regarded as transferred or granted for valuable or other consideration.

(7) In subsection (1)(a) and (c), references to transfer or grant by way of gift include transfer or grant for the purpose of—

(a) constituting a trust under which the settlor does not retain the whole of the beneficial interest, or
(b) uniting the bare legal title and the beneficial interest in property held under a trust under which the settlor did not, on constitution, retain the whole of the beneficial interest.

(8) For the purposes of subsection (1)(g)—
(a) a legal mortgage is protected if it takes effect on its creation as a mortgage to be protected by the deposit of documents relating to the mortgaged estate, and
(b) a first legal mortgage is one which, on its creation, ranks in priority ahead of any other mortgages then affecting the mortgaged estate.

(9) In this section—
"land" does not include mines and minerals held apart from the surface;
"vesting assent" has the same meaning as in the Settled Land Act 1925 (c. 18).

This section makes provision for the circumstances when an unre- **C4.1**
gistered estate must be registered. Mines and minerals held apart from the surface are excepted.[4] The extent of this section may be extended by order: section 5. The events which trigger compulsory registration are:—

Subsection (1)(a): The transfer of a "qualifying estate" in the **C4.1.1**
circumstances set forth in subsections (1)(a)(i) or (ii). "Valuable consideration" includes interests which have a negative value (subsection (6)) but excludes marriage consideration or a nominal consideration in money: section 132(1).

"Gift" is extended to include the matters in subsection (7). Thus a settlement by S to trustees on trust for S and B would amount to a gift triggering registration. Transfers to trustees on a bare trust would not.

A "vesting assent" is defined in SLA 1925, s. 117(xxxi): subs. (9).[5]

A "qualifying estate" means a freehold or leasehold estate in land for a term which at the time of transfer, grant or creation has more than seven years to run: subsection (2). A transfer by operation of law (*e.g.* vesting in a trustee in bankruptcy) is not a triggering transfer (subsection (3)). Neither is an assignment of a mortgage term or the assignment or surrender of a term of years to the immediate reversioner where merger would occur: subsection (4).

Subsection (1)(b): the transfer of an unregistered legal estate where **C4.1.2**
section 171A of the Housing Act 1985 applies: *i.e.* where a person ceases to be a secure tenant by reason of his lessor's disposal of an interest in the dwelling-house in question to a landlord who does not satisfy the landlord condition for secure tenancies as stipulated in Housing Act 1985, s. 80 (a private sector landlord).

Subsection (1)(c): the grant out of a qualifying estate (defined in **C4.1.3**
subsection (2)) of a term of years of more than seven years from the date of grant for valuable or other consideration or by way of gift or

---

[4] See s. 4(9).

[5] "Vesting assent" means the instrument whereby a personal representative after the death of a tenant for life or statutory owner or the survivor of two or more tenants for life or statutory owners vests settled land in a person entitled as tenant for life or statutory owner.

pursuant to a court order. See notes to subs. (1), *supra.* A mortgage by way of demise or sub-demise does not trigger compulsory registration: subsection (5).[6] A PPP lease is excluded from these provisions: section 90(2).

C4.1.4 Subsection (1)(d): the grant out of a qualifying estate (defined in subsection (2)) of a term of years taking effect in possession more than three months after the date of grant. There is no requirement as to the length of the term so granted. This provision is designed to end the pre-existing difficulties that such leases only took effect as overriding interests (LRA 1925, s. 70(1)(k)) and thus could be difficult to spot since the lessee would not be in possession.

C4.1.5 Subsection (1)(e), (f): Reflect the pre-existing law.

C4.1.6 Subsection (1)(g): The creation of a protected first legal mortgage of a qualifying estate. A legal mortgage is protected and comprises a first legal mortgage in the circumstances set forth in subsection (8).

C4.1.7 Subsection (9): Excludes mines and minerals held apart from the surface from the definition of "land". "Mines and minerals" are defined: section 132(1).

5 Power to extend section 4

A5.1 (1) The Lord Chancellor may be order—

(a) amend section 4 so as to add to the events on the occurrence of which the requirement of registration applies such relevant event as he may specify in the order, and
(b) make such consequential amendments of any provision of, or having effect under, any Act as he thinks appropriate.

(2) For the purposes of subsection (1)(a), a relevant event is an event relating to an unregistered legal estate which is an interest of any of the following kinds—

(a) an estate in land,
(b) a rentcharge,
(c) a franchise, and

[6] See notes to section 3(5), *supra*.

(d) a profit à prendre in gross.

(3) The power conferred by subsection (1) may not be exercised so as to require the title to an estate granted to a person as a mortgagee to be registered.

(4) Before making an order under this section the Lord Chancellor must consult such persons as he considers appropriate.

Section 5 permits the Lord Chancellor by order (and having consulted such persons as he considers appropriate) to amend section 4 in order to add additional events which trigger compulsory registration. This power extends to making consequential amendments of any provision of or having effect under any act as appropriate. This power is subject to the limitation stated in subsection (3). **C5.1**

6 Duty to apply for registration of title

(1) If the requirement of registration applies, the responsible estate owner, or his successor in title, must, before the end of the period for registration, apply to the registrar to be registered as the proprietor of the registrable estate. **A6.1**

(2) If the requirement of registration applies because of section 4(1)(g)—

(a) the registrable estate is the estate charged by the mortgage, and
(b) the responsible estate owner is the owner of that estate.

(3) If the requirement of registration applies otherwise than because of section 4(1)(g)—

(a) the registrable estate is the estate which is transferred or granted, and
(b) the responsible estate owner is the transferee or grantee of that estate.

(4) The period for registration is two months beginning with the date on which the relevant event occurs, or such longer period as the registrar may provide under subsection (5).

(5) If on the application of any interested person the registrar is satisfied that there is good reason for

doing so, he may by order provide that the period for registration ends on such later date as he may specify in the order.

(6) Rules may make provision enabling the mortgagee under any mortgage falling within section 4(1)(g) to require the estate charged by the mortgage to be registered whether or not the mortgagor consents.

C6.1 "Requirement of registration": defined s. 132(1)

Where compulsory registration is necessary "the responsible estate owner" (defined in subsection 3(b) as the transferee or grantee of the estate transferred or granted except where the obligation to register arises under section 4(1)(g) in which case the responsible estate owner is the mortgagor: subsection (2)) must apply to be registered as proprietor of the registrable estate (being the estate transferred, granted or owned: see subsections (2) and (3)) before the end of the period for registration. That period is two months from the occurrence of the relevant event, unless extended by the registrar under subsection (5): subsection (4). The extension of time by the registrar can be retrospective: section 7(3). Section 7 makes provision in the event of non-compliance. Rules may be made enabling a mortgagee who must register that interest by virtue of section 4(1)(g) to cause the mortgaged estate to be registered without the mortgagor's consent. No rules have, as yet, been made.

7 Effect of non-compliance with section 6

A7.1 (1) If the requirement of registration is not complied with, the transfer, grant or creation becomes void as regards the transfer, grant or creation of a legal estate.

(2) On the application of subsection (1)—

(a) in a case falling within section 4(1)(a) or (b), the title to the legal estate reverts to the transferor who holds it on a bare trust for the transferee, and

(b) in a case falling within section 4(1)(c) to (g), the grant or creation has effect as a contract made for valuable consideration to grant or create the legal estate concerned.

(3) If an order under section 6(5) is made in a case where subsection (1) has already applied, that application of the subsection is to be treated as not having occurred.

(4) The possibility of reverter under subsection (1) is to be disregarded for the purposes of determining whether a fee simple is a fee simple absolute.

Subsection (1): A failure to comply with the obligation to register imposed by section 6 renders the transfer, grant or creation of a legal estate void. **C7.1**

Subsection (2): Where a transfer of a legal estate is void, the transferor holds the estate on a bare trust for the transferee. Where a legal interest is granted or created in a case falling within section 4(1)(c)–(g), the grant or creation avoided operates as a contract for valuable consideration to grant or create the legal estate concerned. **C7.1.1**

Subsection (4): This provision precludes the possibility that a void transfer of a fee simple absolute could give rise to a determinable fee and thus not of a legal estate within Law of Property Act 1925, s. 1. **C7.1.2**

8 Liability for making good void transfers, etc.

If a legal estate is retransferred, regranted or recreated because of a failure to comply with the requirement of registration, the transferee, grantee or, as the case may be, the mortgagor— **A8.1**

(a) is liable to the other party for all the proper costs of and incidental to the retransfer, regrant or recreation of the legal estate, and

(b) is liable to indemnify the other party in respect of any other liability reasonably incurred by him because of the failure to comply with the requirement of registration.

Where a disposition has to be repeated because of a failure to register the same, the responsible estate owner in default is liable to the other party for all the proper costs of and incidental to the repetition of the transfer and must indemnify that party in the terms set forth in section 8(b). **C8.1**

Classes of title

9 Titles to freehold estates[7]

(1) In the case of an application for registration under this Chapter of a freehold estate, the classes of title with which the applicant may be registered as proprietor are— **A9.1**

[7] See *Ruoff & Roper*, paras 5.01–5.09.

(a) absolute title,
(b) qualified title, and
(c) possessory title;

and the following provisions deal with when each of the classes of title is available.

(2) A person may be registered with absolute title if the registrar is of the opinion that the person's title to the estate is such as a willing buyer could properly be advised by a competent professional adviser to accept.

(3) In applying subsection (2), the registrar may disregard the fact that a person's title appears to him to be open to objection if he is of the opinion that the defect will not cause the holding under the title to be disturbed.

(4) A person may be registered with qualified title if the registrar is of the opinion that the person's title to the estate has been established only for a limited period or subject to certain reservations which cannot be disregarded under subsection (3).

(5) A person may be registered with possessory title if the registrar is of the opinion—

(a) that the person is in actual possession of the land, or in receipt of the rents and profits of the land, by virtue of the estate, and
(b) that there is no other class of title with which he may be registered.

C9.1 The Act does not alter the substance of the position currently prevailing under the Land Registration Act 1925.

C9.1.1 Subsection (1): Provision is made for title to a freehold estate to continue to be classified absolute, qualified or possessory on registration. The effect of registration is provided for in section 11. Title may be upgraded in accordance with section 62.

C9.1.2 Subsection (2): This permits the registrar to classify a title as absolute in circumstances where he is of the opinion that a willing buyer could be properly advised to accept it.

C9.1.3 Subsection (3): In applying subsection (2), the registrar can disregard the fact that the title would be open to objection if he considers the defect would not cause the holding under the title to be disturbed. Thus even defective titles can be registered as absolute if the requirements of this subsection are satisfied.

Subsection (4): If the defect is such that the registrar cannot form the opinion required by subsection (3), or title can only be established for limited period, it will be registered as qualified. Such titles are, in practice, rare. **C9.1.4**

Subsection (5): In default of obtaining either an absolute or qualified title, an individual in actual possession of the land or in receipt of the rents and profits therefrom may be registered with possessory title. Such title is usually only entered where the applicant has been in adverse possession for a period exceeding 12 years or is, for some other reason, unable to prove title. **C9.1.5**

10 Titles to leasehold estates[8]

(1) In the case of an application for registration under this Chapter of a leasehold estate, the classes of title with which the applicant may be registered as proprietor are— **A10.1**

(a) absolute title,
(b) good leasehold title,
(c) qualified title, and
(d) possessory title;

and the following provisions deal with when each of the classes of title is available.

(2) A person may be registered with absolute title if—

(a) the registrar is of the opinion that the person's title to the estate is such as a willing buyer could properly be advised by a competent professional adviser to accept, and
(b) the registrar approves the lessor's title to grant the lease.

(3) A person may be registered with good leasehold title if the registrar is of the opinion that the person's title to the estate is such as a willing buyer could properly be advised by a competent professional adviser to accept.

---

[8] See *Ruoff-Roper*, paras 5.01 and 5.10–5.18.

(4) In applying subsection (2) or (3), the registrar may disregard the fact that a person's title appears to him to be open to objection if he is of the opinion that the defect will not cause the holding under the title to be disturbed.

(5) A person may be registered with qualified title if the registrar is of the opinion that the person's title to the estate, or the lessor's title to the reversion, has been established only for a limited period or subject to certain reservations which cannot be disregarded under subsection (4).

(6) A person may be registered with possessory title if the registrar is of the opinion—

(a) that the person is in actual possession of the land, or in receipt of the rents and profits of the land, by virtue of the estate, and

(b) that there is no other class of title with which he may be registered.

C10.1 The Act does not alter the substance of the position currently prevailing under the Land Registration Act 1925.

C10.1.1 Subsection (1): The 4 classes of title to leasehold estates remain as before.

C10.1.1A Subsection (2): Title may be classified as absolute where the registrar is of the opinion that a willing buyer would be properly advised to accept it and he approves the lessor's title to grant the lease. Subsection (4) applies.

C10.1.2 Subsection (3): Title may be classified as good leasehold in circumstances where it could be registered with absolute title but the superior title is neither registered nor deduced. Subsection (4) applies.

C10.1.3 Subsection (4): The registrar may register a title as either absolute or good leasehold if he is of the opinion that any defect therein is such as will not cause the holding under the title to be disturbed.

C10.1.4 Subsection (5): Qualified title is given where either the applicant's title or the superior title have only been established for a limited period or is subject to reservations that the registrar cannot disregard under subsection (4).

C10.1.5 Subsection (6): an individual in actual possession of the land or in receipt of the rents and profits therefrom may be registered with possessory title. Such title is usually only entered where the applicant has been in adverse possession for a period exceeding 12 years or is, for some other reason, unable to prove title.

Effect of first registration

11 Freehold estates

(1) This section is concerned with the registration of a person under this Chapter as the proprietor of a freehold estate. **A11.1**

(2) Registration with absolute title has the effect described in subsections (3) to (5).

(3) The estate is vested in the proprietor together with all interests subsisting for the benefit of the estate.

(4) The estate is vested in the proprietor subject only to the following interests affecting the estate at the time of registration—

- (a) interests which are the subject of an entry in the register in relation to the estate,
- (b) unregistered interests which fall within any of the paragraphs of Schedule 1, and
- (c) interests acquired under the Limitation Act 1980 (c. 58) of which the proprietor has notice.

(5) If the proprietor is not entitled to the estate for his own benefit, or not entitled solely for his own benefit, then, as between himself and the persons beneficially entitled to the estate, the estate is vested in him subject to such of their interests as he has notice of.

(6) Registration with qualified title has the same effect as registration with absolute title, except that it does not affect the enforcement of any estate, right or interest which appears from the register to be excepted from the effect of registration.

(7) Registration with possessory title has the same effect as registration with absolute title, except that it does not affect the enforcement of any estate, right or interest adverse to, or in derogation of, the

proprietor's title subsisting at the time of registration or then capable of arising.

C11.1 Subsections (1), (2): Where a person is registered as a proprietor of a freehold estate with absolute title on first registration, the following apply:—

C11.1.1 Subsection (3): The estate is vested in the proprietor together with all interests subsisting for its benefit (*e.g.* easements etc.)

C11.1.2 Subsection (4): On registration, the estate is subject only to (a) interests subsisting on the register against that estate; (b) overriding interests (Schedule 1)[9]; and (c) interests acquired under the Limitation Act 1980 of which the proprietor has notice.

Subsection (4)(c) is new. Subject to the transitional provisions (Schedule 12, paragraph 7),[10] the reduction of the categories of overriding interests (see Schedule 1) means that the rights of the adverse possessor ("AP") in the following example would not, under the Act, be overriding. Suppose AP adversely possesses unregistered land and extinguishes the title of the paper owner ("PO") after 12 years and thus acquires ownership. AP then abandons the land and PO purports to convey to a third party ("TP"), thus triggering TP's compulsory registration. Under subsection 11(4)(c), TP takes free of AP's rights unless he has knowledge of them. If TP has knowledge and is registered, AP can obtain alteration of the register (Schedule 4, paragraphs 2 and 5)[11] since TP is bound by AP's rights. Moreover, since this will not amount to rectification,[12] TP will not be indemnified. Since *ex hypothesi*, TP is aware of AP's rights, no injustice should occur.

C11.1.3 Subsection (5): Where the proprietor holds the estate on trust, it is vested in him but, as between himself and the persons beneficially entitled thereto, subject to such of their interests of which he has notice.

C11.1.4 Subsections (6), (7): Provides for the effect of registration with qualified and possessory titles respectively.

12 Leasehold estates

A12.1 (1) This section is concerned with the registration of a person under this Chapter as the proprietor of a leasehold estate.

---

[9] See para. SC1.0 *et seq.*, *infra*.

[10] See paras S12.1.4, *infra*.

[11] See paras S4.1.2, S4.1.3, *infra*.

[12] See paras S4.1, *infra*.

(2) Registration with absolute title has the effect described in subsections (3) to (5).

(3) The estate is vested in the proprietor together with all interests subsisting for the benefit of the estate.

(4) The estate is vested subject only to the following interests affecting the estate at the time of registration—

- (a) implied and express covenants, obligations and liabilities incident to the estate,
- (b) interests which are the subject of an entry in the register in relation to the estate,
- (c) unregistered interests which fall within any of the paragraphs of Schedule 1, and
- (d) interests acquired under the Limitation Act 1980 (c. 58) of which the proprietor has notice.

(5) If the proprietor is not entitled to the estate for his own benefit, or not entitled solely for his own benefit, then, as between himself and the persons beneficially entitled to the estate, the estate is vested in him subject to such of their interests as he has notice of.

(6) Registration with good leasehold title has the same effect as registration with absolute title, except that it does not affect the enforcement of any estate, right or interest affecting, or in derogation of, the title of the lessor to grant the lease.

(7) Registration with qualified title has the same effect as registration with absolute title except that it does not affect the enforcement of any estate, right or interest which appears from the register to be excepted from the effect of registration.

(8) Registration with possessory title has the same effect as registration with absolute title, except that it does not affect the enforcement of any estate, right or interest adverse to, or in derogation of, the proprietor's title subsisting at the time of registration or then capable of arising.

Subsections (1), (2): Where a person is registered as a proprietor of a leasehold estate with absolute title on first registration, the following apply:— **C12.1**

C12.1.1 Subsection (3): The estate is vested in the proprietor together with all interests subsisting for its benefit (*e.g.* easements, etc.)

C12.1.2 Subsection (4): On registration, the estate is subject only to (a) implied and express covenants, obligations and liabilities incident to the estate; (b) interests subsisting on the register against that estate; (c) overriding interests (Schedule 1); and (d) interests acquired under the Limitation Act 1980 of which the proprietor has notice: see notes to section 11(4)(c), *supra*. "Notice" has its usual meaning and will include matters of which TP ought to have discovered from reasonable inspections and inquiries.[13]

C12.1.3 Subsection (5): Where the proprietor holds the estate on trust, it is vested in him but, as between himself and the persons beneficially entitled thereto, subject to such of their interests of which he has notice.

C12.1.4 Subsection (6), (7) and (8): Provides for the effect of registration with good leasehold, qualified and possessory titles.

Dependent estates

13 Appurtenant rights and charges

Rules may—

A13.1 (a) make provision for the registration of the proprietor of a registered estate as the proprietor of an unregistered legal estate which subsists for the benefit of the registered estate;

(b) make provision for the registration of a person as the proprietor of an unregistered legal estate which is a charge on a registered estate.

C13.1 The rules which may be made by order pursuant to section 128 may provide for the circumstances contained in section 13(a) (*e.g.* the grant of a legal estate such as an easement over unregistered land) and (b) (*e.g.* where, on first registration, the land is already subject to a legal mortgage). No rules have, as yet, been made.

---

[13] The Act draws a clear distinction in circumstances where "notice" means "actual notice"—see Schedule 3, paragraphs 2(c)(ii); 3(1)(a) *infra*.

Supplementary

14 Rules about first registration

Rules may—

(a) make provision about the making of applications for registration under this Chapter; **A14.1**

(b) make provision about the functions of the registrar following the making of such an application, including provision about—

(i) the examination of title, and
(ii) the entries to be made in the register where such an application is approved;

(c) make provision about the effect of any entry made in the register in pursuance of such an application.

No rules have, as yet, been made. **C14.1**

Chapter 2

Cautions against First Registration

A caution against first registration enables a person with a right to lodge one (section 15) with a mechanism by which he will be informed of an application for the first registration of the land in question. Currently such cautions are recorded on an index map[14] which may be searched. This system will continue: section 68(1). A caution against first registration will be the only type of caution capable of creation once the Act is brought into force. Cautions against dealings will be incapable of creation. Similarly, inhibitions are prospectively abolished. **C15.0**

15 Right to lodge

(1) Subject to subsection (3), a person may lodge a caution against the registration of title to an unregistered legal estate if he claims to be— **A15.1**

(a) the owner of a qualifying estate, or
(b) entitled to an interest affecting a qualifying estate.

---

[14] LRR 1925, r. 8.

(2) For the purposes of subsection (1), a qualifying estate is a legal estate which—

(a) relates to land to which the caution relates, and

(b) is an interest of any of the following kinds—

(i) an estate in land,

(ii) a rentcharge,

(iii) a franchise, and

(iv) a profit à prendre in gross.

(3) No caution may be lodged under subsection (1)—

(a) in the case of paragraph (a), by virtue of ownership of—

(i) a freehold estate in land, or

(ii) a leasehold estate in land granted for a term of which more than seven years are unexpired;

(b) in the case of paragraph (b), by virtue of entitlement to such a leasehold estate as is mentioned in paragraph (a)(ii) of this subsection.

(4) The right under subsection (1) is exercisable by application to the registrar.

C15.1 Subsection (1): Subject to subsection (3), a caution against first registration may be entered against the title of unregistered land on application to the registrar (subsection (4)) in accordance with such rules[15] as may be made by a person who is the owner of a qualifying estate (defined in subsection (2)) or such person who is entitled to an interest affecting such an estate. Such an interest is an adverse right affecting the title to that estate: section 132(3)(b). A person affected by lodgement may object (section 73) and the matter may be referred to the Adjudicator. The cautioner is under a duty to act reasonably, the breach of which sounds in damages: section 77.

C15.1.1 Subsection (2): See notes to section 2(a).[16]

C15.1.2 Subsection (3): A person is unable to lodge a caution in circumstances where he should cause the interest to registered; a caution is not an

---

[15] None have, as yet, been made.

[16] See para. C2.1.1, *supra*.

alternative to first registration. Transitional provisions contained in Schedule 12, paragraph 14(1) provide that subsection (3) will not come into force for two years from the day on which section 15 is brought into force. Special provisions apply in relation to cautions against first registration of demesne land.[17]

16 Effect

(1) Where an application for registration under this Part relates to a legal estate which is the subject of a caution against first registration, the registrar must give the cautioner notice of the application and of his right to object to it. **A16.1**

(2) The registrar may not determine an application to which subsection (1) applies before the end of such period as rules may provide, unless the cautioner has exercised his right to object to the application or given the registrar notice that he does not intend to do so.

(3) Except as provided by this section, a caution against first registration has no effect and, in particular, has no effect on the validity or priority of any interest of the cautioner in the legal estate to which the caution relates.

(4) For the purposes of subsection (1), notice given by a person acting on behalf of an applicant for registration under this Part is to be treated as given by the registrar if—
  (a) the person is of a description provided by rules, and
  (b) notice is given in such circumstances as rules may provide.

Subsection (1): The registrar must notify the cautioner (defined in section 22 as the person who lodged the caution or such other person as the rules[18] may provide) of the application for first registration and of his right to object to it. **C16.1**

Subsection (2): Determination of the application for first registration must not occur before the end of the period to be prescribed in the **C16.1.1**

---

[17] See paras A81.1 *et seq.*, *infra*.

[18] None have, as yet, been made.

rules unless the cautioner objects or withdraws his caution. If the cautioner objects, the Registrar must refer the matter to the Adjudicator unless he is satisfied the objection is groundless: section 73(6). If the cautioner does nothing within the prescribed period, the first registration will proceed: section 18(4).

C16.1.2 Subsection (3): A caution only has effect as stated in section 16; it does not effect the validity or priority of any interest of the cautioner.

C16.1.3 Subsection (4): Allows persons other than the registrar specified by the rules and acting for the applicant for first registration to give notice to the cautioner under subsection (1). Thus the procedure of first registration can be expedited with the cautioner being given notice directly rather than only by the registry. It is anticipated that solicitors and licensed conveyancers will have such a right.[19]

17 Withdrawal

A17.1 The cautioner may withdraw a caution against first registration by application to the registrar.

18 Cancellation

A18.1 (1) A person may apply to the registrar for cancellation of a caution against first registration if he is—

(a) the owner of the legal estate to which the caution relates, or

(b) a person of such other description as rules may provide.

(2) Subject to rules, no application under subsection (1)(a) may be made by a person who—

(a) consented in such manner as rules may provide to the lodging of the caution, or

(b) derives title to the legal estate by operation of law from a person who did so.

(3) Where an application is made under subsection (1), the registrar must give the cautioner notice of the application and of the effect of subsection (4).

(4) If the cautioner does not exercise his right to object to the application before the end of such period as

[19] Law Com No. 271, para. 87, p. 476.

rules may provide, the registrar must cancel the caution.

Subsection (1): The owner of the legal estate to which the caution relates and such others as may be permitted by the rules can apply for the cancellation of a caution unless (and subject to the rules) they consented to its lodgement or derive title from someone who did: subsection (2). It is anticipated that the category of those who may apply will include mortgagees, receivers and such others who have an interest in the estate affected and that a person who consented to the lodgement of caution may apply for its cancellation if circumstances change: for example, where it was lodged to protect an interest that has expired by effluxion of time (*e.g* an option for a limited period).[20] **C18.1**

Subsection (3): The registrar must put the cautioner on notice of the application and of the effect of subsection (4). **C18.1.1**

Subsection (4): Unless the cautioner exercises his right to object to the application within such time as is prescribed in the rules, the registrar must cancel the caution. If the cautioner does object, the provisions of section 73 apply unless the matter is disposed of by consent or the registrar is satisfied that it is groundless. **C18.1.2**

19 Cautions register

(1) The registrar must keep a register of cautions against first registration. **A19.1**

(2) Rules may make provision about how the cautions register is to be kept and may, in particular, make provision about—

(a) the information to be included in the register,
(b) the form in which information included in the register is to be kept, and
(c) the arrangement of that information.

The establishment of a separate register is a new requirement. Cautions against first registration are required to be recorded on the index that is and will continue to be maintained under section 68. **C19.1**

20 Alteration of register by court

(1) The court may make an order for alteration of the cautions register for the purpose of— **A20.1**

---

[20] Law Com No. 271, para. 89, p. 477.

(a) correcting a mistake, or
(b) bringing the register up to date.

(2) An order under subsection (1) has effect when served on the registrar to impose a duty on him to give effect to it.

(3) Rules may make provision about—

(a) the circumstances in which there is a duty to exercise the power under subsection (1),
(b) the form of an order under that subsection, and
(c) service of such an order.

C20.1 Sections 20 and 21 relate to the alteration of the cautions register established under section 19. Alteration of the register of title is provided for in Schedule 4.[21]

C20.1.1 Subsection (1): The Court may order the alteration of the register to correct a mistake or to bring the register up to date. Such an order has effect when served on the registrar: subsection (2).

C20.1.2 Subsection (3): Makes provision for rules to govern when and how the powers under the section may be exercised.

21 Alteration of register by registrar

A21.1 (1) The registrar may alter the cautions register for the purpose of—

(a) correcting a mistake, or
(b) bringing the register up to date.

(2) Rules may make provision about—

(a) the circumstances in which there is a duty to exercise the power under subsection (1),
(b) how the cautions register is to be altered in exercise of that power,
(c) applications for the exercise of that power, and
(d) procedure in relation to the exercise of that power, whether on application or otherwise.

---

[21] See paras SC4.0 *et seq.*, *infra*.

(3) Where an alteration is made under this section, the registrar may pay such amount as he thinks fit in respect of any costs reasonably incurred by a person in connection with the alteration.

Similar provision is made for where the register of cautions is altered by the registrar. **C21.1**
Subsection (4): Further, the registrar may make a payment in accordance with subsection (4).

22 Supplementary

In this Chapter, "the cautioner", in relation to a caution against first registration, means the person who lodged the caution, or such other person as rules may provide. **A22.1**

Part 3

Dispositions of Registered Land

Powers of disposition

The Act adopts four principles:—

(1) The "owner" (section 24) shall be taken to have unfettered powers of disposition subject to (2) (section 26(1)); **C23.0**

(2) If the owner's powers to dispose are, in fact, limited that fact should be recorded in the register, otherwise (1) applies (section 26(2)).

(3) Absent any entry in the register, a disponee can assume that the owner's powers of disposition are unfettered (section 26 (1)).

(4) If the owner's powers are, in fact, limited and there is no entry in the register, the disponee's title will be incapable of disturbance. The disponor, on the other hand, remains liable for any improper disposal and the disponee may be liable in certain circumstances (section 26(3)).

23 Owner's powers

(1) Owner's powers in relation to a registered estate consist of— **A23.1**

(a) power to make a disposition of any kind permitted by the general law in relation to an interest of that description, other than a mortgage by demise or sub-demise, and

(b) power to charge the estate at law with the payment of money.

(2) Owner's powers in relation to a registered charge consist of—

(a) power to make a disposition of any kind permitted by the general law in relation to an interest of that description, other than a legal submortgage, and

(b) power to charge at law with the payment of money indebtedness secured by the registered charge.

(3) In subsection (2)(a), "legal sub-mortgage" means—

(a) a transfer by way of mortgage,

(b) a sub-mortgage by sub-demise, and

(c) a charge by way of legal mortgage.

C23.1 Subsection (1): An owner (defined in section 24) of a registered estate can make any disposition in relation to that estate as is permitted by the general law and to charge the same with payment of money. To this, there is one exception. The Act prospectively abolishes mortgages by demise and sub-demise[22] and accordingly amends the Law of Property Act 1925, ss. 85 and 86 (Schedule 11). Thus, in future security taken over land will only consist of charges expressed to be by way of legal mortgage or charges to secure the payment of money (which latter charges have the same effect as the former—see section S1).

C23.1.1 Subsection (2): An owner of a registered charge can make any disposition in relation to that estate as is permitted by the general law in relation to an interest of the description which he owns together with the power stated in subsection (2)(b) to charge the charge with the payment of money indebtedness. However, the ability to do this by making a disposition by way of legal sub-mortgage (defined in subsection (3)) is precluded. In future, a legal sub-charge will only be capable of creation in accordance with subsection (2)(b). This method is not new: LRR, 1925, r. 163.

24 Right to exercise owner's powers

A24.1 A person is entitled to exercise owner's powers in relation to a registered estate or charge if he is—

---

[22] Such mortgages are practically obsolete in any event: Law Com No.271, para. 4.7, p. 65.

(a) the registered proprietor, or

(b) entitled to be registered as the proprietor.

This section prescribes who are "owners" capable of exercising the powers bestowed by the Act. **C24.1**

25 Mode of exercise

(1) A registrable disposition of a registered estate or charge only has effect if it complies with such requirements as to form and content as rules may provide. **A25.1**

(2) Rules may apply subsection (1) to any other kind of disposition which depends for its effect on registration.

The use of prescribed registry forms is not new and they will expand in number. This provision and the power to make rules relating thereto will have an increased importance on the introduction of electronic conveyancing. No rules have, as yet, been made. **C25.1**

26 Protection of disponees

(1) Subject to subsection (2), a person's right to exercise owner's powers in relation to a registered estate or charge is to be taken to be free from any limitation affecting the validity of a disposition. **A26.1**

(2) Subsection (1) does not apply to a limitation—

(a) reflected by an entry in the register, or
(b) imposed by, or under, this Act.

(3) This section has effect only for the purpose of preventing the title of a disponee being questioned (and so does not affect the lawfulness of a disposition).

Subsection (1): Unless subject to a limitation on the register or one imposed by the Act (subsection (2))[23] a person's right to exercise the owner's powers is to be taken to be free from any limitation affecting the validity of that disposition but only for the purpose of preventing **C26.1**

[23] *e.g.* sections 24(2); 25.

the title of the disponee being brought into question. In future, limitations entered in the register will have to be protected by restriction (see section 40) since cautions and inhibitions are prospectively abolished.

C26.1.1 Subsection (3): The section does not render the disposition otherwise lawful. Thus, a valid transfer under section 26 to a disponee by trustees in breach of trust will not preclude the beneficiaries pursuing their remedies against the errant trustees or, if the disponee can be fixed with the requisite knowledge, against the disponee for, by way of example, knowing receipt of trust property.

Registrable dispositions

C27.0 Section 27 is important. It specifies those dispositions which must be completed by registration; a failure to complete a disposition by registration precludes it from operating at law.[24] Once electronic conveyancing is in operation, the importance of this principle will decline—section 93 disapplies section 27, making an electronic disposition of no effect in law or equity until registered.

27 Dispositions required to be registered

A27.1 (1) If a disposition of a registered estate or registered charge is required to be completed by registration, it does not operate at law until the relevant registration requirements are met.

(2) In the case of a registered estate, the following are the dispositions which are required to be completed by registration—

(a) a transfer,

(b) where the registered estate is an estate in land, the grant of a term of years absolute—

(i) for a term of more than seven years from the date of the grant,

(ii) to take effect in possession after the end of the period of three months beginning with the date of the grant,

(iii) under which the right to possession is discontinuous,

---

[24] It is thus similar to LRA 1925, ss. 18 and 21.

(iv) in pursuance of Part 5 of the Housing Act 1985 (c. 68) (the right to buy), or
(v) in circumstances where section 171A of that Act applies (disposal by landlord which leads to a person no longer being a secure tenant),

(c) where the registered estate is a franchise or manor, the grant of a lease,
(d) the express grant or reservation of an interest of a kind falling within section 1(2)(a) of the Law of Property Act 1925 (c. 20), other than one which is capable of being registered under the Commons Registration Act 1965 (c. 64),
(e) the express grant or reservation of an interest of a kind falling within section 1(2)(b) or (e) of the Law of Property Act 1925, and
(f) the grant of a legal charge.

(3) In the case of a registered charge, the following are the dispositions which are required to be completed by registration—

(a) a transfer, and
(b) the grant of a sub-charge.

(4) Schedule 2 to this Act (which deals with the relevant registration requirements) has effect.

(5) This section applies to dispositions by operation of law as it applies to other dispositions, but with the exception of the following—

(a) a transfer on the death or bankruptcy of an individual proprietor,
(b) a transfer on the dissolution of a corporate proprietor, and
(c) the creation of a legal charge which is a local land charge.

(6) Rules may make provision about applications to the registrar for the purpose of meeting registration requirements under this section.

(7) In subsection (2)(d), the reference to express grant does not include grant as a result of the operation of section 62 of the Law of Property Act 1925 (c. 20).

C27.1 Subsection (1): This general principle will, as electronic conveyancing takes hold, cease to operate since dispositions communicated to the registrar electronically will occur and be registered simultaneously. In relation to those dispositions, this subsection is disapplied: section 93(4).

C27.1.1 Subsection (2): " 'Registered estate' means a legal estate the title to which is entered in the register other than a legal charge: section 132(1). A "legal estate" is defined in Law of Property Act 1925, s. 1[25] s. 132(1). The section applies to dispositions by operation of law except those specified in subsection (5).

Subsection (2)(a): Schedule 2, paragraph 2 requires the transferee or his successor in title to be registered as proprietor; in instances where the transfer is of part of a registered estate, the rules may make provision as to the entries that are to be made as against that estate. No rules have, as yet, been made.

Subsection (2)(b): Schedule 2 paragraph 3 requires the grantee or his successor in title to be registered as proprietor and a notice in respect of the lease entered in the register. A disposition of a lease of seven years or less that does not satisfy any of the requirements of subsection (2(b)(ii)–(v) will not require registration. PPP leases are also excluded: section 90(3).

Subsection (2)(c): Schedule 2, paragraph 4 makes like provision with regard to grants of leases of more than seven years out of a franchise or manor, as paragraph 3 does in relation to a grant within subsection (2)(b); Schedule 2 paragraph 5 requires (in relation to leases of less than seven years) only the entry of a notice in the register. Further, where a disposition occurs which consists of the creation of an interest within Law of Property Act 1925, s. (1)(2)(a), (b) or (e)[26] and Schedule 2 paragraph 4 does not apply, Schedule 2 paragraph 7 does. This paragraph requires notice in respect of the interest to be entered on the register and (if the interest benefits a registered estate) the registered proprietor of that estate to be entered in the register as proprietor.

Subsection (2)(d): LPA 1925, s. 1(2)(a) refers to "an easement, right or privilege in or over land for an interest equivalent to a fee simple absolute in possession or a term of years absolute". In practice this means easements and profits à prendre. The exclusion of interests registered under the Commons Registration Act 1965 ensures harmony with section 1(1) of that Act. Subsection (7) also ensures that a grant by operation of LPA 1925, s. 62 (general words implied in conveyances) does not trigger the operation of this sub-section. Schedule 2, paragraph 6 provides that where a disposition of or the creation of a legal rentcharge or *profit à prendre* in gross occurs for an interest equivalent

---

[25] See App. 1, *infra*.

[26] *ibid.*

to a term of seven years or more, the grantee or his successor in title must be entered in the register and a notice entered in respect of the interest created. Schedule 2, paragraph 7 can apply: see above.

Subsection (2)(e): Schedule 2, paragraph 6 applies in relation to dispositions not exceeding seven years from the date of creation. Schedule 2 paragraph 7 can apply: see above.

Subsection (2)(f): A local land charge is excluded (subsection (5(c)) and binds a disponee without registration: Schedule 3, paragraph 6. The exception to this is a local land charge which secures the payment of money; this cannot be realised until registered as a charge: section 55.

Subsection (3): Schedule 2, paragraph 10 provides the registration requirement in relation to a transfer of a registered charge and paragraph 11 in relation to a transfer of a sub-charge. **C27.1.2**

Subsection (5): The personal representatives or Public Trustee (in the case of a transfer on death), the Official Receiver or trustee in bankruptcy (in the case of a transfer on bankruptcy) or the Crown or (if applicable) the appropriate Royal Duchy (in the case of dissolution of a corporate proprietor) can apply under Schedule 4 for the register to be brought up to date and to reflect their ownership of the estate even though there is no requirement for them to do so in order to comply with section 22(1). **C27.1.3**

Subsection (6): Rules may make provision as to how applications are to be made for registration. No rules have, as yet, been made. **C27.1.4**

Effect of dispositions on priority[27]

The Act does not substantially alter the current law. It states a clear principle (section 28) which is subject to a number of important exceptions (sections 29 and 30). As the extent of electronic conveyancing advances, the register will become conclusive as to the priority of interests which are expressly created since they will, in order to be created, have to be registered simultaneously. **C28.0**

Notice

The doctrine of notice has, with some limited exceptions, no place under the Act. This state of affairs accords with the principal objective of the Act, namely to enable conveyancing inquiries to be conducted on line. The exceptions are:—

---

[27] For provisions concerning rights of pre-emption, see section 115; for equities, see section 116.

(1) on first registration, interests acquired under the Limitation Act 1980[28]

(2) Inland Revenue charges under section 31[29]

(3) certain dispositions on bankruptcy: section 86(5)[30]

(4) certain overriding interests, in relation to which the disponee's knowledge is relevant as to whether he is bound by such an interest.[31]

28 Basic rule

A28.1 (1) Except as provided by sections 29 and 30, the priority of an interest affecting a registered estate or charge is not affected by a disposition of the estate or charge.

(2) It makes no difference for the purposes of this section whether the interest or disposition is registered.

C28.1 "Interest affecting a registered estate or charge" includes references to an adverse right affecting title: section 130(3)(b). This and the following sections concerning the effect of dispositions on priority reflect but also alter the pre-existing law. This section lays down the starting point, *subject to the Act*. Regardless of whether an interest affecting a registered estate or charge is registered or not (subsection (2)), the priority of that interest is not affected by any disposition: *i.e.* priority will be determined according to the date of creation. There is no question of having to determine whether the equities are equal. Needless to say, the Act does make further provision.

29 Effect of registered dispositions: estates

A29.1 (1) If a registrable disposition of a registered estate is made for valuable consideration, completion of the disposition by registration has the effect of postponing to the interest under the disposition any interest

---

[28] See ss. 11(4)(c); 12(4)(d), *supra*.

[29] See paras A31.1 *et seq.*, *infra*.

[30] See paras A86.1 *et seq.*, *infra*.

[31] Sched. 3, para. 2(1)(c); *ibid.*, para. 3(i) in both cases if the interest was latent (*i.e.* would not have been obvious on a reasonably careful inspection), a purchaser takes free in the absence of *actual* knowledge: see paras SC3.1.1, *infra*.

affecting the estate immediately before the disposition whose priority is not protected at the time of registration.

(2) For the purposes of subsection (1), the priority of an interest is protected—

(a) in any case, if the interest—

(i) is a registered charge or the subject of a notice in the register,
(ii) falls within any of the paragraphs of Schedule 3, or
(iii) appears from the register to be excepted from the effect of registration, and

(b) in the case of a disposition of a leasehold estate, if the burden of the interest is incident to the estate.

(3) Subsection (2)(a)(ii) does not apply to an interest which has been the subject of a notice in the register at any time since the coming into force of this section.

(4) Where the grant of a leasehold estate in land out of a registered estate does not involve a registrable disposition, this section has effect as if—

(a) the grant involved such a disposition, and
(b) the disposition were registered at the time of the grant.

Subsection (1): Where a "registrable disposition" occurs (*i.e.*, one that requires registration under section 27: section 132(1)) for "valuable consideration",[32] completion by registration of that disposition gives the disposition priority over and postpones to that disposition any interest affecting the estate immediately before the disposition which was not protected at the time of that registration. Thus interests created by a disponee after transfer to him but before registration will not be defeated by this provision since they will not have affected the estate immediately before the disposition. The section however has an impact on unpaid vendor's liens. Such a lien arises on exchange of contracts and thus the purchaser will take free of it when the registrable **C29.1**

[32] Excludes marriage or a nominal consideration in money: section 132(1).

disposition occurs unless it is protected on the register by the vendor by notice against his own title prior to the transfer.

C29.1.1 Subsection (2): Protection is conferred on an interest which satisfies the requirements under this subsection. In summary, they are (i) a registered charge or by entry of a notice of the register; (ii) overriding interests (Schedule 3) which have not, at any time, been protected on the register following the bringing into force of this section (subsection (3)); (iii) interests which appear to be excepted from the effect of registration: see sections 11(6), (7); 12(6), (7) and (8). Subsection (2)(b) protects such burdens which are incidental to a leasehold estate such as covenants, which cannot be protected by notice in any event: section 33(c).

C29.1.2 Subsection (4): This applies the priority rule contained in subsection (1) to leases of seven years or less and replicates the pre-existing law.

30 Effect of registered dispositions: charges

A30.1 (1) If a registrable disposition of a registered charge is made for valuable consideration, completion of the disposition by registration has the effect of postponing to the interest under the disposition any interest affecting the charge immediately before the disposition whose priority is not protected at the time of registration.

(2) For the purposes of subsection (1), the priority of an interest is protected—

(a) in any case, if the interest—

(i) is a registered charge or the subject of a notice in the register,

(ii) falls within any of the paragraphs of Schedule 3, or

(iii) appears from the register to be excepted from the effect of registration, and

(b) in the case of a disposition of a charge which relates to a leasehold estate, if the burden of the interest is incident to the estate.

(3) Subsection (2)(a)(ii) does not apply to an interest which has been the subject of a notice in the register at any time since the coming into force of this section.

This section makes like provision in relation to registrable dispositions of registered charges as section 29 makes in relation to such dispositions of registered estates. **C30.1**

31 Inland revenue charges

The effect of a disposition of a registered estate or charge on a charge under section 237 of the Inheritance Tax Act 1984 (c. 51) (charge for unpaid tax) is to be determined, not in accordance with sections 28 to 30 above, but in accordance with sections 237(6) and 238 of that Act (under which a purchaser in good faith for money or money's worth takes free from the charge in the absence of registration). **A31.1**

Under the Inheritance Tax Act 1984 ("IHTA") a charge is imposed on specified property in respect of unpaid tax on the value transferred by a chargeable transfer. A disposition of that property takes subject to that charge (IHTA, 237(6)) except where the disposal is registered land and the charge is not protected in the register *and* the purchaser is in good faith for consideration other than nominal consideration in money or money's worth (IHTA, s. 272). This section preserves the Inland Revenue's priority in relation to such charges in accordance with that Act by disapplying the provisions of sections 28–30. **C31.1**

Part 4

Notices and Restrictions

This part of the Act concerns the protection of what were termed "minor interests" under the Land Registration Act 1925. **C32.0**

Cautions against dealings and inhibitions are prospectively abolished. Certain transitional arrangements relating to existing entries of this nature are made by Schedule 12. Their roles are taken by the restrictions and notices which may be entered under the Act.

A *notice* protects an interest in registered land where it is intended to bind any person who acquires the land (*e.g.* a restrictive covenant or the burden of an easement).

A *restriction* regulates the circumstances in which a disposition may be the subject of an entry in the register: see section 40 (2).

In relation to both notices and restrictions unilaterally imposed, the Act provides a mechanism by which they may be challenged. The duty to act reasonably imposed by section 77 applies.

Pending land actions, writs, orders and deeds of arrangement[33-35] have been protected historically by the entry of a caution against dealings in the register. The abolition of such cautions requires a different scheme: see section 87. In outline, the new scheme requires deeds of arrangement or orders appointing a receiver or sequestrator to be protected by the entry of a restriction.[36] A pending land action or a writ or order affecting land will be capable of protection by the entry of a restriction or a notice as appropriate. None of these matters can amount to an overriding interest.[36a]

Notices

32 Nature and effect

A32.1 (1) A notice is an entry in the register in respect of the burden of an interest affecting a registered estate or charge.

(2) The entry of a notice is to be made in relation to the registered estate or charge affected by the interest concerned.

(3) The fact that an interest is the subject of a notice does not necessarily mean that the interest is valid, but does mean that the priority of the interest, if valid, is protected for the purposes of sections 29 and 30.

C32.1 This section provides for the nature and effect of a notice entered in the register.

Subsection (3): The entry of a notice does not affect the validity or otherwise of the matter which it is designed to protect. It is simply the statutory device by which the Act enables that matter to be recorded in the register and thus obtain protection under sections 29 and 30.

33 Excluded interests

A33.1 No notice may be entered in the register in respect of any of the following—

(a) an interest under—

[33-35] See Land Charges Act 1972, ss. 5(1)(a), 6(1)(a)(b).

[36] See s. 87(2).

[36a] See s. 87(3).

(i) a trust of land, or
(ii) a settlement under the Settled Land Act 1925 (c. 18),

(b) a leasehold estate in land which—

(i) is granted for a term of years of three years or less from the date of the grant, and
(ii) is not required to be registered,

(c) a restrictive covenant made between a lessor and lessee, so far as relating to the demised premises,

(d) an interest which is capable of being registered under the Commons Registration Act 1965 (c. 64), and

(e) an interest in any coal or coal mine, the rights attached to any such interest and the rights of any person under section 38, 49 or 51 of the Coal Industry Act 1994 (c. 21).

When read in conjunction with section 32, the Act defines the scope of those interests which cannot be protected by notice negatively by prescribing that one cannot be entered in relation to the matters listed in this section. **C33.1**

Paragraph (a): None of the interests under a trust of land or a strict settlement should concern the purchaser, whose only interest is to ensure that they are overreached. Accordingly, the appropriate entry is a restriction on the register to ensure that any rights are overreached by requiring a transfer to be executed by the requisite trustees. **C33.1.1**

Paragraph (b): The period of three years was chosen since it is anticipated that once electronic conveyancing is in place, the seven year threshold for registration will be reduced.[37] A leasehold interest of three years or less of someone in actual occupation could amount to an overriding interest in any event: Schedule 3, paragraph 2. **C33.1.2**

Paragraph (c): Such covenants are normally apparent from the lease and, in any event in cases where they are incident to the estate, such covenants are protected: section 29(2). The limitation is confined to those "relating to the demised premises" and thus will not affect, for example, covenants between lessor and lessee relating to other property owned by the lessor. **C33.1.3**

---

[37] Law Com No. 271, para. 6.11, p. 96.

C33.1.4 Paragraph (d): These interests are overriding interests in relation to first registration (Schedule 1, paragraph 7) and on any disposition thereafter (Schedule 3, paragraph 7).

C33.1.5 Paragraph (e): Since mapping and locating such rights is impossible, they are excluded from being capable of protection by a notice in the register. This reasoning also applies in relation to PPP leases, see section 90(4).

34 Entry on application

A34.1 (1) A person who claims to be entitled to the benefit of an interest affecting a registered estate or charge may, if the interest is not excluded by section 33, apply to the registrar for the entry in the register of a notice in respect of the interest.

(2) Subject to rules, an application under this section may be for—

(a) an agreed notice, or
(b) a unilateral notice.

(3) The registrar may only approve an application for an agreed notice if—

(a) the applicant is the relevant registered proprietor, or a person entitled to be registered as such proprietor,
(b) the relevant registered proprietor, or a person entitled to be registered as such proprietor, consents to the entry of the notice, or
(c) the registrar is satisfied as to the validity of the applicant's claim.

(4) In subsection (3), references to the relevant registered proprietor are to the proprietor of the registered estate or charge affected by the interest to which the application relates.

C34.1 Subsection (1), (2): An application may be made for the entry of an agreed notice or a unilateral notice. An agreed notice can only be entered in the circumstances set out in subsection (3). In relation to a unilateral notice, sections 35 and 36 apply.

C34.1.1 Subsection (3): Clearly if the registrar is satisfied as to the validity of a claim, he can enter a notice. Further, it is anticipated that the rules will enable the register to enter agreed notices in relation to the matters which, under the Land Registration Act 1925 can be entered in the register without the proprietor's consent (notices under the Family Law Act 1996 or orders under the Landlord and Tenant Act 1987 or Access to Neighbouring Land Act 1992).[38] No rules have, as yet, been made.

35 Unilateral notices

(1) If the registrar enters a notice in the register in pursuance of an application under section 34(2)(b) ("a unilateral notice"), he must give notice of the entry to— **A35.1**

(a) the proprietor of the registered estate or charge to which it relates, and
(b) such other persons as rules may provide.

(2) A unilateral notice must—

(a) indicate that it is such a notice, and
(b) identify who is the beneficiary of the notice.

(3) The person shown in the register as the beneficiary of a unilateral notice, or such other person as rules may provide, may apply to the registrar for the removal of the notice from the register.

Subsection (1): When entered, the registrar must give notice thereof to the proprietor and those affected, *e.g.* the liquidator of the registered proprietor.[39] The duty to act reasonably imposed by section 77 applies, breach of which sounds in damages. **C35.1**

Subsection (3): The beneficiary (or such other persons who may be prescribed by the rules) can apply for the removal of the notice. **C35.1.1**

36 Cancellation of unilateral notices

(1) A person may apply to the registrar for the cancellation of a unilateral notice if he is— **A36.1**

(a) the registered proprietor of the estate or charge to which the notice relates, or
(b) a person entitled to be registered as the proprietor of that estate or charge.

---

[38] *ibid.*, paras 175–177, p. 491.
[39] *ibid.*, para. 179, p. 491.

(2) Where an application is made under subsection (1), the registrar must give the beneficiary of the notice of the application and of the effect of subsection (3).

(3) If the beneficiary of the notice does not exercise his right to object to the application before the end of such period as rules may provide, the registrar must cancel the notice.

(4) In this section—

"beneficiary', in relation to a unilateral notice, means the person shown in the register as the beneficiary of the notice, or such other person as rules may provide;

"unilateral notice" means a notice entered in the register in pursuance of an application under section 34(2)(b).

C36.1 Subsection (1), (2): Provides who may apply to cancel a unilateral notice (defined in subsection (4)) and the registrar's duty on receipt of such an application.

C36.1.1 Subsection (3): Inactivity by the beneficiary (defined in subsection (4)) of the notice will result in its cancellation. Otherwise he can object pursuant to section 73 and, absent consensual disposal, the matter must be referred to the Adjudicator.

37 Unregistered interests

A37.1 (1) If it appears to the registrar that a registered estate is subject to an unregistered interest which—

(a) falls within any of the paragraphs of Schedule 1, and
(b) is not excluded by section 33,

he may enter a notice in the register in respect of the interest.

(2) The registrar must give notice of an entry under this section to such persons as rules may provide.

C37.1 The registrar retains a right to enter a notice in relation to matters which would, on first registration, constitute overriding interests unless precluded by section 33 from entering a notice. Such a discretion is consistent with the policy of the Act and reflects and broadens the discretion under Land Registration Act 1925, s. 70(3). No rules have, as yet, been made.

38 Registrable dispositions

Where a person is entered in the register as the proprietor of an interest under a disposition falling within section 27(2)(b) to (e), the registrar must also enter a notice in the register in respect of that interest. **A38.1**

This section imposes a statutory duty on the registrar to enter a notice against the registered estate burdened by the disposition falling with section 27(2)(b)–(e). **C38.1**

39 Supplementary

Rules may make provision about the form and content of notices in the register. **A39.1**

No rules have, as yet, been made. Standard forms should be anticipated. **C39.1**

Restrictions

40 Nature

(1) A restriction is an entry in the register regulating the circumstances in which a disposition of a registered estate or charge may be the subject of an entry in the register. **A40.1**

(2) A restriction may, in particular—

(a) prohibit the making of an entry in respect of any disposition, or a disposition of a kind specified in the restriction;

(b) prohibit the making of an entry—

(i) indefinitely,

(ii) for a period specified in the restriction, or

(iii) until the occurrence of an event so specified.

(3) Without prejudice to the generality of subsection (2)(b)(iii), the events which may be specified include—

(a) the giving of notice,
(b) the obtaining of consent, and
(c) the making of an order by the court or registrar.

(4) The entry of a restriction is to be made in relation to the registered estate or charge to which it relates.

C40.1 Subsection (1): A restriction regulates the disposition of a registered estate and is entered in the register in relation to the registered estate or charge to which it relates (subsection (4)). A restriction cannot therefore be entered in relation to unregistered estates and thus cannot affect the creation or disposition of unregistered estates.

C40.1.1 Subsection (2): The matters a restriction may prohibit are contained in subsections (2) and (3).

Subsection (2)(a): A blanket restriction envisaged in this subsection would be appropriate in support of a freezing injunction. A restriction of a specified kind would be appropriate where certain transactions were outside the powers of the registered proprietor.

Subsection (2)(b): An indefinite prohibition by restriction would be appropriate where the registered proprietor had no powers to enter into a transaction. A prohibition for a specified period may arise where the registered proprietor could not dispose of an interest prior to a certain date. A restriction until the occurrence of a specified event may be necessary in order to require any of the steps specified in subsection (3) to be taken or performed.

41 Effect

A41.1 (1) Where a restriction is entered in the register, no entry in respect of a disposition to which the restriction applies may be made in the register otherwise than in accordance with the terms of the restriction, subject to any order under subsection (2).

(2) The registrar may by order—

(a) disapply a restriction in relation to a disposition specified in the order or dispositions of a kind so specified, or
(b) provide that a restriction has effect, in relation to a disposition specified in the order or dispositions of a kind so specified, with modifications so specified.

(3) The power under subsection (2) is exercisable only on the application of a person who appears to the

registrar to have a sufficient interest in the restriction.

Subsection (1): A restriction thus precludes an entry in the register which would be contrary to the terms of the restriction. This rule can be disapplied by an order under subsection (2). **C41.1**

Subsections (2), (3): The registrar can disapply the provisions of a restriction in whole (subsection (2)(a)) or in part (subsection (2)(b)) upon the application of a person with sufficient interest in the restriction. The registrar's power extends to specific restrictions and those of a generic type. It is envisaged that the registrar may exercise these powers in circumstances where, for example, a named individual whose consent to a disposition is required has disappeared.[40] **C41.1.1**

42 Power of registrar to enter

(1) The registrar may enter a restriction in the register if it appears to him that it is necessary or desirable to do so for the purpose of— **A42.1**

(a) preventing invalidity or unlawfulness in relation to dispositions of a registered estate or charge,

(b) securing that interests which are capable of being overreached on a disposition of a registered estate or charge are overreached, or

(c) protecting a right or claim in relation to a registered estate or charge.

(2) No restriction may be entered under subsection (1)(c) for the purpose of protecting the priority of an interest which is, or could be, the subject of a notice.

(3) The registrar must give notice of any entry made under this section to the proprietor of the registered estate or charge concerned, except where the entry is made in pursuance of an application under section 43.

(4) For the purposes of subsection (1)(c), a person entitled to the benefit of a charging order relating

---

[40] *ibid.*, para. 195, p. 494.

to an interest under a trust shall be treated as having a right or claim in relation to the trust property.

C42.1 Subsection (1): The registrar *may* enter a restriction if it is necessary or desirable for any of the purposes set out in paragraphs (a), (b) or (c).

Subsection (1)(a): A restriction would prevent "invalidity" in circumstances where a registered proprietor has limited powers of disposition which, if the restriction were not entered, would otherwise appear to be unfettered under the provisions of sections 26 or 52[41]; "unlawfulness" would clearly extend to dispositions that would otherwise be in breach of contract (*e.g.* of sale or a pre-emption right) or breach of trust.

Subsection (1)(b): Interests under a trust of land or under a settlement are only overreached if the proceeds of sale are paid to two trustees or a trust corporation. By entering a restriction, for example, requiring payment of capital monies in circumstances where the interests of the beneficiaries will be overreached, the disponee and the beneficiaries are protected. If two or more persons are registered as proprietors of a registered estate, such a restriction must be entered in accordance with section 44.

Subsection (1)(c): Such a right or claim may arise under a resulting or constructive trust by reason of a contribution by a person who is not the registered proprietor to the costs of acquisition of the registered estate. See also subsection (4).

C42.1.1 Subsection (2): This limits the registrar's power to enter a restriction. A restriction cannot be utilised for *protecting the priority* of an interest which is (or could be) protected by the entry of a notice. As with cautions under the Land Registration Act 1925, a restriction does not confer priority; it merely provides a means of determining how a registered estate may be dealt with. Subsection (2) only precludes the entry of a restriction in order to protect priority; it does not preclude the entry of a restriction and a notice in relation to the same matter. Thus where a notice is required to protect priority and a restriction is necessary to govern the disposition of the registered estate, both can be entered: *e.g.* where a right of pre-emption has been granted. Both the priority of that right and the manner of its exercise require protection and both a notice and a restriction would thus be appropriate.

C42.1.2 Subsection (4): Under section 2 of the Charging Orders Act 1979, the beneficial interest of a debtor under any trust can be the subject of a charging order. Subsection (4) declares such an order to be "a right or claim" in relation to the trust property and thus capable or protection by a restriction under subsection (1)(c).

---

[41] *ibid.*, para. 197, p. 494.

43 Applications

(1) A person may apply to the registrar for the entry of a restriction under section 42(1) if— **A43.1**

- (a) he is the relevant registered proprietor, or a person entitled to be registered as such proprietor,
- (b) the relevant registered proprietor, or a person entitled to be registered as such proprietor, consents to the application, or
- (c) he otherwise has a sufficient interest in the making of the entry.

(2) Rules may—

- (a) require the making of an application under subsection (1) in such circumstances, and by such person, as the rules may provide;
- (b) make provision about the form of consent for the purposes of subsection (1)(b);
- (c) provide for classes of person to be regarded as included in subsection (1)(c);
- (d) specify standard forms of restriction.

(3) If an application under subsection (1) is made for the entry of a restriction which is not in a form specified under subsection (2)(d), the registrar may only approve the application if it appears to him—

- (a) that the terms of the proposed restriction are reasonable, and
- (b) that applying the proposed restriction would—
  - (i) be straightforward, and
  - (ii) not place an unreasonable burden on him.

(4) In subsection (1), references to the relevant registered proprietor are to the proprietor of the registered estate or charge to which the application relates.

Subsection (1): Clearly states the categories of persons entitled to apply for the entry of a restriction. "Relevant registered proprietor" is defined in subsection (4). **C43.1**

C43.1.1 Subsection (2): Makes provision for rules to regulate how a person entitled to apply for the entry of restriction may do so and (in the case of subsection (1)(c)) permits the rules to specify the classes of persons who shall be regarded as having "sufficient interest" in the making of the entry. No rules have, as yet, been made.

Subsection (2)(a): The provision to require the entry of a restriction reflects the practice under, for example, the Land Registration Rules 1925, rr. 59A and 106A(1) (where trustees of land have limited powers) and r. 124(1) (where a corporation becomes a no-exempt charity).

Subsection (2)(c): Permits the rules to specify those individuals which are to be regarded as *included* in subsection (1)(c) and thus any rules made will not limit the scope of that subsection. It is suggested that the rules may cover beneficiaries under a trust of land; the donee of a special power of appointment in relation to registered land; where the land is held on charitable trust, the Charity Commission; where land is administered by the Church Commissioners, the Church Commission or a receiver, administrative receiver, administrator or sequestrator appointed in relation to a registered estate.[42]

C43.1.2 Subsection (3): Subsection (2)(d) permits the prescription of standard forms of restriction. Subsection (3) permits the entry of a non-standard restriction if subsection (3)(a) and (b) are satisfied. One should anticipate that standard form restrictions will quickly emerge and be encouraged.

44 Obligatory restrictions

A44.1 (1) If the registrar enters two or more persons in the register as the proprietor of a registered estate in land, he must also enter in the register such restrictions as rules may provide for the purpose of securing that interests which are capable of being overreached on a disposition of the estate are overreached.

(2) Where under any enactment the registrar is required to enter a restriction without application, the form of the restriction shall be such as rules may provide.

C44.1 Subsection (1): This section *requires* the entry of a restriction in all cases where two or more persons are registered as proprietors. No form of restriction has been prescribed but one should be anticipated.

---

[42] *ibid.*, para. 205, p. 496.

Subsection (2): For example, section 86(4) (replacing bankruptcy inhibitions). Also Housing Act 1988, ss.81(1), 133(9); Local Government and Housing Act 1989, s.37(8); Charities Act 1993 ss.37(8), 39 (1B) (each as amended by Schedule 11).

45 Notifiable applications

(1) Where an application under section 43(1) is notifiable, the registrar must give notice of the application, and of the right to object to it, to— **A45.1**

(a) the proprietor of the registered estate or charge to which it relates, and
(b) such other persons as rules may provide.

(2) The registrar may not determine an application to which subsection (1) applies before the end of such period as rules may provide, unless the person, or each of the persons, notified under that subsection has exercised his right to object to the application or given the registrar notice that he does not intend to do so.

(3) For the purposes of this section, an application under section 43(1) is notifiable unless it is—

(a) made by or with the consent of the proprietor of the registered estate or charge to which the application relates, or a person entitled to be registered as such proprietor,
(b) made in pursuance of rules under section 43(2)(a), or
(c) an application for the entry of a restriction reflecting a limitation under an order of the court or registrar, or an undertaking given in place of such an order.

This section protects the registered proprietor from the unjustified entry of a restriction against the registered estate. **C45.1**

Subsection (1): Unless the application is by consent of the persons stated in subsection 3(a) or mandatory (subsection 3(b)) or reflects an order of the Court or registrar or an undertaking given in lieu of such an order (subsection 3(c)), the registrar must give notice of the application and the right to object to it to the registered proprietor and such other persons as the rules may provide. No rules have, as yet, been made but it is anticipated that registered chargees and other persons **C45.1.1** who have a direct interest in any disposition of the property will be included.[43] The provisions regarding objections are contained in sections 73 and 108.

C45.1.2 Subsection (2): No application can be determined until the procedure concerning any objections has been completed or the registered proprietor has indicated his consent.

46 Power of court to order entry

A46.1 (1) If it appears to the court that it is necessary or desirable to do so for the purpose of protecting a right or claim in relation to a registered estate or charge, it may make an order requiring the registrar to enter a restriction in the register.

(2) No order under this section may be made for the purpose of protecting the priority of an interest which is, or could be, the subject of a notice.

(3) The court may include in an order under this section a direction that an entry made in pursuance of the order is to have overriding priority.

(4) If an order under this section includes a direction under subsection (3), the registrar must make such entry in the register as rules may provide.

(5) The court may make the exercise of its power under subsection (3) subject to such terms and conditions as it thinks fit.

C46.1 Subsection (1): The Court may, subject to subsection (2), order the entry of a restriction in the register in order to protect a right or claim in relation to a registered estate or charge. It is envisaged that such an order may be made in circumstances where the Court would currently order an inhibition.[44] Thus, for example, such an order may be given in support of a freezing injunction or as a part of the relief granted in a claim for a declaration as to the beneficial ownership of land where that land is registered in the sole name of another individual.

C46.1.1 Subsection (2): See section 42(2) above and the notes thereto.

C46.1.2 Subsections (3), (4) and (5): These subsections allow the Court to confer overriding priority on an entry in the register pursuant to its

---

[43] *ibid.*, para. 209, p. 497.

[44] *ibid.*, para. 6.51, p. 113. *Ruoff & Roper*, para. 37–01 *et seq.*

order. Thus the Court may give priority over entries made during the priority period bestowed by section 72 if it thinks fit and its order in this regard should be clear. It may also impose terms and conditions not only as to the provisions of the restriction but generally. It is envisaged that these may include such matters as requiring the indemnification of a bona fide purchaser who has suffered loss as a result of the order or the payment of money into court or costs etc.[45]

47 Withdrawal

A person may apply to the registrar for the withdrawal of a restriction if— **A47.1**

(a) the restriction was entered in such circumstances as rules may provide, and

(b) he is of such a description as rules may provide.

Provision is thus made for the withdrawal of a restriction. No rules have, as yet, been made. **C47.1**

PART 5

CHARGES

The Act provides for charges over land. It prospectively abolishes the ability to create mortgages by way of demise or sub-demise and amends the law in relation to tacking and further advances. It makes provision for the priority of charges (section 48). **C48.0**

After the Act is brought into force, a legal mortgage will only be capable of creation by a charge expressed to be by way of legal mortgage or by a charge to secure the payment of money. Their effect will be the same (section 51).

"Charge" is broadly defined in section 132 (1).

The Act makes provision for the protection of disponees: 132(2) (section 52)).

Equitable charges remain capable of creation as permitted by the general law.[46]

Relative priority

48 Registered charges

(1) Registered charges on the same registered estate, or on the same registered charge, are to be taken to rank as between themselves in the order shown in the register. **A48.1**

---

[45] *ibid.*, para. 218, p. 498.

[46] See *Cousins on the Law of Mortgages* (2nd ed., 2001), paras 2, 5–01 *et seq.*

(2) Rules may make provision about—

(a) how the priority of registered charges as between themselves is to be shown in the register, and

(b) applications for registration of the priority of registered charges as between themselves.

C48.1 "Charge" and "registered charge" defined section 132 (1).

Subsection (1): Priority is thus recorded as between registered charges on the same registered estate or charge in the order shown on the register. The provisions concerning the priority of a registered charge in relation to prior charges are set out in sections 29 and 30.

Subsection (2): The mechanics of how priority is shown on the register and how applications are to be made is left to the rules. None have, as yet, been made.

49 Tacking and further advances

A49.1 (1) The proprietor of a registered charge may make a further advance on the security of the charge ranking in priority to a subsequent charge if he has not received from the subsequent chargee notice of the creation of the subsequent charge.

(2) Notice given for the purposes of subsection (1) shall be treated as received at the time when, in accordance with rules, it ought to have been received.

(3) The proprietor of a registered charge may also make a further advance on the security of the charge ranking in priority to a subsequent charge if—

(a) the advance is made in pursuance of an obligation, and

(b) at the time of the creation of the subsequent charge the obligation was entered in the register in accordance with rules.

(4) The proprietor of a registered charge may also make a further advance on the security of the charge ranking in priority to a subsequent charge if—

(a) the parties to the prior charge have agreed a maximum amount for which the charge is security, and

(b) at the time of the creation of the subsequent charge the agreement was entered in the register in accordance with rules.

(5) Rules may—

(a) disapply subsection (4) in relation to charges of a description specified in the rules, or

(b) provide for the application of that subsection to be subject, in the case of charges of a description so specified, to compliance with such conditions as may be so specified.

(6) Except as provided by this section, tacking in relation to a charge over registered land is only possible with the agreement of the subsequent chargee.

This section sets out the only four methods by which a chargee can advance further sums on an existing charge and obtain priority for those additional sums by relying on the security of that existing charge over any later charges. **C49.1**

Subsection (1): First, a further advance will obtain priority if the chargee has no notice of any subsequent charge. Provision is made for the rules to prescribe the form and content of any notice and the manner of service (see Schedule 10, paragraph 5). None have, as yet, been made. **C49.1.1**

Subsection (2): Whatever the rules prescribe, notice is deemed to have been given when, in accordance with the rules, it ought to have been received. This mechanism will allow subsequent chargees to serve notice and reflects the current practice of lenders who would rather rely on their common law rights than the procedure laid down in the Land Registration Act 1925. The new provision will divest the registrar of responsibility to serve notice of a subsequent charge on the prior chargee as is currently required under Land Registration Act, 1925, s. 30(1), and end a system which is not used because of the inherent disadvantage that if any advances are made by the prior chargee during any delay at the registry in giving notice, those advances acquire priority. **C49.1.2**

Subsection (3): Secondly, advances made in accordance with a pre-existing obligation which is entered in the register in accordance with the rules at the time of the creation of the subsequent charge will acquire priority. **C49.1.3**

Subsection (4): Thirdly, the parties can agree a "maximum amount for which the charge is security" and, if that sum is entered in the register **C49.1.4** in accordance with the rules at the time of the creation of the subsequent charge, subsequent advances will acquire priority over the later charge provided the maximum sum is not exceeded. The "maximum amount" must include principal, interest and costs for which the charge is security.[47] Subsection (5) provides for the rules which may limit the availability of such "maximum amount charges" or subject them to certain specified conditions. This method is new. No rules have, as yet, been made.

C49.1.5 Subsection (6): Fourthly, advances made by a prior chargee with the consent of later chargees can, by consent, acquire priority.

50 Overriding statutory charges: duty of notification

A50.1 If the registrar enters a person in the register as the proprietor of a charge which—

(a) is created by or under an enactment, and

(b) has effect to postpone a charge which at the time of registration of the statutory charge is—

(i) entered in the register, or
(ii) the basis for an entry in the register,

he must in accordance with rules give notice of the creation of the statutory charge to such person as rules may provide.

C50.1 This section provides for notice to be given by the registrar to a registered chargee of the creation of a subsequent statutory charge where that statutory charge has the effect of postponing the earlier registered charge. Examples of statutory charges are those imposed by a street works authority for expenses incurred or a local authority for the expenses of repairing and improving houses.[48] Local land charges are considered in section 55.

---

[47] Law Com No. 271, para. 7.34, p. 131. This may ensure that amongst primary lenders this option is not popular although continental lenders do use this method.

[48] See *Ruoff & Roper*, 23–33 *et seq*. No rules have, as yet been made. Doubt has been expressed over whether such charges are compatible with Article 1 of the First Protocol to the European Convention on Human Rights: Law Com No. 271, para. 7.41, p. 134. The current rules deal with the priority of such charges on an *ad hoc* basis. It is envisaged this approach will continue pending judicial determination of the point: *ibid*.

Powers as chargee

51 Effect of completion by registration

On completion of the relevant registration requirements, a charge created by means of a registrable disposition of a registered estate has effect, if it would not otherwise do so, as a charge by deed by way of legal mortgage. **A51.1**

Section 23(1) preserves the registered proprietor's power to make any disposition permitted by the general law other than a mortgage by demise or sub-demise and also permits him to "charge the estate at law with the payment of money": see section 23(1)(b)". Section 51 causes any charge created by means of a registrable disposition to have the effect (if it would not otherwise do so) on completion of the relevant registration requirements as a charge by way of legal mortgage and thus bestows on the chargee all the rights and remedies that such a charge enjoys.[49] Thus a charge under section 23(1)(b) is equivalent to a charge by way of legal mortgage. **C51.1**

52 Protection of disponees

(1) Subject to any entry in the register to the contrary, the proprietor of a registered charge is to be taken to have, in relation to the property subject to the charge, the powers of disposition conferred by law on the owner of a legal mortgage. **A52.1**

(2) Subsection (1) has effect only for the purpose of preventing the title of a disponee being questioned (and so does not affect the lawfulness of a disposition).

This section extends, in the case of registered land, the protection afforded to purchasers by Law of Property Act 1925, s. 104(2) and (3). **C52.1**

Subsection (1): This section makes similar provision to that contained in section 26 in relation to dispositions of registered land. Unless stated to the contrary in the register, a proprietor of a registered charge is taken to have all the powers conferred on the owner of a legal mortgage.[50] **C52.1.1**

---

[49] As to which, see *Ruoff & Roper*, paras 23–42; 24–01; 24–11 *et seq.*

[50] *ibid.*

C52.1.2 Subsection (2): The section does not protect the disponor in instances where the disposition is without authority. Thus, where a power of sale is purportedly exercised in circumstances where it has not arisen, the chargor's remedies are preserved even though (assuming there is no entry in the register to the contrary) the transfer to the disponee is unimpeachable.

53 Powers as sub-chargee

A53.1 The registered proprietor of a sub-charge has, in relation to the property subject to the principal charge or any intermediate charge, the same powers as the sub-chargor.

C53.1 This section extends the current scope of Land Registration Rules 1925, r. 163(2) by granting to the registered proprietor of a sub-charge the same powers as the sub-chargor in circumstances where the property is subject to a principal or intermediate charge.[51]

Realisation of security

54 Proceeds of sale: chargee's duty

A54.1 For the purposes of section 105 of the Law of Property Act 1925 (c. 20) (mortgagee's duties in relation to application of proceeds of sale), in its application to the proceeds of sale of registered land, a person shall be taken to have notice of anything in the register immediately before the disposition on sale.

C54.1 Law of Property Act 1925, s. 105 provides that money which is received on a sale by the mortgagee is held (after the discharge of any prior encumbrances to which the sale is not made subject or the payment into court of an equivalent sum) by the mortgagee on trust to be applied first, in payment of all costs charges and expenses properly incurred by him as incident to the sale or any attempted sale or otherwise; secondly, in discharge of the mortgage money, interest and costs and other money (if any) due under the mortgage; and thirdly, the residue is to be paid to the person entitled to the mortgage property or authorised to give a receipt for the proceeds of sale of that property. The "person entitled to the mortgage property" means, in cases where there is a subsequent charge, the later chargee and so the mortgagee selling must hold the proceeds on trust for those chargees of which, if the land is unregistered, he has actual, constructive or imputed notice.

---

[51] *ibid.*, para. 24–10.

Whereas registration in the Land Charges Register amounts to actual notice[52] registration in the register does not. Section 54, by imposing on the mortgagee when discharging his duty "notice of anything in the register immediately before the disposition on sale", creates an obligation on him to search the register when discharging his duty under Law of Property Act, s. 105.

55 Local land charges

A charge over registered land which is a local land charge may only be realised if the title to the charge is registered. **A55.1**

This section reflects the law under Land Registration Act 1925.[53] An inability to enforce a charge governed by this section does not preclude it from binding any disponee by reason of its status as an overriding interest: Schedule 3, paragraph 6. **C55.1**

Miscellaneous

56 Receipt in case of joint proprietors

Where a charge is registered in the name of two or more proprietors, a valid receipt for the money secured by the charge may be given by— **A56.1**

(a) the registered proprietors,

(b) the survivors or survivor of the registered proprietors, or

(c) the personal representative of the last survivor of the registered proprietors.

This section reflects the provisions of the Land Registration Act 1925, section 32.[54] **C56.1**

57 Entry of right of consolidation

Rules may make provision about entry in the register of a right of consolidation in relation to a registered charge. **A57.1**

No rules have, as yet, been made. Consolidation is the right of a mortgagee, absent provision to the contrary,[55] to prevent the redemption of one mortgage unless another or others are redeemed simultaneously.[56] **C57.1**

---

[52] LPA 1925, s. 198.

[53] See *Ruoff & Roper*, para. 7–08.

[54] *ibid.*, para. 23–29.

[55] LPA, 1925, s. 93(1).

[56] See *Ruoff & Roper*, para. 23–41.

PART 6

REGISTRATION: GENERAL

Registration as proprietor

58 Conclusiveness

A58.1 (1) If, on the entry of a person in the register as the proprietor of a legal estate, the legal estate would not otherwise be vested in him, it shall be deemed to be vested in him as a result of the registration.

(2) Subsection (1) does not apply where the entry is made in pursuance of a registrable disposition in relation to which some other registration requirement remains to be met.

"Register" and "legal estate" defined s. 132(1).

C58.1 Subsection (1): This preserves the fundamental principle of registration that the person in whose name the estate is registered is deemed to be the legal proprietor. It reflects the position under the Land Registration Act 1925.[57] Thus a forged transfer which results in the registration of the transferee will not preclude the transferee from dealing with the registered estate, albeit that rectification may lie.[58]

C58.1.1 Subsection (2): This creates an exception to the principle in subsection (1). Thus where there is a registrable disposition and some further requirement remains to be met (see section 27 and Schedule 2), the legal estate is not vested in the registered proprietor.[59]

---

[57] As to which and the historical development of this position, see *Ruoff & Roper*, para. 2–07.

[58] *ibid.*, para. 2–18.

[59] An example would be where X applies to be registered as the grantee of a term of years. The lease is registered under its own title but the registrar fails to enter notice of the lease on the superior freehold title. In those circumstances, subsection (2) will preclude the operation of section 58(1) and the legal estate will not vest in X, although X will obtain an equitable estate. X's remedy is to apply for the mistake to be corrected under para. 5(a) of Sched. 4: Law Com No. 271, para. 255, p. 503.

59 Dependent estates

(1) The entry of a person in the register as the proprietor of a legal estate which subsists for the benefit of a registered estate must be made in relation to the registered estate. **A59.1**

(2) The entry of a person in the register as the proprietor of a charge on a registered estate must be made in relation to that estate.

(3) The entry of a person in the register as the proprietor of a sub-charge on a registered charge must be made in relation to that charge.

"Legal estate"; "Charge" and "Sub-charge" defined section 132(1). Without this section requiring the registration of the estates in the manner prescribed, the register and its operation would become unduly cumbersome. **C59.1**

Subsection (1): Thus where a dominant tenement enjoys an easement over another registered estate, that easement (which is a legal estate under the Law of Property Act 1925) must be registered against both the dominant and servient tenements. **C59.1.1**

Subsection (2): The proprietor of a registered charge must be so registered against the title to the estate over which the charge is held. **C59.1.2**

Subsection (3): Similarly, the proprietor of a sub-charge on a registered charge must be so registered in relation to the latter charge. **C59.1.3**

Boundaries

60 Boundaries

(1) The boundary of a registered estate as shown for the purposes of the register is a general boundary, unless shown as determined under this section. **A60.1**

(2) A general boundary does not determine the exact line of the boundary.

(3) Rules may make provision enabling or requiring the exact line of the boundary of a registered estate to be determined and may, in particular, make provision about—

(a) the circumstances in which the exact line of a boundary may or must be determined,
(b) how the exact line of a boundary may be determined,
(c) procedure in relation to applications for determination, and
(d) the recording of the fact of determination in the register or the index maintained under section 68.

(4) Rules under this section must provide for applications for determination to be made to the registrar.

C60.1 Subsections (1), (2): These reflect the "general boundaries rule"[60] currently contained in the Land Registration Rules 1925 r. 278 (as amended). Thus, unless the boundary is fixed pursuant to subsection (3), the register is not conclusive and merely indicative of the boundaries in question.

C60.1.1 Subsection (3): Provides for the mechanism under which the boundaries of a registered estate can, subject to section 61, be made conclusive. Whilst such a provision exists in the Land Registration Rules 1925[61] it is rarely used.[62] It is envisaged that this power will be used more frequently because modern mapping techniques make the exercise less demanding and the subsection prescribes for the rules to provide when the exact line of the boundary *must* be determined.[63] The ability to compel the determination of the boundaries is new.[64] It remains to be seen whether this provision causes an increase in the number of boundaries determined by HM Land Registry.

C60.1.2 Subsection (4): No rules have, as yet, been made.

61 Accretion and diluvion

A61.1 (1) The fact that a registered estate in land is shown in the register as having a particular boundary does not affect the operation of accretion or diluvion.

---

[60] See *Ruoff & Roper*, para. 4–17 *et seq.*

[61] Land Registration Rules 1925, r. 276.

[62] See *Ruoff & Roper*, para. 4–22.

[63] *e.g.* where an application for registration is made by a squatter: Law Com No. 271, para. 9.13, p. 185.

[64] *ibid.*, para. 264–265, p. 504.

(2) An agreement about the operation of accretion or diluvion in relation to a registered estate in land has effect only if registered in accordance with rules.

"Land" defined section 132(1). "Land" includes "land covered with water". **C61.1**

Subsection (1): This section provides an exception to the conclusive nature of any boundaries fixed in accordance with section 60(3). Land abutting water is susceptible to gradual erosion or increase by the deposit of silts etc at the water's edge. Thus the boundary may not be static and land acquired by accretion or lost by diluvion will result in the movement of the boundaries of the registered estate, as appropriate. **C61.1.1**

Subsection (2): This can be excluded by agreement if it is registered in accordance with the rules. None have, as yet, been made. **C61.1.2**

Quality of title

62 Power to upgrade title

(1) Where the title to a freehold estate is entered in the register as possessory or qualified, the registrar may enter it as absolute if he is satisfied as to the title to the estate. **A62.1**

(2) Where the title to a leasehold estate is entered in the register as good leasehold, the registrar may enter it as absolute if he is satisfied as to the superior title.

(3) Where the title to a leasehold estate is entered in the register as possessory or qualified the registrar may—

(a) enter it as good leasehold if he is satisfied as to the title to the estate, and

(b) enter it as absolute if he is satisfied both as to the title to the estate and as to the superior title.

(4) Where the title to a freehold estate in land has been entered in the register as possessory for at least twelve years, the registrar may enter it as absolute if he is satisfied that the proprietor is in possession of the land.

(5) Where the title to a leasehold estate in land has been entered in the register as possessory for at least twelve years, the registrar may enter it as good leasehold if he is satisfied that the proprietor is in possession of the land.

(6) None of the powers under subsections (1) to (5) is exercisable if there is outstanding any claim adverse to the title of the registered proprietor which is made by virtue of an estate, right or interest whose enforceability is preserved by virtue of the existing entry about the class of title.

(7) The only persons who may apply to the registrar for the exercise of any of the powers under subsections (1) to (5) are—

(a) the proprietor of the estate to which the application relates,
(b) a person entitled to be registered as the proprietor of that estate,
(c) the proprietor of a registered charge affecting that estate, and
(d) a person interested in a registered estate which derives from that estate.

(8) In determining for the purposes of this section whether he is satisfied as to any title, the registrar is to apply the same standards as those which apply under section 9 or 10 to first registration of title.

(9) The Lord Chancellor may by order amend subsection (4) or (5) by substituting for the number of years for the time being specified in that subsection such number of years as the order may provide.

C62.1 "Proprietor in possession" defined in section 131.

Under the Land Registration Act 1925, s. 77, the registrar has similar powers.[65] In upgrading title, the registrar must be satisfied to the same standards as required under section 9: subsection (8). An "upgrade" may be granted if the registrar is satisfied that the circumstances which initially dictated a limited title no longer exist and subsection (6) does not apply. An application can only be made by those persons specified in subsection (7). A person who suffers loss by the "upgrade" of the

[65] See *Ruoff & Roper*, para. 14–01 *et seq.*

title is regarded as having suffered loss by reason of the rectification of the register and is entitled to an indemnity: Schedule 8, paragraph 1(2).

Subsection (1): A proprietor is registered with qualified or possessory title in relation to a freehold estate in the circumstances set forth in section 9(4) or (5). **C62.1.1**

Subsection (2): A proprietor is registered with good leasehold title in circumstances set forth in section 10(3). **C62.1.2**

Subsection (3): A proprietor is registered with possessory or qualified title in relation to a leasehold estate in the circumstances set forth in section 10(5) and (6). **C62.1.3**

Subsection (4): A proprietor who has been registered with possessory title for at least 12 years may be registered with absolute title if the registrar is satisfied that the proprietor is in possession of the land. Registration with possessory title does not necessarily mean that all other interests in the land are extinguished; however, where such title has been registered for 12 years, it is envisaged that the scope for a successful challenge is significantly reduced by reason of the operation of the Limitation Act 1980, ss. 15 and 17 and thus an "upgrade" is justifiable.[66] The 12-year period is subject to amendment by order: subsection (9). **C62.1.4**

Subsection (5): Similar provisions and considerations apply in relation to an "upgrade" of a leasehold estate. **C62.1.5**

Subsection (6): The registrar cannot upgrade title whilst there is an outstanding claim adverse to the title of the registered proprietor. **C62.1.6**

Subsection (7): The classes of applicant are clearly stated and self-explanatory. Subsection (7) would allow a lessee whose title was limited by reason of the status of the lessor's title (see section 10(5)) to apply to upgrade both. **C62.1.7**

63 Effect of upgrading title

(1) On the title to a registered freehold or leasehold estate being entered under section 62 as absolute, the proprietor ceases to hold the estate subject to any estate, right or interest whose enforceability was **A63.1**

---

[66] Law Com No. 271, para. 279, p. 507.

preserved by virtue of the previous entry about the class of title.

(2) Subsection (1) also applies on the title to a registered leasehold estate being entered under section 62 as good leasehold, except that the entry does not affect or prejudice the enforcement of any estate, right or interest affecting, or in derogation of, the title of the lessor to grant the lease.

C63.1 Subsection (1): On registration with an absolute title, all other estates, rights or interest that were preserved by the former registration by the operation of sections 11 or 12 are extinguished. A person suffering loss thereby may be entitled to an indemnity: Schedule 8, paragraph 1(2).

C63.1.1 Subsection (2): Applies subsection (1) to upgrades to good leasehold title save that such an upgrade will not affect or prejudice the enforcement of any estate right or interest affecting or in derogation of the title of the lessor to grant the lease.

64 Use of register to record defects in title

A64.1 (1) If it appears to the registrar that a right to determine a registered estate in land is exercisable, he may enter the fact in the register.

(2) Rules may make provision about entries under subsection (1) and may, in particular, make provision about—

(a) the circumstances in which there is a duty to exercise the power conferred by that subsection,

(b) how entries under that subsection are to be made, and

(c) the removal of such entries.

C64.1 This provision is new. No rules have, as yet, been made. It is envisaged that this provision will operate, in particular, to cases concerning rentcharges. If X wishes to purchase a registered freehold estate from Y subject to a rentcharge in favour of Z which is in arrears and thus Z's right of re-entry has arisen, X may be prepared to run the risk of Z re-entering. However, his title is, in law, bad. If such a feature is apparent to the registrar he may or depending on the rules he must enter it in the register and thus alert any successors in title to X.[67] It is envisaged

[67] Law Com No. 271, para. 290, p. 509.

that the terms of a network access agreement may require the purchaser's solicitor or licensed conveyancer to disclose specified information to the Registry.[68]

Alteration of register

65 Alteration of register

Schedule 4 (which makes provision about alteration of the register) has effect. **A65.1**

Information etc.

66 Inspection of the registers etc

(1) Any person may inspect and make copies of, or of any part of— **A66.1**

(a) the register of title,
(b) any document kept by the registrar which is referred to in the register of title,
(c) any other document kept by the registrar which relates to an application to him, or
(d) the register of cautions against first registration.

(2) The right under subsection (1) is subject to rules which may, in particular—

(a) provide for exceptions to the right, and
(b) impose conditions on its exercise, including conditions requiring the payment of fees.

Given the policy underlying the Act which requires the register to be as inclusive as possible, the ability to inspect it and documents referred to in it is of cardinal importance. This section enshrines the concept of the "open register" introduced by the Land Registration Act 1988. It also broadens it as provided in section 66(1)(b). **C66.1**

Whilst the right bestowed by subsection (1) is broader than that currently enjoyed under the Land Registration Act 1925, section 112 it is envisaged that the rules which may qualify those rights (see subsection (2)) will do so in order to protect private information. No rules have, as yet, been made. This power to inspect would make the

---

[68] *ibid.*, para. 9.35, p. 192.

property market much more transparent; for example obtaining all the necessary information with regard to rent reviews may be much more straightforward. How the desire by one party to keep certain information private and another desire to inspect it are to be resolved remains to be seen.

67 Official copies of the registers etc

A67.1 (1) An official copy of, or of a part of—

(a) the register of title,
(b) any document which is referred to in the register of title and kept by the registrar,
(c) any other document kept by the registrar which relates to an application to him, or
(d) the register of cautions against first registration,

is admissible in evidence to the same extent as the original.

(2) A person who relies on an official copy in which there is a mistake is not liable for loss suffered by another by reason of the mistake.

(3) Rules may make provision for the issue of official copies and may, in particular, make provision about—

(a) the form of official copies,
(b) who may issue official copies,
(c) applications for official copies, and
(d) the conditions to be met by applicants for official copies, including conditions requiring the payment of fees.

C67.1 Subsection (1): Official copies of all the items which section 66 grants a right to inspect are admissible in evidence to the same extent as the original. The terminology that is employed under the Land Registration Act 1925 has changed slightly; "office copies" has been replaced by "official copies".

C67.1.1 Subsection (2): Whilst the person who relies on the official copy is not liable for the loss suffered by another by reason of any mistake therein, the person suffering the loss is entitled to an indemnity: Schedule 8, paragraph 1(d).

Subsection (3): No rules have, as yet, been made. Schedule 5, paragraph 1(2)(d) will, on the advent of electronic conveyancing, permit persons with a network access agreement to issue official copies. C67.1.2
See also section 120 (conclusiveness of filed copies).

68 Index

(1) The registrar must keep an index for the purpose of enabling the following matters to be ascertained in relation to any parcel of land— A68.1

(a) whether any registered estate relates to the land,
(b) how any registered estate which relates to the land is identified for the purposes of the register,
(c) whether the land is affected by any, and, if so what, caution against first registration, and
(d) such other matters as rules may provide.

(2) Rules may—

(a) make provision about how the index is to be kept and may, in particular, make provision about—

(i) the information to be included in the index,
(ii) the form in which information included in the index is to be kept, and
(iii) the arrangement of that information;

(b) make provision about official searches of the index.

The current obligation to maintain the Index is contained in the Land Registration Rules 1925, r. 8. No rules have, as yet, been made. C68.1

69 Historical information

(1) The registrar may on application provide information about the history of a registered title. A69.1

(2) Rules may make provision about applications for the exercise of the power conferred by subsection (1).

(3) The registrar may—

(a) arrange for the provision of information about the history of registered titles, and
(b) authorise anyone who has the function of providing information under paragraph (a) to have access on such terms as the registrar thinks fit to any relevant information kept by him.

C69.1 Currently the registrar may, if good reason is shown, permit a person to inspect the historical record kept at the registry. This section embodies that practice. Historical information can be desirable in many circumstances (*e.g.* to determine whether land has, at any time, been in common ownership in order to determine a claim to a quasi-easement, for example). No rules have, as yet, been made. It is envisaged that the rules will limit the categories of persons who may apply for historical information and that such an enquiry should never become routine.[69]

70 Official searches

A70.1 Rules may make provision for official searches of the register, including searches of pending applications for first registration, and may, in particular, make provision about—

(a) the form of applications for searches,

(b) the manner in which such applications may be made,

(c) the form of official search certificates, and

(d) the manner in which such certificates may be issued.

C70.1 No rules have, as yet, been made. It is envisaged that on the advent of electronic conveyancing those with network access agreements may be authorised to issue official search certificates: Schedule 5, paragraph 1(2)(c). For searches with priority protection, see section 72.

Applications

71 Duty to disclose unregistered interests

Where rules so provide—

---

[69] Law Com No. 271, para. 311, p. 512.

(a) a person applying for registration under Chapter 1 of Part 2 must provide to the registrar such information as the rules may provide about any interest affecting the estate to which the application relates which— **A71.1**

(i) falls within any of the paragraphs of Schedule 1, and
(ii) is of a description specified by the rules;

(b) a person applying to register a registrable disposition of a registered estate must provide to the registrar such information as the rules may provide about any unregistered interest affecting the estate which—

(i) falls within any of the paragraphs of Schedule 3, and
(ii) is of description specified by the rules.

This provision is part of those which aim to make the register as inclusive as possible. By this route the extent of any interests that could otherwise be overriding will be reduced in number and recorded in the register. **C71.1**

Subject to the rules (which have, as yet, to be made) an applicant for registration under Chapter 1 of Part 2 of the Act (first registration) is placed under an obligation to provide the registrar with such information as required relating to any interest affecting the estate that falls within any of the paragraphs of Schedule 1[70] or is specified by the rules.

Where an applicant seeks to register a registrable disposition, an obligation is imposed on him in like terms save that the information he must provide concerns any unregistered interest affecting the estate which falls within any of the paragraphs of Schedule 3[71] or is specified by the rules.

72 Priority protection

(1) For the purposes of this section, an application for an entry in the register is protected if— **A72.1**

(a) it is one to which a priority period relates, and
(b) it is made before the end of that period.

(2) Where an application for an entry in the register is protected, any entry made in the register during the

---

[70] See para. SC1.0 *et seq.*, *infra*.

[71] See para. SC3.0 *et seq.*, *infra*.

priority period relating to the application is postponed to any entry made in pursuance of it.

(3) Subsection (2) does not apply if—

(a) the earlier entry was made in pursuance of a protected application, and

(b) the priority period relating to that application ranks ahead of the one relating to the application for the other entry.

(4) Subsection (2) does not apply if the earlier entry is one to which a direction under section 46(3) applies.

(5) The registrar may defer dealing with an application for an entry in the register if it appears to him that subsection (2) might apply to the entry were he to make it.

(6) Rules may—

(a) make provision for priority periods in connection with—

(i) official searches of the register, including searches of pending applications for first registration, or

(ii) the noting in the register of a contract for the making of a registrable disposition of a registered estate or charge;

(b) make provision for the keeping of records in relation to priority periods and the inspection of such records.

(7) Rules under subsection (6)(a) may, in particular, make provision about—

(a) the commencement and length of a priority period,

(b) the applications for registration to which such a period relates,

(c) the order in which competing priority periods rank, and

(d) the application of subsections (2) and (3) in cases where more than one priority period relates to the same application.

C72.1 An office copy under the Land Registration Act 1925 is only a statement of the entries existing in the register on the date it bears and since third party rights may intervene between that date and the completion of any disposition of the registered estate, a period of security (*i.e.* priority) over any such third party rights is necessary. This is currently bestowed by an official search with priority.[72] The Act makes the following provisions in relation to priority protection:—

Subsection (1): Provides the definition of a protected application, being an application for an entry in the register to which a priority period relates and which is made prior to the expiry of that period. **C72.1.1**

Subsection (2): The protection afforded to a protected application is to postpone any third party entry in the register made during the priority period to any entry made in pursuance of that application during that period. To this, there are two exceptions:— **C72.1.2**

Subsection (3): First, subsection (2) does not apply where the third party entry was itself made in pursuance of a priority application and that priority period takes precedence. **C72.1.3**

Subsection (4): Secondly, if the third party entry is made pursuant to an order of the court bestowing priority on it: section 46(3). **C72.1.4**

Subsection (5): This enables the registrar to wait until the end of a priority period before making an entry in the register. **C72.1.5**

Subsection (6): Rules may be made concerning the provision for priority periods and the keeping of records relating to those periods and their inspection. None have, as yet, been made. **C72.1.6**

Subsection (7): Enables rules to be made in particular about certain matters. No rules have, as yet, been made. **C72.1.7**

73 Objections

(1) Subject to subsections (2) and (3), anyone may object to an application to the registrar. **A73.1**

(2) In the case of an application under section 18, only the person who lodged the caution to which the application relates, or such other person as rules may provide, may object.

(3) In the case of an application under section 36, only the person shown in the register as the beneficiary

[72] See *Ruoff & Roper*, para. 30–01 *et seq.*

of the notice to which the application relates, or such other person as rules may provide, may object.

(4) The right to object under this section is subject to rules.

(5) Where an objection is made under this section, the registrar—

(a) must give notice of the objection to the applicant, and

(b) may not determine the application until the objection has been disposed of.

(6) Subsection (5) does not apply if the objection is one which the registrar is satisfied is groundless.

(7) If it is not possible to dispose by agreement of an objection to which subsection (5) applies, the registrar must refer the matter to the adjudicator.

(8) Rules may make provision about references under subsection (7).

C73.1 This section sets out the framework in accordance with which objections may be made to the registrar concerning any application to him.[73] References in the Act to "the right to object" are references to the right under this section: section 132(3).

C73.1.1 Subsection (1): Enables anyone to object to the registrar, subject to subsections (2) and (3).

C73.1.2 Subsection (2): Where the application is for cancellation of a caution, only the cautioner or such other person as the rules may provide may object. No rules have, as yet, been made.

C73.1.3 Subsection (3): Where the application is for the cancellation of a unilateral notice, only the person shown in the register to be the beneficiary of the notice or such other person as the rules may provide may object. No rules have, as yet, been made.

C73.1.4 Subsection (4): No rules have, as yet, been made.

---

[73] Of which there are many—see sections. 3, 4, 15, 18, 27, 34, 35, 36, 43, 47, 48, 60, 62, 67, 70, Schedule 5 paragraph 1, Schedule 6 paragraphs 1, 6 and section 106(2). The manner in which these applications may be made is subject to such rules as may be prescribed: Schedule 10, paragraph 6.

Subsection (5): Unless the registrar is satisfied that the objection is "groundless" (subsection (6)) he must give notice to the applicant and may not determine the application until the objection has been determined Rules (as yet to be made) may specify the form, content and manner of service in relation to such notices: Schedule 10, paragraph 5. Determination must be by agreement or by reference to the adjudicator: subsection (7). Rules may be made concerning references to the adjudicator: subsection (8). None have, as yet, been made. **C73.1.5**

74 Effective date of registration

An entry made in the register in pursuance of— **A74.1**

(a) an application for registration of an unregistered legal estate, or

(b) an application for registration in relation to a disposition required to be completed by registration,

has effect from the time of the making of the application.

Rules may be made concerning the form and content of applications under the Act and, in particular, when such an application is taken to be made: Schedule 10, paragraph 6. Clearly, this section provides for the inevitable delay between receipt of an application for the registration of an unregistered estate or a disposition of a registered estate and the appropriate entry in the register.[74] With the advent and growth of electronic conveyancing, this section will become less and less relevant since disposition and registration will be simultaneous: see section 93. **C74.1**

Proceedings before the registrar

75 Production of documents

(1) The registrar may require a person to produce a document for the purposes of proceedings before him. **A75.1**

(2) The power under subsection (1) is subject to rules.

(3) A requirement under subsection (1) shall be enforceable as an order of the court.

---

[74] Currently provided for by LRR 1925, rr. 24, 42, 83 and 85.

(4) A person aggrieved by a requirement under subsection (1) may appeal to a county court, which may make any order which appears appropriate.

C75.1 "Court" is defined section 132(3)(a).

C75.1.1 Subsection (1): The power given by this subsection is subject to rules which have, as yet, to be made: subsection (2).

C75.1.2 Subsection (3): The requirement by the registrar is enforceable as if an order of the High Court or county court.

C75.1.3 Subsection (4): An appeal from the registrar's requirement is to the county court, which may make such order as appears appropriate.

76 Costs

A76.1 (1) The registrar may make orders about costs in relation to proceedings before him.

(2) The power under subsection (1) is subject to rules which may, in particular, make provision about—

(a) who may be required to pay costs,
(b) whose costs a person may be required to pay,
(c) the kind of costs which a person may be required to pay, and
(d) the assessment of costs.

(3) Without prejudice to the generality of subsection (2), rules under that subsection may include provision about—

(a) costs of the registrar, and
(b) liability for costs thrown away as the result of neglect or delay by a legal representative of a party to proceedings.

(4) An order under subsection (1) shall be enforceable as an order of the court.

(5) A person aggrieved by an order under subsection (1) may appeal to a county court, which may make any order which appears appropriate.

"Court" defined section 132(3)(a).

C76.1 Subsection (1): Subject to rules made under subsection (2) (which have, as yet, to be made), the registrar can make costs orders in relation to proceedings before him. It is anticipated that the rules will permit those costs to be summarily assessed.

Subsection (3): Those rules are permitted to include provision about the costs of the registrar and costs against a party's legal representative incurred by reason of his neglect or delay. **C76.1.1**

Subsection (4), (5): A costs order is enforceable as if an order of the High Court of county court. An appeal from the registrar's requirement is to the county court, which may make such order as appears appropriate. **C76.1.2**

Miscellaneous

77 Duty to act reasonably

(1) A person must not exercise any of the following rights without reasonable cause— **A77.1**

- (a) the right to lodge a caution under section 15,
- (b) the right to apply for the entry of a notice or restriction, and
- (c) the right to object to an application to the registrar.

(2) The duty under this section is owed to any person who suffers damage in consequence of its breach.

Subsection (1): Cautions against first registration can be entered unilaterally pursuant to section 15. Unilateral notices and restrictions can be entered in accordance with sections 35 and 43. A right to object to an application can be made under section 73. All these features of the Act have significant potential to cause disruption to conveyancing transactions and occasion loss. This subsection declares that a person exercising those rights must not do so without reasonable cause. **C77.1**

Subsection (2): An absence of reasonable cause amounts to a breach of statutory duty which sounds in damages. **C77.1.1**

78 Notice of trust not to affect registrar

The registrar shall not be affected with notice of a trust. **A78.1**

The registrar is not to be affected by notice of any trust; his concern is only with the entries in the register. **C78.1**

Part 7

Special cases

The Crown

79 Voluntary registration of demesne land

A79.1 (1) Her Majesty may grant an estate in fee simple absolute in possession out of demesne land to Herself.

(2) The grant of an estate under subsection (1) is to be regarded as not having been made unless an application under section 3 is made in respect of the estate before the end of the period for registration.

(3) The period for registration is two months beginning with the date of the grant, or such longer period as the registrar may provide under subsection (4).

(4) If on the application of Her Majesty the registrar is satisfied that there is a good reason for doing so, he may by order provide that the period for registration ends on such later date as he may specify in the order.

(5) If an order under subsection (4) is made in a case where subsection (2) has already applied, that application of the subsection is to be treated as not having occurred.

C79.1 "Demesne Land" defined section 132(1), (2).

Within England and Wales, all land is owned by the Crown and those holding under it merely hold an estate in the land.[75] Whilst most land is occupied and held by tenants of the Crown either directly or indirectly, substantial areas and classes of land are held by the Crown in demesne (*i.e.* as Sovereign or lord paramount in which it no estate has been granted). Examples of such land include:

(a) the foreshore around England and Wales save where it has been granted or vested in a private owner;

[75] See Megarry & Wade, *The Law of Real Property* (6th ed. 2000), paras 2–001 *et seq.*

(b) land which has passed by way of escheat to the Crown;

(c) ancient land of the Crown which have never been granted away;

(d) land under the management of the Crown Estate Commissioners;

(e) the Crown's Private Estate;

(f) the Royal Duchies of Cornwall and Lancaster.

Subsection (1): Subject to subsection (3), this subsection overcomes the difficulties inherent in a system of land registration which only permits the registration of estates in that land. This subsection enables Her Majesty to grant to Herself an estate in fee simple out of demesne land and thus for the same to be capable of registration. **C79.1.1**

"Demesne Land" means land belonging to Her Majesty in right of the Crown which is not held for an estate in fee simple absolute in possession and does not include land in relation to which a freehold estate therein has determined (*i.e.* escheated) but in relation to which there has been no act of entry or management by the Crown: sections 132(1), (2).

The departure afforded by this subsection is revolutionary and permits for the first time the registration of land vested in the Crown and for the Crown to enjoy the benefits bestowed by the Act. It also brings much closer the goal of total registration.

Subsection (2): Whilst the Registrar can extend time in accordance with subsection (4), the grant of an estate under subsection (1) is not to be regarded as having been made unless an application for voluntary registration under section 3 is made in respect of the estate before the end of the period for registration, being two months beginning with the date of the grant: subsection (3). Thus an inadvertent creation of a fee simple cannot occur. **C79.1.2**

Subsection (5): If the Registrar extends time pursuant to subsection (4), that will not invalidate the application for voluntary registration by reason of the failure to register within the initial period. This is so even if the period is extended after the expiry of the period for registration. **C79.1.3**

80 Compulsory registration of grants out of demesne land

(1) Section 4(1) shall apply as if the following were included among the events listed— **A80.1**

(a) the grant by Her Majesty out of demesne land of an estate in fee simple absolute in possession, otherwise than under section 79;

(b) the grant by Her Majesty out of demesne land of an estate in land—

(i) for a term of years absolute of more than seven years from the date of the grant, and

(ii) for valuable or other consideration, by way of gift or in pursuance of an order of any court.

(2) In subsection (1)(b)(ii), the reference to grant by way of gift includes grant for the purpose of constituting a trust under which Her Majesty does not retain the whole of the beneficial interest.

(3) Subsection (1) does not apply to the grant of an estate in mines and minerals held apart from the surface.

(4) The Lord Chancellor may by order—

(a) amend this section so as to add to the events in subsection (1) such events relating to demesne land as he may specify in the order, and

(b) make such consequential amendments of any provision of, or having effect under, any Act as he thinks appropriate.

(5) In its application by virtue of subsection (1), section 7 has effect with the substitution for subsection (2) of—

"(2) On the application of subsection (1), the grant has effect as a contract made for valuable consideration to grant the legal estate concerned".

C80.1 Section 4 (1) provides for compulsory registration on the *transfer* of or the *grant* out of an estate in fee simple of a term of years absolute with more than seven years to run. Accordingly it does not provide for the compulsory registration of grants out of demesne land. This section does by compelling grants by Her Majesty to third parties (*i.e.* not to Herself pursuant to section 79) to be registered.

C80.1.1 Subsection (1): It utilises the mechanism prescribed for compulsory registration of transfers or grants out of an estate in fee simple on a term of years absolute with more than seven years to run by including in the provisions of section 4(1) those set out at section 80(1) (a) and (b). They are analogous to the provisions set forth in section 4. Therefore whilst Her Majesty may grant Herself an estate in fee simple out of demesne land and choose whether voluntarily to register that, a grant of a fee simple absolute in possession or a term of years as specified in section 80 will trigger compulsory registration.

Subsection (2): A grant out of demesne land of a term of years absolute of more than seven years from the date of grant by way of gift includes a grant for the purpose of constituting a trust under which Her Majesty does not retain the whole of the beneficial interest. **C80.1.2**

Subsection (3): Subsection (1) does not apply to the grant of an estate in mines and minerals held apart from the surface. **C80.1.3**

Subsection (4): The Lord Chancellor may, by order in accordance with section 128 amend subsection (1) and the events which give rise to compulsory registration of grants out of demesne land. Similar powers exist in relation to section 4: section 5. **C80.1.4**

Subsection (5): The effect of subsection (5) is that if a grant is required to be registered within the period for registration stipulated by section 6 (being two months beginning with the date on which the relevant event occurs or such longer period as the Registrar may provide: section 6(4)) and is not, it takes effect as a contract made for valuable consideration to grant the legal estate concerned. **C80.1.5**

81 Demesne land: cautions against first registration

(1) Section 15 shall apply as if demesne land were held by Her Majesty for an unregistered estate in fee simple absolute in possession. **A81.1**

(2) The provisions of this Act relating to cautions against first registration shall, in relation to cautions lodged by virtue of subsection (1), have effect subject to such modifications as rules may provide.

Since demesne land does not constitute an "unregistered legal estate" for the purposes of section 15, there is (absent this section) no provision for a caution against first registration. However this section provides as follows: **C81.1**

Subsection (1): It deems the demesne land to be held by Her Majesty for an unregistered estate in fee simple absolute in possession. **C81.1.1**

C81.1.2 Subsection (2): Rules may be made concerning cautions against first registration of demesne land. None have, as yet, been made. The policy limiting cautions against first registration is that they should not become a substitute for registration; accordingly, section 15(3) precludes the entry of a caution against first registration by an individual who is otherwise compelled to apply for registration. This feature of the Act is to be brought in slowly. The transitional provision in relation to section 15(3) is that it shall not come into force for the period of two years beginning with the day on which section 15 is brought into force: Schedule 12, paragraph 14(1). Paragraph 14(3) of Schedule 12 disapplies that provision in relation to section 81. It is envisaged that because the Crown has historically not been able to register demesne land and further, because of the extent of that land, it will take a substantial period of time for it to be registered. Thus paragraph 15 of Schedule 12 allows a period of 10 years beginning with the day on which section 15 comes into force (or such longer period as may be provided for by rules)[76] for cautions against first registration to be lodged. This ability extends not only to the Crown but also to such other persons as may have an interest in demesne land.[77]

C81.1.3 Subsection (2): Rules may be made in order to modify the provision of the Act in relation to cautions against first registration of demesne land. No rules have, as yet, been made.

82 Escheat etc

A82.1 (1) Rules may make provision about—

(a) the determination of a registered freehold estate in land, and

(b) the registration of an unregistered freehold legal estate in land in respect of land to which a former registered freehold estate in land related.

(2) Rules under this section may, in particular—

(a) make provision for determination to be dependent on the meeting of such registration requirements as the rules may specify;

(b) make provision for entries relating to a freehold estate in land to continue in the register,

---

[76] It is envisaged that this period will be extended: Law Com No. 271, para. 11.18, p. 245.

[77] *e.g.* an incumbrance of land that has escheated: *Attorney-General of Ontario v. Mucu* (1883) 8 App. Cas. 767, 772.

notwithstanding determination, for such time as the rules may provide;

(c) make provision for the making in the register in relation to a former freehold estate in land of such entries as the rules may provide;

(d) make provision imposing requirements to be met in connection with an application for the registration of such an unregistered estate as is mentioned in subsection (1)(b).

Escheat occurs upon the determination of the legal estate in fee simple.[78] The feudal lord from whom the land is held (the Crown or the Duchies of Cornwall or Lancaster) thereby becomes entitled to the land freed from the estate that previously existed in it. However, escheat does not determine the subsisting charges or other encumbrances that bound the defunct fee simple absolute although the paramount lord will not be subject to the liabilities that affected the defunct fee simple absolute unless and until he takes possession or control of it or brings proceedings for its recovery. The most common incident of escheat is where the Crown disclaims land that has passed it as *bona vacantia* on the dissolution of a limited company. Under the current law, an estate which has escheated will be removed from the register because it no longer exists since it will have vested back in the paramount lord. Such a state of affairs would, (if it prevailed under the Act) be contrary to its objective to make the register as inclusive as possible. **C82.1**

Voluntary registration would not assist since the act of voluntary registration by the Crown or the relevant Duchy would amount to an act of management, subjecting the Crown or that Duchy to the liabilities attaching to the property. Accordingly, section 82 provides for rules to be made to ensure that any estate which has escheated remains registered.

Subsection (1): Rules may be made in accordance with this section although none have, as yet, been made. It is envisaged that the rules that will be made will ensure that an estate which has escheated will remain in the register until such time as there is a disposition of the land by the Crown or the relevant Duchy or by order of the Court.[79] It is envisaged that rules under this provision would operate as follows: where a registered fee simple absolute escheats, the Treasury Solicitor **C82.1.1**

---

[78] Some 500 estates escheat each year: Law Com No. 271, para. 11.22, p. 247. Escheat most frequently occurs upon disclaimer by a trustee in bankruptcy or a liquidator or as a result of the Treasury Solicitor disclaiming land that has passed by way of *bona vacantia*.

[79] Law Com No. 271, para. 369, p. 523.

(or, if he disclaims) the Crown Estate or a Royal Duchy (in other cases) will apply for the entry of restriction in the register. Such restriction is likely to prohibit the entry of a disposition in the register unless it is made by order of the Court or by or on the direction of the Crown Estate or the relevant Royal Duchy. When such a disposition is made, it will necessarily create a new fee simple and it will be registered with a new title number. The old title will then be closed. Any encumbrances which will form the title of the subject and which will subsist in relation to the new estate will be entered in the register of the new title.[80]

C82.1.2 Subsection (2): The rules, when made, may specifically provide for the matters detailed in paragraph (a)–(d).

83 Crown and Duchy land: representation

A83.1 (1) With respect to a Crown or Duchy interest, the appropriate authority—

(a) may represent the owner of the interest for all purposes of this Act,

(b) is entitled to receive such notice as that person is entitled to receive under this Act, and

(c) may make such applications and do such other acts as that person is entitled to make or do under this Act.

(2) In this section—

"the appropriate authority" means—

(a) in relation to an interest belonging to Her Majesty in right of the Crown and forming part of the Crown Estate, the Crown Estate Commissioners;

(b) in relation to any other interest belonging to Her Majesty in right of the Crown, the government department having the management of the interest or, if there is no such department, such person as Her Majesty may appoint in writing under the Royal Sign Manual;

(c) in relation to an interest belonging to Her Majesty in right of the Duchy of Lancaster, the Chancellor of the Duchy;

---

[80] *ibid.*, para. 370, p. 523.

(d) in relation to an interest belonging to the Duchy of Cornwall, such person as the Duke of Cornwall, or the possessor for the time being of the Duchy of Cornwall, appoints;

(e) in relation to an interest belonging to a government department, or held in trust for Her Majesty for the purposes of a government department, that department;

"Crown interest" means an interest belonging to Her Majesty in right of the Crown, or belonging to a government department, or held in trust for Her Majesty for the purposes of a government department;

"Duchy interest" means an interest belonging to Her Majesty in right of the Duchy of Lancaster, or belonging to the Duchy of Cornwall;

"interest" means any estate, interest or charge in or over land and any right or claim in relation to land.

Subsection (1): Section 83 provides which "appropriate authority" may represent the owner of the interest for all purposes of the Act and is entitled to receive such notices or make such applications as the Act provides. **C83.1**

Subsection (2): "The appropriate authority" for the purposes of subsection (1) is defined as set out in the subsection. **C83.1.1**

84 Disapplication of requirements relating to Duchy land

Nothing in any enactment relating to the Duchy of Lancaster or the Duchy of Cornwall shall have effect to impose any requirement with respect to formalities or enrolment in relation to a disposition by a registered proprietor. **A84.1**

This section saves the Duchy of Lancaster or the Duchy of Cornwall from having to comply with the complex conveyancing requirements imposed on them by various nineteenth century Acts of Parliament in cases where the land is registered. In such circumstances they need only comply with the provisions of the Act and not the provisions of the Duchy of Cornwall Act 1844, Duchy of Lancaster Land Act 1855 or the Duchy of Cornwall Management Acts 1863–1982.[81] **C84.1**

---

[81] See *Ruoff & Roper* para. 10–19.

85 Bona vacantia

A85.1 Rules may make provision about how the passing of a registered estate or charge as bona vacantia is to be dealt with for the purposes of this Act.

C85.1 No rules have, as yet, been made.

Pending actions etc.

86 Bankruptcy

A86.1 (1) In this Act, references to an interest affecting an estate or charge do not include a petition in bankruptcy or bankruptcy order.

(2) As soon as practicable after registration of a petition in bankruptcy as a pending action under the Land Charges Act 1972 (c. 61), the registrar must enter in the register in relation to any registered estate or charge which appears to him to be affected a notice in respect of the pending action.

(3) Unless cancelled by the registrar in such manner as rules may provide, a notice entered under subsection (2) continues in force until—

(a) a restriction is entered in the register under subsection (4), or
(b) the trustee in bankruptcy is registered as proprietor.

(4) As soon as practicable after registration of a bankruptcy order under the Land Charges Act 1972, the registrar must, in relation to any registered estate or charge which appears to him to be affected by the order, enter in the register a restriction reflecting the effect of the Insolvency Act 1986 (c. 45).

(5) Where the proprietor of a registered estate or charge is adjudged bankrupt, the title of his trustee in bankruptcy is void as against a person to whom a registrable disposition of the estate or charge is made if—

(a) the disposition is made for valuable consideration,

(b) the person to whom the disposition is made acts in good faith, and

(c) at the time of the disposition—

(i) no notice or restriction is entered under this section in relation to the registered estate or charge, and

(ii) the person to whom the disposition is made has no notice of the bankruptcy petition or the adjudication.

(6) Subsection (5) only applies if the relevant registration requirements are met in relation to the disposition, but, when they are met, has effect as from the date of the disposition.

(7) Nothing in this section requires a person to whom a registrable disposition is made to make any search under the Land Charges Act 1972.

Subsection (1): The general rules concerning priority contained in sections 28–30 of the Act do not include a petition in bankruptcy or bankruptcy order, since neither of these comprises an "interest affecting an estate or charge". Accordingly section 86 applies. **C86.1**

Subsection (2): Currently, when a petition is filed, the Court forthwith sends to the Registrar notice of the petition for registration in the register of pending actions.[82] This will continue under the Act. As soon as practicable after registration of that petition, the Registrar must enter a notice in the register in relation to any registered estate or charge which appears to him to be affected. This system works since the registrar is responsible for maintaining both the register of Land Charges and the register of title. If it *appears* to him that an estate or charge is affected, he will enter a notice. **C86.1.1**

Subsection (3): Unless cancelled by the Registrar in accordance with the rules (which have, as yet, to be made) a notice entered under subsection (2) continues in force until a bankruptcy order is made or the trustee in bankruptcy is registered as a proprietor. It can be anticipated that the rules will provide for the vacation or the cancellation of the notice in circumstances where the petition is dismissed. **C86.1.2**

Subsection (4): This subsection provides for the entry of a restriction reflecting the limitation imposed on the disposition of a bankrupt's **C86.1.3**

[82] Insolvency Rules 1986, r. 6.43.

property following upon his bankruptcy. Section 284 of the Insolvency Act 1986 provides that where a person is adjudged bankrupt, any disposition of property made by him in the period to which section 284 applies (which is the period beginning with the day of the presentation of the petition and ending with the vesting under Chapter IV of Part IX of that Act in the bankrupt's trustee) is void except to the extent that it is or was an act with the consent of the Court or is or was subsequently ratified by the Court. That provision is subject to limitations contained in section 284(4) of the Insolvency Act 1986 which precludes a remedy against any person in respect of any property or payment which he received before the commencement of the bankruptcy in good faith, for value without notice that the petition had been presented or in respect of any interest in property which he derives from an interest in respect of which there is, by virtue of the subsection, no remedy. The bankruptcy of an individual commences on the day on which the bankruptcy order is made.[83–84] Subsection (5) of the Act follows the provisions of section 284(4) of the Insolvency Act 1986 and makes provision for the circumstances in which the title of the trustee in bankruptcy is void against a person to whom a registrable disposition of an estate or charge is made in the circumstances set out in the sub-paragraphs contained in the subsection. It thus replicates the protection afforded to disponees in good faith.

C86.1.4 Subsection (6): The registration requirements are set out in section 27 and Schedule 2 of the Act.

C86.1.5 Subsection (7): A person to whom a registerable disposition is made is not required to make a search under the Land Charges Act 1972 and thus any entry in the register of pending actions can have no direct effect; accordingly the obligation is imposed upon the Registrar to enter a notice in relation to the registered estate or charge in accordance with subsection (2).

87 Pending land actions, writs, orders and deeds of arrangement

A87.1 (1) Subject to the following provisions, references in this Act to an interest affecting an estate or charge include—

(a) a pending land action within the meaning of the Land Charges Act 1972,

(b) a writ or order of the kind mentioned in section 6(1)(a) of that Act (writ or order

[83–84] Insolvency Act 1986, s. 278.

affecting land issued or made by any court for the purposes of enforcing a judgment or recognisance),

(c) an order appointing a receiver or sequestrator, and

(d) a deed of arrangement.

(2) No notice may be entered in the register in respect of—

(a) an order appointing a receiver or sequestrator, or

(b) a deed of arrangement.

(3) None of the matters mentioned in subsection (1) shall be capable of falling within paragraph 2 of Schedule 1 or 3.

(4) In its application to any of the matters mentioned in subsection (1), this Act shall have effect subject to such modifications as rules may provide.

(5) In this section, "deed of arrangement" has the same meaning as in the Deeds of Arrangement Act 1914 (c. 47).

Since cautions against dealings are prospectively abolished, new provision is required for pending land actions, writs, orders and deeds of arrangement since hitherto all these matters have been protected by the entry of a caution. The new provisions are as follows:—

Subsection (1): Subject to any rules made under subsection (4), this is brought about by extending the definition of "an interest affecting an estate or charge" to include the matters set forth in sub-paragraph (a)–(d) and thus permitting the entry of a notice under section 32. **C87.1**

Sub-paragraph (a): A "pending land action" means any action or proceedings pending in Court relating to land or any interest in or charge on the land: Land Charges Act 1972 s. 17(1).

Sub-paragraph (b): Section 6(1)(a) of the Land Charges Act 1972 refers to "any writ or order affecting land issued or made by any Court for the purpose of enforcing a judgment or recognisance".

Sub-paragraph (d): Such a deed comprises a written agreement of a designated class made by, for or in respect of the affairs of a debtor (a) for the benefit of his creditors generally or (b) who was insolvent at the date of the execution of the instrument for the benefit of any three or more of his creditors otherwise in pursuance of the law for the time being in force relating to that bankruptcy.

The designated classes of (d) are an assignment of property; a deed of or agreement for a composition; in cases where creditors of the debtor obtain any control over his property or business, a deed of inspectorship entered into for the purpose of carrying on or winding up a business; a letter of licence authorising the debtor or any other person to manage, carry on, realise or dispose of the business with a view to the payment of debts; and any agreement or instrument entered into for the purpose of carrying on or winding up the debtor's business or authorising the debtor or any other person to manage, carry on, realise or dispose of the debtor's business with a view to the payment of his debts.

Such deeds are seldom utilised and indeed, the Act has been recommended for repeal.[85]

C87.1.1 Subsection (2): Since no notice may be entered in relation to an order appointing a Receiver or Sequestrator or a Deed of Arrangement, these can only be protected by entry of a restriction. A pending land action or a writ or order of the kind mentioned in section 6(1)(a) of the Land Charges Act 1972 may be protected by the entry of a notice or a restriction or, where appropriate, both.

C87.1.2 Subsection (3): Schedule 1 provides for unregistered interests which override first registration; Schedule 3 provides for unregistered interests which override registered dispositions. Paragraph 2 of those schedules concerns the interest of persons in actual occupation. The effect of this subsection is that none of the interests affecting an estate or charge set out in section 87(1) are capable of being protected by reason of the actual occupation of the person having the benefit of any of them. They cannot override first registration or a registered disposition unless protected by the appropriate entry in the register.

C87.1.3 Subsection (4): Rules may provide for the modification of the Act in relation to the matters mentioned in subsection (1). None have, as yet, been made.

Miscellaneous

88 Incorporeal hereditaments

A88.1 In its application to—

(a) rentcharges,

---

[85] See Report of the Review Committee into Insolvency Law and Practice (Cmnd. 8558).

(b) franchises,

(c) *profits à prendre* in gross, or

(d) manors,

this Act shall have effect subject to such modification as rules may provide.

This section allows rules to be made which may modify the provisions of the Act in relation to its application to the four classes of incorporeal hereditaments specified in the section. No rules have, as yet, been made. **C88.1**

89 Settlements

(1) Rules may make provision for the purposes of this Act in relation to the application to registered land of the enactments relating to settlements under the Settled Land Act 1925 (c. 18). **A89.1**

(2) Rules under this section may include provision modifying any of those enactments in its application to registered land.

(3) In this section, "registered land" means an interest the title to which is, or is required to be, registered.

The Land Registration Act 1925 makes extensive provision in relation to settled land.[86] Since no new settlements have been capable of creation after December 31, 1996, the significance of settled land will accordingly diminish further. Accordingly the provisions under the Act in relation to settled land are to be contained in the rules which have, as yet, to be made. **C89.1**

90 PPP leases relating to transport in London

(1) No application for registration under section 3 may be made in respect of a leasehold estate in land under a PPP lease. **A90.1**

(2) The requirement of registration does not apply on the grant or transfer of a leasehold estate in land under a PPP lease.

(3) For the purposes of section 27, the following are not dispositions requiring to be completed by registration—

---

[86] See *Ruoff & Roper*, para. 30–01 *et seq.*

(a) the grant of a term of years absolute under a PPP lease;

(b) the express grant of an interest falling within section 1(2) of the Law of Property Act 1925 (c. 20), where the interest is created for the benefit of a leasehold estate in land under a PPP lease.

(4) No notice may be entered in the register in respect of an interest under a PPP lease.

(5) Schedules 1 and 3 have effect as if they included a paragraph referring to a PPP lease.

(6) In this section, "PPP lease" has the meaning given by section 218 of the Greater London Authority Act 1999 (c. 29) (which makes provision about leases created for public-private partnerships relating to transport in London).

C90.1 A "PPP Lease" is defined in section 90(6). Section 90 prohibits the registration of any PPP lease relating to transport in London, whether voluntarily or as a result of the requirement for registration. Moreover any such lease is not deemed to be a disposition requiring registration under section 27 nor is it capable of protection on the register by the entry of a notice. It will, however, constitute an overriding interest which overrides first registration and subsequent registered dispositions: see section 90(5). The reason for the exclusion of PPP leases is simple; it is anticipated that if any are granted they will be for a relatively short period and will be virtually inalienable. Accordingly, it is considered that the costs of producing accurate plans to attach to such leases would be enormous and disproportionate to any benefits that may accrue in such an exercise.

PART 8

ELECTRONIC CONVEYANCING

C91.0 As stated above[87] the objective of the Act is to enable dispositions of registered land to be conducted electronically. It is in order to assist this objective that the register is to be made as inclusive as possible of all rights and interests that exist in relation to registered land save where it is impossible so to do (*e.g.* rights acquired by proprietary estoppel or

[87] See paras 1.001 and 3.001 *et seq.*

prescription). This part of the Act and Schedule 5 set out the provisions in relation to the implementation and management of the process of electronic conveyancing. They will, in due course be supplemented by rules, which will contain most of the detail. No rules have, as yet, been made. Draft rules for consultation are expected to be published soon.

91 Electronic dispositions: formalities

(1) This section applies to a document in electronic form where— **A91.1**

(a) the document purports to effect a disposition which falls within subsection (2), and
(b) the conditions in subsection (3) are met.

(2) A disposition falls within this subsection if it is—

(a) a disposition of a registered estate or charge,
(b) a disposition of an interest which is the subject of a notice in the register, or
(c) a disposition which triggers the requirement of registration,

which is of a kind specified by rules.

(3) The conditions referred to above are that—

(a) the document makes provision for the time and date when it takes effect,
(b) the document has the electronic signature of each person by whom it purports to be authenticated,
(c) each electronic signature is certified, and
(d) such other conditions as rules may provide are met.

(4) A document to which this section applies is to be regarded as—

(a) in writing, and
(b) signed by each individual, and sealed by each corporation, whose electronic signature it has.

(5) A document to which this section applies is to be regarded for the purposes of any enactment as a deed.

(6) If a document to which this section applies is authenticated by a person as agent, it is to be

regarded for the purposes of any enactment as authenticated by him under the written authority of his principal.

(7) If notice of an assignment made by means of a document to which this section applies is given in electronic form in accordance with rules, it is to be regarded for the purposes of any enactment as given in writing.

(8) The right conferred by section 75 of the Law of Property Act 1925 (c. 20) (purchaser's right to have the execution of a conveyance attested) does not apply to a document to which this section applies.

(9) If subsection (4) of section 36A of the Companies Act 1985 (c. 6) (execution of documents) applies to a document because of subsection (4) above, subsection (6) of that section (presumption of due execution) shall have effect in relation to the document with the substitution of "authenticated" for "signed".

(10) In this section, references to an electronic signature and to the certification of such a signature are to be read in accordance with section 7(2) and (3) of the Electronic Communications Act 2000 (c. 7).

C91.1 Subsection (1): A document which is in electronic form and purports to effect a disposition in subsection (2) and which satisfies the conditions in subsection (3) is a document to which section 91 applies.

C91.1.1 Subsection (2): A disposition which complies with subsections (2)(a), (b), (c) and which is of a kind specified by the rules, is a disposition within this subsection. It is anticipated that in due course there will be a prescribed form of electronic disposition for all dispositions that could be made in electronic form under this section. Such forms are likely to be similar to those that have been successfully employed in paper form since 1997 in relation to applications for registration: see Schedule 1 to the Land Registration Rules 1925.[88]

C91.1.2 Subsection (3)(a): The document must provide for the time and date when it takes effect. Since a document in electronic form is not a deed

---

[88] Law Com No. 271 para. 402, p. 529.

(but is merely regarded for the purposes of any enactment as such: subsection (5)), the concept of delivery is therefore inapplicable and thus a document in an electronic form must clearly state the time and date when it takes effect.

Subsection (3)(b): References to an electronic signature are to be read in accordance with section 7(2) and (3) of the Electronic Communications Act 2000: see subsection 10. The obligation is for the electronic signature to be applied in order to authenticate the document in electronic form by each person *by whom it purports to be authenticated.* Thus in instances where both the disponor and the disponee are required to execute the document in electronic form, both must append their electronic signature. **C91.1.3**

Subsection (3)(c): "Certification" has the meaning given to it in section 7(3) of the Electronic Communications Act 2000: subsection 10. Clearly such a requirement is necessary in order to ensure security. **C91.1.4**

Subsection (3)(d): Compliance is required with such conditions as the rules may provide. Such a provision leaving detail to subordinate legislation provides flexibility in what is a novel form of documentation and clearly can be utilised to the fullest advantage. However, it does mean that the detail is currently unknown since no rules have, as yet, been made. **C91.1.5**

Subsection (4): Where a document in electronic form complies with subsections (1), (2), and (3), it is to be regarded as (a) in writing and (b) signed by each individual and sealed by each corporation whose electronic signature it has. Thus this subsection deems the document to comply not only with the statutory requirements of formality imposed by the Electronic Communications Act 2000 but also to those required by the common law. It thus enables the execution of documents in electronic form by corporations which can only do so by the affixing of a seal and, provided the appropriate signatures are appended, enables the electronic execution of documents by those corporations which take advantage of section 36A(4) the Companies Act 1985 which provides that "a document signed by a director and the secretary . . ., or by two directors . . ., and expressed (in whatever form) to be executed by the company has the same effect as if it were executed under the common seal of the company". **C91.1.6**

Subsection (5): As indicated, this subsection provides that a document in electronic form to which this section applies is only *regarded* for the purposes of any enactment as a deed; thus the rule at common law that an agent can only execute a deed on behalf of his or her principal if authorised so do to by deed has no application. **C91.1.7**

C91.1.8 Subsection (6): Certain provisions[89] require the principal's authority to his agent to be in writing. This subsection precludes any challenge to the authority of an agent only on the basis that his authority was not conferred upon him in *writing*. It will not preclude any challenge to the authority of the agent on any other grounds.

C91.1.9 Subsection (7): Under the Act, it is possible to dispose of an interest which is the subject of a notice in the register (s.91(2)(b)). If such a disposition amounts to an assignment of, for example a debt or legal chose in action (such as an option or an estate contract), the provisions of the Law of Property Act 1925, s. 136 require the giving of "express notice *in writing* of the assignment to the debtor or other contracting party". This subsection provides that electronic notices of an arrangement made in a form to which this section applies are to be regarded for the purposes of any enactment as given in writing and thus will, for example, satisfy section 136.

C91.1.10 Subsection (8): The right of a purchaser to have a conveyance attested, at his expense, is thought to be very seldom exercised, in any event.[90]

C91.1.11 Subsection (9): Section 36A(6) of the Companies Act 1985 provides that "in favour of a purchaser a document shall be deemed to have been duly executed by a company if it purports to be signed by a director and the secretary of the company or by two directors of the company, and, where it makes clear on its face that it is intended by the person or persons making it to be a deed, to have been delivered upon it being executed". Subsection (9) permits the extension of that protection for purchasers in circumstances where the document is "authenticated" with the electronic signature of the relevant persons pursuant to section 91(3) in circumstances where it would not otherwise be "signed" within the meaning of section 36A of the Companies Act 1985.

C91.1.12 Subsection (10): Section 7(2) of the Electronic Communications Act 2000 provides that an electronic signature "is so much of anything in electronic form as:

(i) is incorporated into or logically associated with any electronic communication or electronic data; and

(ii) purports to be incorporated or associated for the purpose of being used in establishing the authenticity of the communication or data, the integrity of the communication or data, or both."

---

[89] *e.g.* LPA 1925, s. 53(1)(a).

[90] Law Com No. 271, para. 414, p. 532.

Section 7(3) of the Electronic Communications Act 2000 provides that "an electronic signature incorporated into or associated with a particular electronic communication or particular electronic data is certified by any person if that person (whether before or after the making of the communication) has made a statement confirming that:

(i) the signature;

(ii) a means of producing, communicating or verifying the signature, or

(iii) a procedure applied to the signature,

is (either alone or in combination with other factors) a valid means of establishing the authenticity of the communication or data, the integrity of the communication or data, or both".

92 Land registry network

(1) The registrar may provide, or arrange for the provision of, an electronic communications network for use for such purposes as he thinks fit relating to registration or the carrying on of transactions which— **A92.1**

(a) involve registration, and
(b) are capable of being effected electronically.

(2) Schedule 5 (which makes provision in connection with a network provided under subsection (1) and transactions carried on by means of such a network) has effect.

The Land Registry Network will provide the means by which electronic conveyancing will be conducted. Schedule 5[91] governs the manner in which that network will operate and it may be supplemented by rules, as appropriate: see paragraphs 1(3); 2(3); 3(3); 11(3). No rules have, as yet, been made. **C92.1**

93 Power to require simultaneous registration

(1) This section applies to a disposition of— **A93.1**

(a) a registered estate or charge, or
(b) an interest which is the subject of a notice in the register,

---

[91] See paras SC5.0 *et seq.*, *infra*.

where the disposition is of a description specified by rules.

(2) A disposition to which this section applies, or a contract to make such a disposition, only has effect if it is made by means of a document in electronic form and if, when the document purports to take effect—

(a) it is electronically communicated to the registrar, and
(b) the relevant registration requirements are met.

(3) For the purposes of subsection (2)(b), the relevant registration requirements are—

(a) in the case of a registrable disposition, the requirements under Schedule 2, and
(b) in the case of any other disposition, or a contract, such requirements as rules may provide.

(4) Section 27(1) does not apply to a disposition to which this section applies.

(5) Before making rules under this section the Lord Chancellor must consult such persons as he considers appropriate.

(6) In this section, "disposition", in relation to a registered charge, includes postponement.

C93.1 This section contains a power to make electronic conveyancing compulsory and to require that electronic dispositions should be simultaneously registered. It is envisaged that this power will not be exercised lightly.[92] The two elements which can be compulsorily enforced are the use of electronic conveyancing and the requirement that disposition should be made and registered simultaneously.

The power to make electronic conveyancing compulsory is considered desirable in order to minimise the confusion and difficulties of running two conveyancing systems in tandem and also to bring about the anticipated costs savings that electronic conveyancing will bestow. Since "chain management" is a feature of electronic conveyancing, the existence of one paper-based link in that chain will be sufficient to slow

---

[92] Law Com No. 271, para. 41, p. 533.

the whole process down to the speed of the slowest conveyancer. Thus it is considered desirable for a power of coercion to be included in the Act to require conveyancing to be conducted electronically although the hope is expressed that solicitors and licensed conveyancers will choose to conduct conveyancing electronically in view of the advantages that it has to offer.[93] It is not anticipated that making electronic conveyancing compulsory will happen immediately.[93a]

The simultaneous registration of dispositions is considered desirable because it will ensure the accuracy and the conclusiveness of the register, so far as is possible. Network transaction rules will be made to ensure that a transaction and its registration coincide but the concern is expressed that if, due to some mischance in a particular case this does not happen, the transaction might still then have some effect between the parties (as it would now) even though it was not registered. This would undermine the objective of making the register conclusive as to priority and therefore it is thought necessary to have a statutory provision that will ensure a transaction can have no effect unless simultaneously registered in circumstances where that is required.[94]

Subsection (1): This subsection enables the provisions of section 93 to be brought in gradually by rules, which have (as yet) to be made. Such rules will require to be made after consultation: subsection (5). "Disposition" is defined in subsection (6). **C93.1.1**

Subsection (2): This section provides for such a disposition as is specified by the rules or a contract to make such a disposition only to have effect if (1) it is made by means of a document in electronic form and (2) if, when the document purports to have effect, subsections (a) and (b) are complied with. **C93.1.2**

Subsection (3): The "relevant registration requirements" for the purposes of subsection (2)(b) are specified. When brought into effect, subsection (2) will end the lapse of time between the transaction and its registration and thus preclude the creation of or disposal of rights and interests off the register by making their creation or disposal and registration simultaneous and, in the absence of registration, ineffective. It will thus preclude the creation of third party rights in the interim or the loss or destruction of the as-yet-to-be-registered interest.[95] The register will then become conclusive of the priority of any interests in registered land. Whilst the Act provides for priority to be determined **C93.1.3**

---

[93] *ibid.*, para. 422, p. 534.

[93a] See para. 3.005, *supra*. Also see para. SC5.1.1.1, *infra*.

[94] *ibid.*, para. 423, p. 534.

[95] See *Brown & Root Technology Limited v. Sun Alliance & London Assurance Company* [2001] Ch. 733.

by reference to the creation of an interest in land (as currently prevails under the Land Registration Act 1925), the implementation of section 93 will mean that since creation and registration will coincide, the register will, in effect, be conclusive as to the priority of competing interests which have been expressly created.

C93.1.4 Subsection (4): Since section 93 requires a disposition to have no effect until the registration requirements are met, it is necessary to disapply section 27(1).

C94.1 Such a system would complement a system of electronic conveyancing and would allow for the simultaneous movement of funds and the deduction of stamp duty and registry fees.

94 Electronic settlement

A94.1 The registrar may take such steps as he thinks fit for the purpose of securing the provision of a system of electronic settlement in relation to transactions involving registration.

95 Supplementary

Rules may—

A95.1 (a) make provision about the communication of documents in electronic form to the registrar;

(b) make provision about the electronic storage of documents communicated to the registrar in electronic form.

C95.1 No rules have, as yet, been made. It is anticipated that they are likely to be technical in character and, from time-to-time, to change to reflect developments in information technology.[96]

Part 9

Adverse Possession

C96.0 The provisions of the Act in relation to the acquisition of title to registered land by adverse possession severely limit and make more difficult an adverse possessor's ability to obtain title by adverse possession. Indeed, it abolishes an individual's ability to acquire adverse

---

[96] Law Com No. 271, para. 430, p. 535.

possession of an estate in land by possession alone. Instead, it permits an adverse possessor who has adversely possessed registered land for a period of 10 years or more to apply to be registered as proprietor. If, on that application, he succeeds, that is the end of the matter. On the other hand, if he does not, the registered proprietor has a period of two years in which to take certain steps in order to protect his title. If he does so within that period, the claim to adverse possession may be defeated. If he does not, the adverse possessor is entitled to be registered in his stead on a second application. Consideration was given to the abolition of the concept of adverse possession in relation to the acquisition of title to registered land but it was considered that an ability to acquire ownership by adverse possession should remain for reason of public policy. For example, in circumstances where the registered proprietor dies or simply disappears and the property is adversely possessed in his absence, a total abolition of the doctrine would prevent that land from returning to commercial application and would thus be sterilised.[97]

The structure of the statutory provisions concerning adverse possession in relation to registered land is as follows:—

(1) Section 95 disapplies the provisions of the Limitation Act 1980 in relation to registered land;

(2) Schedule 6 provides for the circumstances in which an adverse possessor may apply to be registered as proprietor of registered land in substitution for the registered proprietor;

(3) Section 97 deals with defences to an action for possession of land;

(4) Schedule 12 provides for certain transitional provisions from the pre-existing law to that set out in the Act.

96 Disapplication of periods of limitation

(1) No period of limitation under section 15 of the Limitation Act 1980 (c. 58) (time limits in relation to recovery of land) shall run against any person, other than a chargee, in relation to an estate in land or rentcharge the title to which is registered. **A96.1**

(2) No period of limitation under section 16 of that Act (time limits in relation to redemption of land) shall run against any person in relation to such an estate in land or rentcharge.

(3) Accordingly, section 17 of that Act (extinction of title on expiry of time limit) does not operate to

[97] See Law Com No. 271, para. 433, p. 536.

extinguish the title of any person where, by virtue of this section, a period of limitation does not run against him.

C96.1 Subsection (1): No period of limitation under section 15 of the Limitation Act 1980 is capable of running against any person other than a chargee in relation to a *registered* estate in land or a registered rentcharge. This gives rise to a number of consequences:—

(1) Unless the individual in question is a chargee or the period in question relates to an estate in land or rentcharge which is *unregistered*, no period of limitation under section 15 of the Limitation Act 1980 can run. Thus subsection (3) provides that section 17 of the Limitation Act 1980 does not operate to extinguish the title of the registered proprietor in circumstances where a period of limitation under the latter Act does not run against him;

(2) The exclusion of a chargee from the provisions of subsection (1) means that a chargee's rights to recover possession or to foreclose remains subject to the provisions of the Limitation Act 1980.

C96.1.1 Subsection (3): The disapplication of a period of limitation under section 15 is confined to instances where the title is registered. Accordingly, the Limitation Act 1980 will continue to apply to the following situations:—

(a) Where the land is not registered. Thus, for example, where an adverse possessor has been in adverse possession against the tenant under a lease which was granted prior to the Act coming into force for a term of 21 years or less[98] prior to the Act coming into force. Once the Act is in force, unregistered leases will be confined to those of seven years or less and thus will not be capable of being barred by adverse possession since the requisite period is 12 years; those of seven years or more will require the title to be registered[99] and thus will fall within the provisions of section 95.

(b) A licensee or tenant-at-will will continue to be bound by the Limitation Act 1980 in relation to any claim that he may bring against an adverse possessor of land, since neither will be registered proprietors of an estate in land.

---

[98] See *Ruoff & Roper*, para. 21–11 such a lease is not required to be registered.

[99] See sections 3(3) and 4(1).

(c) Where a right of re-entry becomes exercisable in respect of a term of years absolute or a fee simple for breach of condition or on the occurrence of some other event, that right will not be excluded from the operation of the Limitation Act 1980 since a right of re-entry is not an estate in land.[1]

(d) Where an adverse possessor ("AP1") has obtained title to land by reason of a period of adverse possession of 12 years or more and he is dispossessed by a second adverse possessor ("AP2"), AP2 must rely upon the provisions of the Limitation Act 1980 in order to obtain title because the title of AP1 will not have been registered and thus will be outside the provisions of section 95(1).

Subsection (2): This section represents a substantial change in the law. **C96.1.2** It precludes a mortgagee who has been in possession of the mortgaged property for a period of 12 years or more from extinguishing the mortgagor's right to redeem the mortgage. Currently section 16 of the Limitation Act 1980 provides for the mortgagor's right to be extinguished. The Act precludes the mortgagee's possession in such circumstances from being adverse since he will either be a tenant under a lease (if the mortgage was made by demise or sub-demise prior to the Act coming into force[2]) or would have the same rights as such a person if the mortgage were charged by way of legal mortgage.[3] Accordingly, possession by a mortgagee cannot be said to be truly adverse since it is attributable to the legal relationship between mortgagor and mortgagee. Accordingly no period of possession of the mortgaged property by the mortgagee will, under the Act, extinguish a mortgagor's right to seek the redemption of the mortgage and the recovery of the land: see subsection (3).

97 Registration of adverse possessor

Schedule 6 (which makes provision about the registration of an adverse possessor of an estate in land or rentcharge) has effect. **A97.1**

Section 97 provides for the application of Schedule 6 to the Act.[4]

98 Defences

(1) A person has a defence to an action for possession of land if— **A98.1**

---

[1] LPA 1925, s. 1(1). See App. 1, *infra*.
[2] LPA 1925, ss. 85 and 86.
[3] LPA 1925, s. 87.
[4] See S6.0 *et seq.*, *infra*.

(a) on the day immediately preceding that on which the action was brought he was entitled to make an application under paragraph 1 of Schedule 6 to be registered as the proprietor of an estate in the land, and

(b) had he made such an application on that day, the condition in paragraph 5(4) of that Schedule would have been satisfied.

(2) A judgment for possession of land ceases to be enforceable at the end of the period of two years beginning with the date of the judgment if the proceedings in which the judgment is given were commenced against a person who was at that time entitled to make an application under paragraph 1 of Schedule 6.

(3) A person has a defence to an action for possession of land if on the day immediately preceding that on which the action was brought he was entitled to make an application under paragraph 6 of Schedule 6 to be registered as the proprietor of an estate in the land.

(4) A judgment for possession of land ceases to be enforceable at the end of the period of two years beginning with the date of the judgment if, at the end of that period, the person against whom the judgment was given is entitled to make an application under paragraph 6 of Schedule 6 to be registered as the proprietor of an estate in the land.

(5) Where in any proceedings a court determines that—

(a) a person is entitled to a defence under this section, or

(b) a judgment for possession has ceased to be enforceable against a person by virtue of subsection (4),

the court must order the registrar to register him as the proprietor of the estate in relation to which he is entitled to make an application under Schedule 6.

(6) The defences under this section are additional to any other defences a person may have.

(7) Rules may make provision to prohibit the recovery of rent due under a rentcharge from a person who has been in adverse possession of the rentcharge.

This section mirrors the provisions of Schedule 6; to the extent that an adverse possessor is able to establish an entitlement to registration under that Schedule, he has a defence to a claim for possession. **C98.1**

Subsection (1): It is a defence to an action for the possession of land if: **C98.1.1**

(a) on the day immediately preceding that on which the action was brought the adverse possessor could apply to be registered as the proprietor of a registered estate in the land on the basis that he had been in adverse possession for the period of 10 years ending on the date of the application and

(b) had he done so (i) the land to which the action related is adjacent to land belonging to the defendant (ii) the exact line of the boundary between the two has not been determined in accordance with any rules under section 60 (iii) for at least 10 years of the period of adverse possession ending on the day immediately preceding that on which the action was brought the defendant reasonably believed that the land to which the action related belonged to him and (iv) the estate to which the action related was registered more than one year prior to the day immediately preceding that on which the action was brought.

Subsection (2): The normal provision that an action on a judgment may be brought within six years beginning with the date of judgment without leave of the Court[5] is abrogated by this subsection which prescribes that a judgment for possession of land ceases to be enforceable at the end of the period of two years beginning with the date of judgment if the proceedings in which the judgment is given were commenced against a person who had been in adverse possession of the estate for the period of 10 years on the day immediately preceding that on which the action was brought. **C98.1.2**

Subsection (3): A person has a defence to an action for possession of land if on the day immediately preceding that on which the action was brought he (a) has been in adverse possession of the land for at least 10 years; (b) has made an application for registration which was rejected and (c) would have been entitled to re-apply to be registered under **C98.1.3**

---

[5] See Limitation Act 1980, s. 24(1); CPR Sched. 1, RSC, O. 46.2(a); *ibid.*, Sched. 2, CCR, O. 26.5(1)(a).

Schedule 6, paragraph 6. The requirements of that paragraph will be satisfied where (a) no steps were taken to terminate the adverse possessor's possession within two years of the rejection of the first application and during that period he has remained in adverse possession; (b) a judgment was obtained against the adverse possessor but was not enforced within two years; or (c) although possession proceedings were brought against the adverse possessor they were discharged or struck out within two years of the rejection of the first application.[6]

C98.1.4 Subsection (4): A judgment will cease to be enforceable against an adverse possessor pursuant to this subsection where:—

(a) he has been in adverse possession of the land for at least 10 years;

(b) he has made an application for registration which was rejected;

(c) the judgment was obtained in possession proceedings against him within two years of that rejection and

(d) two years have elapsed since the judgment was obtained but no steps have been taken to enforce it.[7]

C98.1.5 Subsection (5): Where an individual has a defence pursuant to this section or a judgment has ceased to be enforceable against him the Court *must* order the Registrar to register him as proprietor. Accordingly, a successful defence has the same effect as a successful application by the squatter pursuant to Schedule 6.

C98.1.6 Subsection (6): The defences under section 98 are in addition to any other that an individual may have.

C98.1.7 Subsection (7): It is envisaged that any rules made pursuant to this section will be technical and complex and disproportionate to their importance. Further since the incidence of rentcharges tends to be rather localised (they are most common in Greater Manchester, Lancashire, Sunderland and Bristol), and since most rentcharges will terminate in 2037 pursuant to sections 2 and 3 of the Rentcharges Act 1977, it is thought appropriate for provisions in relation to the prohibition of recovery of rent due under a rentcharge to be contained in the rules.[8]

---

[6] Law Com No. 271, para. 447, p. 539.
[7] *ibid.*, para. 448, p. 539.
[8] Law Com No. 271, para. 451, p. 540.

Part 10

Land Registry

This part of the Act provides for the establishment and management of Her Majesty's Land Registry. It is to be read in conjunction with Schedule 7 (the Land Registry) and Schedule 8 (Indemnities) to the Act. **C99.0**

Administration

99 The land registry

(1) There is to continue to be an office called Her Majesty's Land Registry which is to deal with the business of registration under this Act. **A99.1**

(2) The land registry is to consist of—

(a) the Chief Land Registrar, who is its head, and
(b) the staff appointed by him;

and references in this Act to a member of the land registry are to be read accordingly.

(3) The Lord Chancellor shall appoint a person to be the Chief Land Registrar.

(4) Schedule 7 (which makes further provision about the land registry) has effect.

Subsection (1): Her Majesty's Land Registry remains royally preserved by the Act, having been established as The Office of Land Registry by the Land Transfer Act 1875, s. 106. The Land Registry retains a seal and any document purporting to be sealed with it is admissible in evidence without any further or other proof: Schedule 7, paragraph 5. **C99.1**

Furthermore, the Documentary Evidence Act 1868 applies so that any regulations (including any form or direction) issued by the Registrar or any person authorised to act on his behalf are prima facie evidence of those regulations (including any formal direction) and may be given in all Courts of Justice and in all legal proceedings whatsoever in all or any of the modes mentioned in section 2 of the Act, that is to say:—

(1) By the production or copy of the *London Gazette*, the *Edinburgh Gazette*, the *Dublin Gazette* or any of such Gazettes purporting to contain such regulation;

(2) By the production of a copy of such regulation purported to be printed by the Government printer;

(3) By the production of a copy or extract of the regulations purporting to be specified to be true by the Registrar or any person authorised to act on his behalf. Such a copy or extract may be printed or in manuscript or partly in print and partly in writing. No proof is required of the handwriting or official position of any person certifying, in pursuance of the Act, to the truth of any copy of or extract of any regulation: see Schedule 7, para. 6.

C99.1.1 Subsection (2): No member of the Land Registry is liable in damages for anything done or omitted in the discharge or purported discharge of any function relating to land registration unless it be shown that the act or omission was in bad faith: Schedule 7, paragraph 4. The essential constitution of the Land Registry remains unaltered.

C99.1.2 Subsection (3): The Chief Land Registrar remains an appointee of the Lord Chancellor. He is a disqualified person for the purposes of the House of Commons Disqualification Act 1975 and the Northern Ireland Assembly by virtue of the Northern Ireland Assembly Disqualification Act 1975. He holds office in accordance with the provisions of Schedule 7, paragraph 1. His remuneration is authorised in accordance with Schedule 7, paragraph 2. The Chief Land Registrar has authority to appoint such staff as he wishes and can do so on such terms and conditions as he thinks fit, subject to the approval of the Minister to the Civil Service: Schedule 7, paragraph 3.

100 Conduct of business

A100.1 (1) Any function of the registrar may be carried out by any member of the land registry who is authorised for the purpose by the registrar.

(2) The Lord Chancellor may by regulations make provision about the carrying out of functions during any vacancy in the office of registrar.

(3) The Lord Chancellor may by order designate a particular office of the land registry as the proper office for the receipt of applications or a specified description of application.

(4) The registrar may prepare and publish such forms and directions as he considers necessary or desirable for facilitating the conduct of the business of registration under this Act.

C100.1 Subsection (3): The practice of retaining District Registries with specific geographical responsibilities will remain and it is envisaged that in future specific types of application may be directed to be sent to a particular district registry; for example with applications for first registration becoming increasingly rare, it might be desirable to designate one or more particular land registries to deal with all such applications.[9]

Subsection (4): The practice in recent years has been to publish prescribed forms for a range of transactions involving registered land. This practice will continue and must be expected to grow. **C100.1.1**

101 Annual report

(1) The registrar must make an annual report on the business of the land registry to the Lord Chancellor. **A101.1**

(2) The registrar must publish every report under this section and may do so in such manner as he thinks fit.

(3) The Lord Chancellor must lay copies of every report under this section before Parliament.

This section enshrines the current practice in statute. Moreover that report must be published and laid before Parliament. **C101.1**

Fees and indemnities

102 Fee orders

The Lord Chancellor may with the advice and assistance of the body referred to in section 127(2) (the Rule Committee), and the consent of the Treasury, by order— **A102.1**

(a) prescribe fees to be paid in respect of dealings with the land registry, except under section 69(3)(b) or 105;

(b) make provision about the payment of prescribed fees.

The mechanics for determining the fees which the Land Registry may charge are clearly set out. Section 128(1) enables the fees to differ for different types of transaction. It is envisaged that the current method of **C102.1**

---

[9] Law Com No. 271, para. 462, p. 541.

assessment of fees to change from its present *ad valorem* basis to one based on the work involved in any particular transaction.[10]

103 Indemnities

A103.1 Schedule 8 (which makes provision for the payment of indemnities by the registrar) has effect.

C103.1 The material provisions are contained in Schedule 8.[11]

Miscellaneous

104 General information about land

A104.1 The registrar may publish information about land in England and Wales if it appears to him to be information in which there is legitimate public interest.

C104.1 The Registrar's ability to provide statistical information is authorised by this section; currently the Land Registry issues its Residential Property Price Report quarterly free of charge and it is envisaged that further information will be published in future.

105 Consultancy and advisory services

A105.1 (1) The registrar may provide, or arrange for the provision of, consultancy or advisory services about the registration of land in England and Wales or elsewhere.

(2) The terms on which services are provided under this section by the registrar, in particular terms as to payment, shall be such as he thinks fit.

C105.1 This section is new. It enables the Registrar to act as a free-lance consultant or advisor in relation to the registration of land not only within the jurisdiction but also outside it and to negotiate such terms as to payment as he thinks fit. Further, he may arrange for others to provide those services.

---

[10] Law Com No. 271, para. 469, p. 542.

[11] See para. SC8.0 *et seq.*, *infra*.

106 Incidental powers: companies

(1) If the registrar considers it expedient to do so in connection with his functions under section 69(3)(a), 92(1), 94 or 105(1) or paragraph 10 of Schedule 5, he may— **A106.1**

(a) form, or participate in the formation of, a company, or
(b) purchase, or invest in, a company.

(2) In this section—

"company" means a company within the meaning of the Companies Act 1985 (c. 6);
"invest" means invest in any way (whether by acquiring assets, securities or rights or otherwise).

(3) This section is without prejudice to any powers of the registrar exercisable otherwise than by virtue of this section.

This sections allows the Registrar to incorporate a limited company in connection with his functions under section 69(3)(a) (provision of historical information), section 92(1) (Land Registry Network), section 94 (electronic settlement), section 105(1) (consultancy and advisory service) and paragraph 10 of Schedule 5 (education and training re: Land Registry Network). Subsection (3) preserves the Registrar's powers otherwise than by virtue of this section. **C106.1**

Part 11

Adjudication

This part is new, establishing for the first time, the office of the Adjudicator to Her Majesty's Land Registry. The Adjudicator's role will be to determine disputes referred to him by the Registrar pursuant to section 73(7). The Registrar's judicial role under the Land Registration Act 1925[12] is abolished. Under the current law the Adjudicator's role is partially discharged by the Solicitor to Her Majesty's Land Registry but since he only deals with disputes between parties and not those involving the conduct of the Registry, his remit is necessarily **C107.0**

[12] See *Ruoff & Roper* paras 41–01 *et seq.*

limited. This limitation is not repeated; the Adjudicator has jurisdiction to hear appeals concerning the Registrar's decisions concerning the entry into or termination of a network access agreement. However, the Adjudicator's powers in this regard are not without limitation—this is the only basis upon which he may adjudicate on the conduct of the Registry. For example, a challenge to the Registrar's entry of a restriction would be by way of judicial review. Given the Adjudicator's ability to determine some disputes involving the Land Registry, the need for him to be an independent person outside the structure of the Land Registry is self-evident.

107 The adjudicator

A107.1 (1) The Lord Chancellor shall appoint a person to be the Adjudicator to Her Majesty's Land Registry.

(2) To be qualified for appointment under subsection (1), a person must have a 10 year general qualification (within the meaning of section 71 of the Courts and Legal Services Act 1990 (c. 41)).

(3) Schedule 9 (which makes further provision about the adjudicator) has effect.

C107.1 Subsection (1): The Adjudicator is an appointee of the Lord Chancellor. He may at any time resign his office or be removed by the Lord Chancellor on the ground of incapacity or misbehaviour: Schedule 9, paragraph 1(1), (2). He must retire at 70, although there is the possibility of an annual extension to the age of 75.[13] Otherwise he holds office in accordance with the terms of his appointment and is eligible for reappointment on ceasing to hold office.[14] Paragraph 2 of Schedule 9 provides for his remuneration and the provision of pension. The Adjudicator is disqualified from sitting in the House of Commons or the Northern Ireland Assembly.[15]

C107.1.1 Subsection (2): An individual must have a ten year general qualification within the meaning of section 71 of the Courts and Legal Services Act 1990 to be eligible for appointment as Adjudicator. A "general qualification" within that Act means "a right of audience in relation to any class of proceedings in any part of the Supreme Court, or all proceedings in county courts or magistrates' courts".

---

[13] Sched. 9, para. 1(3).

[14] *ibid.*, para. 4.

[15] *ibid.*, para. 9.

Subsection (3): Schedule 9 enables the Adjudicator to appoint such staff as he wishes on such terms and conditions as he thinks fit, subject to the approval of the Minister for the Civil Service.[16] The Adjudicator has power to delegate any of his functions to any member of his staff save that functions which are not of an administrative character can only be delegated to a member of staff who has a ten year general qualification, as defined above.[17] Provision is made concerning the financing of the Adjudicator and the expenditure incurred in the discharge of his functions.[18] The Adjudicator is subject to the Tribunals and Inquiries Act 1992.[19] Accordingly, the Council on Tribunals is under an obligation to keep under review the constitution and workings of the Adjudicator and from time to time to report thereon. Moreover, the Adjudicator is under an obligation pursuant to section 10 of that Act to give reasons for his decisions. **C107.1.2**

108 Jurisdiction

(1) The adjudicator has the following functions— **A108.1**

(a) determining matters referred to him under section 73(7), and
(b) determining appeals under paragraph 4 of Schedule 5.

(2) Also, the adjudicator may, on application, make any order which the High Court could make for the rectification or setting aside of a document which—

(a) effects a qualifying disposition of a registered estate or charge,
(b) is a contract to make such a disposition, or
(c) effects a transfer of an interest which is the subject of a notice in the register.

(3) For the purposes of subsection (2)(a), a qualifying disposition is—

(a) a registrable disposition, or
(b) a disposition which creates an interest which may be the subject of a notice in the register.

(4) The general law about the effect of an order of the High Court for the rectification or setting aside of a document shall apply to an order under this section.

---

[16] *ibid.*, para. 3.
[17] *ibid.*, para. 2.
[18] *ibid.*, para. 6.
[19] *ibid.*, para. 8.

C108.1 Subsection (1): The Adjudicator's jurisdiction is confined to matters referred to him by the Registrar pursuant to section 73(7) and to hearing appeals from decisions of the Registrar with respect to the entry into or termination of a network access agreement pursuant to Schedule 5.

C108.1.1 Subsection (2): The Adjudicator can, on application, make any order which the High Court could make in relation to the matters specified in sub-paragraphs (a), (b) and (c). "Qualifying disposition" is defined in subsection (3). Thus the Adjudicator has limited powers to rectify or set aside the documentation defined in subsections (2) and (3).

C108.1.2 Subsection (4): The general law concerning the effect of an order for rectification applies to any order that the Registrar may make.[20]

109 Procedure

A109.1 (1) Hearings before the adjudicator shall be held in public, except where he is satisfied that exclusion of the public is just and reasonable.

(2) Subject to that, rules may regulate the practice and procedure to be followed with respect to proceedings before the adjudicator and matters incidental to or consequential on such proceedings.

(3) Rules under subsection (2) may, in particular, make provision about—

(a) when hearings are to be held,
(b) requiring persons to attend hearings to give evidence or to produce documents,
(c) the form in which any decision of the adjudicator is to be given,
(d) payment of costs of a party to proceedings by another party to the proceedings, and
(e) liability for costs thrown away as the result of neglect or delay by a legal representative of a party to proceedings.

C109.1 Subsection (1): Whilst any hearings that the Adjudicator holds shall be in public unless their exclusion is just and reasonable, it is not intended that there should be any requirement for the Adjudicator to hold a

---

[20] See *Ruoff & Roper*, para. 40–11 *et seq.*

hearing unless one or both of the parties wish to have one. It is envisaged that when hearings are to be held they will be the subject of rules (which have, as yet, to be made) under subsection (3). It is envisaged that he may, instead, determine a matter on the papers submitted to him by the parties, as is currently the case when a matter is determined by the Registrar.[21]

Subsection (2), (3): No rules have, as yet, been made. **C109.1.1**

110 Functions in relation to disputes

(1) In proceedings on a reference under section 73(7), the adjudicator may, instead of deciding a matter himself, direct a party to the proceedings to commence proceedings within a specified time in the court for the purpose of obtaining the court's decision on the matter. **A110.1**

(2) Rules may make provision about the reference under subsection (1) of matters to the court and may, in particular, make provision about—

- (a) adjournment of the proceedings before the adjudicator pending the outcome of the proceedings before the court, and
- (b) the powers of the adjudicator in the event of failure to comply with a direction under subsection (1).

(3) Rules may make provision about the functions of the adjudicator in consequence of a decision on a reference under section 73(7) and may, in particular, make provision enabling the adjudicator to determine, or give directions about the determination of—

- (a) the application to which the reference relates, or
- (b) such other present or future application to the registrar as the rules may provide.

(4) If, in the case of a reference under section 73(7) relating to an application under paragraph 1 of Schedule 6, the adjudicator determines that it

---

[21] Law Com No. 271, para. 490, p. 545.

would be unconscionable because of an equity by estoppel for the registered proprietor to seek to dispossess the applicant, but that the circumstances are not such that the applicant ought to be registered as proprietor, the adjudicator—

(a) must determine how the equity due to the applicant is to be satisfied, and
(b) may for that purpose make any order that the High Court could make in the exercise of its equitable jurisdiction.

C110.1 Subsection (1): The Adjudicator retains the power to direct proceedings to be commenced in Court in relation to references to him under section 73(7) of the Act. "Court" means the High Court or the county court. It is envisaged that it may be appropriate for the Adjudicator to direct a reference to the Court in circumstances where a difficult or novel point of law arises; the facts are such that a Court hearing would be more appropriate by reason of their complexity; or there are matters in issue between the parties which the Adjudicator could not himself determine such as ancillary matrimonial issues or an award of damages for breach of the statutory duty imposed by section 77.

C110.1.1 Subsection (2), (3): No rules have, as yet, been made. One can anticipate that the rules would allow the Adjudicator to adjourn an application pending a decision of the Court on any aspect referred to it and, in circumstances where a party is directed to commence proceedings within a specified time in the Court and fails to do so, for the disposal of the application in such manner as appears appropriate.

C110.1.2 Subsection (4): In circumstances where a person who has been in adverse possession of an estate for a period of 10 years or more applies to be registered with title thereto and, on that application, the Adjudicator determines that it will be unconscionable for the registered proprietor to seek to dispossess the applicant but that because of an equity by estoppel the circumstances are not such that the applicant ought to be registered as proprietor, the Adjudicator has authority to determine how the equity due to the applicant is to be satisfied and may, for that purpose, make any order that the High Court could make in the exercise of its equitable jurisdiction.[22]

---

[22] See by way of example the notes to Schedule 6, paragraph 5: paras SC6.1.2.1 *et seq.*, *infra*.

111 Appeals

(1) Subject to subsection (2), a person aggrieved by a decision of the adjudicator may appeal to the High Court. **A111.1**

(2) In the case of a decision on an appeal under paragraph 4 of Schedule 5, only appeal on a point of law is possible.

(3) If on an appeal under this section relating to an application under paragraph 1 of Schedule 6 the court determines that it would be unconscionable because of an equity by estoppel for the registered proprietor to seek to dispossess the applicant, but that the circumstances are not such that the applicant ought to be registered as proprietor, the court must determine how the equity due to the applicant is to be satisfied.

Subsection (1): An individual has an unfettered right of appeal from the Adjudicator to the High Court on both questions of law and fact, unless his decision concerns the determination of an appeal against the decision of the Registrar with respect to the entry into or the termination of a network access agreement: subsection (2). In that instance the appeal is confined to points of law only. The policy behind this distinction is that by reason of the appeal from the Adjudicator being a second appeal, it should be governed by the principles contained in CPR Part 52. However, an appeal from the Adjudicator under subsection (1) can be required, by rules of Court, to be exercisable only with permission.[23] In the light of the framework contained in CPR Part 52 with regard to appeals, it may be anticipated that a requirement for permission will be imposed. Subsection (3) imposes upon the Court on appeal the same duty and latitude imposed upon the Adjudicator pursuant to section 108(4). **C111.1**

112 Enforcement of orders etc

A requirement of the adjudicator shall be enforceable as an order of the court. **A112.1**

"Court" means the High Court or the County Court: s.132(3)(a). Clearly the full range of remedies are available against an individual **C112.1**

[23] Access to Justice Act 1999, s. 54(1).

declining to comply with an order of the Adjudicator, including a committal for contempt.

113 Fees

A113.1 The Lord Chancellor may by order—

(a) prescribe fees to be paid in respect of proceedings before the adjudicator;

(b) make provision about the payment of prescribed fees.

C113.1 No provision has, as yet, been made.

114 Supplementary

A114.1 Power to make rules under this Part is exercisable by the Lord Chancellor.

C114.1 No rules have, as yet, been made.

PART 12

MISCELLANEOUS AND GENERAL

Miscellaneous

115 Rights of pre-emption

A115.1 (1) A right of pre-emption in relation to registered land has effect from the time of creation as an interest capable of binding successors in title (subject to the rules about the effect of dispositions on priority).

(2) This section has effect in relation to rights of pre-emption created on or after the day on which this section comes into force.

C115.1 Subsection (1): Subject to the provisions concerning the effect of dispositions on priority[24] this section declares that a right of pre-emption enjoys priority from the date of its creation but only in relation

---

[24] See sections 28–31, *supra*.

to rights of pre-emption created after the day upon which section 113 is brought into effect: subsection (2). This section will probably alter the law in relation to registered land. For the difficulties created otherwise see *Pritchard v. Briggs*.[25]

116 Proprietary estoppel and mere equities

It is hereby declared for the avoidance of doubt that, in relation to registered land, each of the following— **A116.1**

(a) an equity by estoppel, and

(b) a mere equity,

has effect from the time the equity arises as an interest capable of binding successors in title (subject to the rules about the effect of dispositions on priority).

Subject to the provisions concerning the effect of dispositions on priority[26] an equity by estoppel and a mere equity have effect from the time upon which each arises. **C116.1**

In relation to equities arising by estoppel, the current practice at the Registry is to permit a caution or notice to be entered in relation to such a right upon notification notwithstanding that until a Court gives effect to the claimant's equity, it is an equitable right of an inchoate nature. This section thus confirms the proprietary nature of such an estoppel by declaring that it has effect from the time it arises.

A "mere equity" is difficult to define. An equitable interest is an actual right of property whereas a mere equity is not a right of property but a right, usually of a procedural nature, which is ancillary to some right of property and which limits or qualifies it in some way. Thus, mere equities include the right to have a transaction set aside for fraud, misrepresentation, or undue influence, or to have a document rectified by mistake, or by inserting a repairing covenant.[27] A mere equity also includes a right to seek relief against forfeiture of the lease after a landlord has peaceably re-entered. It is capable under the existing law of being an overriding interest.

In relation to both these, section 114 ensures that they have effect from the time they arise as an interest capable of binding successors in title (subject to sections 28–31) and thus will not be defeated by the purchaser of a later equitable interest in registered land without notice of that equity. In relation to mere equities, it is considered that this probably alters the law.[28]

---

[25] [1980] Ch. 338, CA.

[26] See sections 28–31.

[27] *Snell's Equity* (30th ed., 2000), para. 2–05.

[28] Law Com No. 271, para. 5.36, p. 90.

117 Reduction in unregistered interests with automatic protection

A117.1 (1) Paragraphs 10 to 14 of Schedules 1 and 3 shall cease to have effect at the end of the period of ten years beginning with the day on which those Schedules come into force.

(2) If made before the end of the period mentioned in subsection (1), no fee may be charged for—

(a) an application to lodge a caution against first registration by virtue of an interest falling within any of paragraphs 10 to 14 of Schedule 1, or

(b) an application for the entry in the register of a notice in respect of an interest falling within any of paragraphs 10 to 14 of Schedule 3.

C117.1 Subsection (1): A franchise, a manorial right, a right to rent which was reserved to the Crown on the granting of any freehold estate (whether or not the right is still vested in the Crown), a non-statutory right in respect of an embankment or sea wall or river wall and a right to payment in lieu of tithe will cease to have effect as overriding interests at the conclusion of the period of 10 years beginning with the day on which Schedules 1 and 3 of the Act come into force. This provision relates to those right, which are all of ancient origin and unusual in character. They can be difficult to discover and can, in certain circumstances, be exceptionally onerous. The loss of their overriding status is not as draconian as may appear by reason of the provisions of subsection (2).

C117.1.1 Subsection (2): An individual with the benefit of any of the rights referred to above can, free of charge and prior to the end of the ten year period beginning with the day on which Schedules 1 and 3 come into force apply for either (a) a caution against first registration where the land in question is unregistered in order to protect the right; or (b) apply for the entry in the register of a notice where the land in question is registered.

118 Power to reduce qualifying term

A118.1 (1) The Lord Chancellor may by order substitute for the term specified in any of the following provisions—

(a) section 3(3),

(b) section 4(1)(c)(i) and (2)(b),
(c) section 15(3)(a)(ii),
(d) section 27(2)(b)(i),
(e) section 80(1)(b)(i),
(f) paragraph 1 of Schedule 1,
(g) paragraphs 4(1), 5(1) and 6(1) of Schedule 2, and
(h) paragraph 1 of Schedule 3,

such shorter term as he thinks fit.

(2) An order under this section may contain such transitional provision as the Lord Chancellor thinks fit.

(3) Before making an order under this section, the Lord Chancellor must consult such persons as he considers appropriate.

Subsection (1): The Lord Chancellor can substitute the term specified in any of the provisions set out in the subsection. Broadly speaking these are the periods which trigger or permit registration or which determine the applicability of other rights under the Act (*e.g.* whether certain leases can be overriding interests). In accordance with the policy of the Act, one must anticipate that this power will be exercised in due course to increase in number the range of dispositions that must or can be entered in the register. **C118.1**

Subsection (2), (3): An obligation is imposed for consultation prior to the substitution of any of these periods. No order has, as yet, been made. **C118.1.1**

119 Power to deregister manors

On the application of the proprietor of a registered manor, the registrar may remove the title to the manor from the register. **A119.1**

Since manorial rights are often divorced from the property which formerly comprised the manor and are thus entirely incorporeal, their registration at HM Land Registry confers few practical benefits and causes substantial difficulties. Accordingly, voluntary de-registration is permitted. Clearly, insofar as such rights are no longer associated with land, their deregistration will not offend the objectives of the Act. **C119.1**

120 Conclusiveness of filed copies etc

(1) This section applies where— **A120.1**

(a) a disposition relates to land to which a registered estate relates, and
(b) an entry in the register relating to the registered estate refers to a document kept by the registrar which is not an original.

(2) As between the parties to the disposition, the document kept by the registrar is to be taken—

(a) to be correct, and
(b) to contain all the material parts of the original document.

(3) No party to the disposition may require production of the original document.

(4) No party to the disposition is to be affected by any provision of the original document which is not contained in the document kept by the registrar.

C120.1 This section precludes an individual from impeaching the contents of the register by challenging the documentation upon which it is founded if those documents are not original.

C120.1.1 Subsection (1): The section applies where a disposition relates to land to which a registered estate relates and subsection (1)(b) applies. Thus any disposition relating to land which is registered comes within subsection (1)(a). A lessee of a term of less than seven years (which currently is not registerable) can, if the reversionary interest is registered and subsection (1)(b) is satisfied, rely upon the conclusiveness of filed copies. If the document held by the Registrar is an original, clearly the section will not apply. An original document may be inspected pursuant to section 66 and any rules made thereunder. Schedule 8, paragraph 1(1)(e) permits an individual to be indemnified by the Registrar if he suffers loss by reason of a mistake in a document kept by the Registrar which is not an original and is referred to in the register.

121 Forwarding of applications to registrar of companies

A121.1 The Lord Chancellor may by rules make provision about the transmission by the registrar to the registrar of companies (within the meaning of the Companies Act 1985 (c.6)) of applications under—

(a) Part 12 of that Act (registration of charges), or

(b) Chapter 3 of Part 23 of that Act (corresponding provision for oversea companies).

Section 395 of the Companies Act 1985 provides that subject to the provisions of Chapter 1 of Part XII of the Companies Act 1985, a charge created by a company registered in England and Wales is so far as any security on the company's property or undertaking is conferred by the charge, void against the liquidator or administrator and any creditor of the company unless the prescribed particulars of the charge together with the instrument (if any) by which the charge is created or evidenced are delivered to or received by the registrar of companies for registration in the manner required by Chapter 1 within 21 days after the date of the charge's creation. **C121.1**

If that charge is over land, the provisions of the Act must also be complied with. Registration at either Companies House or at HM Land Registry is not sufficient for the purposes of the other or the requirements of the appropriate enactment. This section anticipates the possibility of a combined application to the Land Registry for registration of a charge over land and for that application to be communicated directly to Companies House for registration pursuant and in accordance with section 395 of the Companies Act 1985. No rules have, as yet, been made.

122 Repeal of Land Registry Act 1862

(1) The Land Registry Act 1862 (c. 53) shall cease to have effect. **A122.1**

(2) The registrar shall have custody of records of title made under that Act.

(3) The registrar may discharge his duty under subsection (2) by keeping the relevant information in electronic form.

(4) The registrar may on application provide a copy of any information included in a record of title made under that Act.

(5) Rules may make provision about applications for the exercise of the power conferred by subsection (4).

The system established by the Land Registry Act 1862 strove to achieve such perfection that it collapsed in ruins.[29] The resultant Royal Commission led to the Land Transfer Act 1875 and the modern system. There are very few subsisting entries under the 1862 Act. Where these **C122.1**

[29] *Ruoff & Roper*, para. 1–09.

exist, they are (wherever possible) brought within the modern system of registration.[30] Clearly this process will continue and, it is envisaged, be facilitated by the rules. None have, as yet, been made.

Offences etc.

123 Suppression of information[31]

A123.1 (1) A person commits an offence if in the course of proceedings relating to registration under this Act he suppresses information with the intention of—

(a) concealing a person's right or claim, or
(b) substantiating a false claim.

(2) A person guilty of an offence under this section is liable—

(a) on conviction on indictment, to imprisonment for a term not exceeding two years or to a fine;
(b) on summary conviction, to imprisonment for a term not exceeding six months or to a fine not exceeding the statutory maximum, or to both.

C123.1 This section applies to the suppression of information with the intention of either concealing a person's right or claim or substantiating a false claim. The offence is capable of commission both in proceedings before the Court and the Adjudicator and also during the course of non-contentious proceedings relating to matters generally under the Act.

124 Improper alteration of the registers

A124.1 (1) A person commits an offence if he dishonestly induces another—

(a) to change the register of title or cautions register, or
(b) to authorise the making of such a change.

(2) A person commits an offence if he intentionally or recklessly makes an unauthorised change in the register of title or cautions register.

---

[30] *ibid.*, para. 9–20.

[31] See also section 75.

(3) A person guilty of an offence under this section is liable—

(a) on conviction on indictment, to imprisonment for a term not exceeding 2 years or to a fine;

(b) on summary conviction, to imprisonment for a term not exceeding six months or to a fine not exceeding the statutory maximum, or to both.

(4) In this section, references to changing the register of title include changing a document referred to in it.

This offence is new. It will be committed by a person who dishonestly induces another to change the register of title or cautions register or induces another to authorise the making of such change. Subsection (4) ensures that references to "changing the register of title" includes changing a document referred to in it. The offence would be committed in circumstances where a person deliberately made a false statement in a document which gave rise to an alteration in the register of title or the cautions register or, in instances where electronic conveyancing applied, where that deliberate and false statement caused an individual with a network access agreement to change the register of title or cautions register since the person with the benefit of that agreement would be authorised to make such a change. **C124.1**

Subsection (2): since the Act anticipates persons other than employees of the registry making alterations to the register of title or cautions register, this offence is new. It covers two situations: first, where an unauthorised person changes the register and does so in the knowledge that he is unauthorised so to do or is reckless as to that fact; secondly, where an authorised person intentionally or recklessly makes a change in the register which he is not authorised to make.

125 Privilege against self-incrimination

(1) The privilege against self-incrimination, so far as relating to offences under this Act, shall not entitle a person to refuse to answer any question or produce any document or thing in any legal proceedings other than criminal proceedings. **A125.1**

(2) No evidence obtained under subsection (1) shall be admissible in any criminal proceedings under this Act against the person from whom it was obtained or that person's spouse.

The section precludes the privilege against self-incrimination assisting an individual in proceedings other than criminal proceedings. Any evidence so obtained is not admissible in criminal proceedings. **C125.1**

Land registration rules

126 Miscellaneous and general powers

A126.1 Schedule 10 (which contains miscellaneous and general land registration rule-making powers) has effect.

C126.1 This applies Schedule 10.[32] No rules have, as yet, been made.

127 Exercise of powers

A127.1 (1) Power to make land registration rules is exercisable by the Lord Chancellor with the advice and assistance of the Rule Committee.

(2) The Rule Committee is a body consisting of—

(a) a judge of the Chancery Division of the High Court nominated by the Lord Chancellor,
(b) the registrar,
(c) a person nominated by the General Council of the Bar,
(d) a person nominated by the Council of the Law Society,
(e) a person nominated by the Council of Mortgage Lenders,
(f) a person nominated by the Council of Licensed Conveyancers,
(g) a person nominated by the Royal Institution of Chartered Surveyors,
(h) a person with experience in, and knowledge of, consumer affairs, and
(i) any person nominated under subsection (3).

(3) The Lord Chancellor may nominate to be a member of the Rule Committee any person who appears to him to have qualifications or experience which would be of value to the committee in considering any matter with which it is concerned.

C127.1 No rules have, as yet, been made.

---

[32] See paras S10.1 *et seq.*, *infra*.

Supplementary

128 Rules, regulations and orders

(1) Any power of the Lord Chancellor to make rules, regulations or orders under this Act includes power to make different provision for different cases. **A128.1**

(2) Any power of the Lord Chancellor to make rules, regulations or orders under this Act is exercisable by statutory instrument.

(3) A statutory instrument containing—

(a) regulations under section 100(2), or
(b) an order under section 100(3), 102 or 113,

is to be laid before Parliament after being made.

(4) A statutory instrument containing—

(a) land registration rules,
(b) rules under Part 11 or section 121,
(c) regulations under paragraph 5 of Schedule 9, or
(d) an order under section 5(1), 62(9), 80(4), 118(1) or 130,

is subject to annulment in pursuance of a resolution of either House of Parliament.

(5) Rules under section 93 or paragraph 1, 2 or 3 of Schedule 5 shall not be made unless a draft of the rules has been laid before and approved by resolution of each House of Parliament.

No rules, regulations or orders have, as yet, been made. **C128.1**

129 Crown application

This Act binds the Crown. **A129.1**

130 Application to internal waters

This Act applies to land covered by internal waters of the United Kingdom which are— **A130.1**

(a) within England or Wales, or

(b) adjacent to England or Wales and specified for the purposes of this section by order made by the Lord Chancellor.

C130.1 "England" means, subject to any alteration of boundaries under Part IV of the Local Government Act 1972, the area comprising of the counties established by section 1 of that Act, Greater London and the Isles of Scilly.[33]

"Wales" means the combined area of the counties which were created by section 20 of the Local Government Act 1972, as originally enacted, but subject to any alteration made under section 73 of that Act (consequential alteration of boundary following alteration of water course):[34]

Subparagraph (a): this paragraph reflects the current practice, that land within local government administrative areas is registerable notwithstanding that it is covered by water.

Subparagraph (b): this provision however enables the Crown (subject to any order by the Lord Chancellor) to register submarine land from the county boundaries to the base lines which define the territorial limits of the United Kingdom pursuant to the Convention on the Territorial Sea of 1958, Article 4. It is envisaged that such an exercise will protect submarine land from encroachment by adverse possessors who might, for example, lay cables or pipelines within internal waters outside the body of any county. It is anticipated that this power will be phased in slowly, if only to avoid overloading the registry.[35]

131 "Proprietor in possession"

A131.1 (1) For the purposes of this Act, land is in the possession of the proprietor of a registered estate in land if it is physically in his possession, or in that of a person who is entitled to be registered as the proprietor of the registered estate.

(2) In the case of the following relationships, land which is (or is treated as being) in the possession of the second-mentioned person is to be treated for the purposes of subsection (1) as in the possession of the first-mentioned person—

(a) landlord and tenant;

---

33 Interpretation Act 1978, Sched. 1.

34 *ibid.*

35 Law Com No. 271, para. 558, p. 557.

(b) mortgagor and mortgagee;
(c) licensor and licensee;
(d) trustee and beneficiary.

(3) In subsection (1), the reference to entitlement does not include entitlement under Schedule 6.

Subsection (1): Clearly the proprietor of a registered estate in land is in possession if he is physically in possession. Moreover, an individual who is entitled to be registered as proprietor of the registered estate is also "in possession" unless that right arises under Schedule 6 (adverse possession). Thus a beneficiary behind a bare trust would be a "proprietor in possession". **C131.1**

Subsection (2): The provisions of this subsection are clear. The ability to treat land as being in the possession of the second-mentioned person means that a landlord, for example, would be in possession where his tenant has sub-let since the tenant will be treated as being in possession by virtue of his relationship with the sub-tenant. **C131.1.1**

132 General interpretation

(1) In this Act— **A132.1**

"adjudicator" means the Adjudicator to Her Majesty's Land Registry;

"caution against first registration" means a caution lodged under section 15;

"cautions register" means the register kept under section 19(1);

"charge" means any mortgage, charge or lien for securing money or money's worth;

"demesne land" means land belonging to Her Majesty in right of the Crown which is not held for an estate in fee simple absolute in possession;

"land" includes—

(a) buildings and other structures,
(b) land covered with water, and
(c) mines and minerals, whether or not held with the surface;

"land registration rules" means any rules under this Act, other than rules under section 93, Part 11, section 121 or paragraph 1, 2 or 3 of Schedule 5;

“legal estate” has the same meaning as in the Law of Property Act 1925 (c. 20);

“legal mortgage” has the same meaning as in the Law of Property Act 1925;

“mines and minerals” includes any strata or seam of minerals or substances in or under any land, and powers of working and getting any such minerals or substances;

“registrar” means the Chief Land Registrar;

“register” means the register of title, except in the context of cautions against first registration;

“registered” means entered in the register;

“registered charge” means a charge the title to which is entered in the register;

“registered estate” means a legal estate the title to which is entered in the register, other than a registered charge;

“registered land” means a registered estate or registered charge;

“registrable disposition” means a disposition which is required to be completed by registration under section 27;

“requirement of registration” means the requirement of registration under section 4;

“sub-charge” means a charge under section 23(2)(b);

“term of years absolute” has the same meaning as in the Law of Property Act 1925 (c. 20);

“valuable consideration” does not include marriage consideration or a nominal consideration in money.

(2) In subsection (1), in the definition of “demesne land”, the reference to land belonging to Her Majesty does not include land in relation to which a freehold estate in land has determined, but in relation to which there has been no act of entry or management by the Crown.

(3) In this Act—

(a) references to the court are to the High Court or a county court,

(b) references to an interest affecting an estate or charge are to an adverse right affecting the title to the estate or charge, and

(c) references to the right to object to an application to the registrar are to the right under section 73.

Subsection (1): "Legal Estate"[37]; "Legal Mortgage"[38]; "Term of Years Absolute"[39] **C132.1**

Final provisions

133 Minor and consequential amendments

Schedule 11 (which makes minor and consequential amendments) has effect. **A133.1**

134 Transition

(1) The Lord Chancellor may by order make such transitional provisions and savings as he thinks fit in connection with the coming into force of any of the provisions of this Act. **A134.1**

---

[37] " 'Legal Estate' means the estates, interest and charges, in or over land (subsisting or created at law) which are by [the Law of Property Act 1925] authorised to subsist or to be created as legal estates": LPA 1925, s. 205(1)(x). As to those authorised to subsist or to be created as legal estates, see App. 1, *infra*.

[38] " 'Legal Mortgage' means a mortgage by demise or sub-demise or a charge by way of legal mortgage and 'legal mortgagee' has a corresponding meaning": LPA 1925, s. 205(1)(xvi).

[39] " 'Term of Years Absolute" means a term of years (taking effect either in possession or in reversion whether or not at a rent) with or without impeachment for waste, subject or not to another legal estate, and either certain or liable to determination by notice, re-entry, operation of law or by a provision for cesser on redemption, or in any other event (other than the dropping of a life, or the determination of a determinable life interest); but does not include any term of years determinable with life or lives or with the cesser of a determinable life interest, nor, if created after the commencement of [the Law of Property Act 1925] a term of years which is not expressed to take effect in possession within 21 years after the creation thereof where required by [the Law of Property Act 1925] to take effect within that period; and in this definition the expression 'term of years' includes a term for less than a year or for a year or years and a fraction of a year from year to year": LPA 1925, s. 205 (1)(xxvii).

(2) Schedule 12 (which makes transitional provisions and savings) has effect.

(3) Nothing in Schedule 12 affects the power to make transitional provisions and savings under subsection (1); and an order under that subsection may modify any provision made by that Schedule.

C134.1 Schedule 12, which has effect pursuant to subsection 2, makes certain transitional provisions and savings but is without prejudice to the Lord Chancellor's power to make, by order, such other transitional provisions and savings as he thinks fit. No order has, as yet, been made.

135 Repeals

A135.1 The enactments specified in Schedule 13 (which include certain provisions which are already spent) are hereby repealed to the extent specified there.

136 Short title, commencement and extent

A136.1 (1) This Act may be cited as the Land Registration Act 2002.

(2) This Act shall come into force on such day as the Lord Chancellor may by order appoint, and different days may be so appointed for different purposes.

(3) Subject to subsection (4), this Act extends to England and Wales only.

(4) Any amendment or repeal by this Act of an existing enactment, other than—

(a) section 37 of the Requisitioned Land and War Works Act 1945 (c. 43), and

(b) Schedule 2A to the Building Societies Act 1986 (c. 53),

has the same extent as the enactment amended or repealed.

C136.1 Subsection (2): No order has, as yet, been made under this subsection.

C136.1.1 Subsection (4): Notwithstanding the geographical limitation imposed by subsection (3), some of the amendments and repeals effected by the Act are needed to extend to other parts of the United Kingdom because the enactment amended or repealed by it do so (*e.g.* the amendments to the House of Commons Disqualification Act 1975).

Schedules

SCHEDULE 1 Sections 11 and 12

Unregistered Interests Which Override First Registration

Unlike the Land Registration Act 1925, the Act distinguishes between those interests which are overriding and bind the registered proprietor upon first registration (Schedule 1) and those which bind the registered proprietor on a registered disposition (Schedule 3).[1] Both these schedules significantly reduce the scope and extent of overriding interests under the Act. This reduction is consistent with the policy behind the Act, which is to ensure that the register is as inclusive as possible and that all rights which exist in relation to registered land are apparent from a search of the register. Clearly, this approach cannot be made absolute, if only on the grounds of public policy. **SC1.0**

Section 11(4) declares that the estate is, on first registration, vested in the registered proprietor subject only to the interests affecting the estate at the time of registration, namely:

(a) interests which are the subject of an entry in the register in relation to the estate,

(b) unregistered interests which fall within any of the paragraphs of schedule 1[2] and

(c) interests acquired under the Limitation Act 1980 of which the proprietor has notice.

Clearly therefore the 15 classes of interest which can constitute overriding interests on first registration comprise matters of importance to any purchaser of land which is to be registered.

Section 12(4) makes similar provision in relation to the interests which affect leasehold estates at the time of registration.

Paragraphs 10, 11, 12 and 14 of Schedule 1 cease to have effect at the end of the period of ten years beginning with the day on which it comes into force[3]; since the interests are capable of protection without charge

---

[1] See para. SC3.0 *et seq.*, *infra*.

[2] And section 90(5) which states that a PPP lease relating to transport in London has effect as if it were including in Schedule 1.

[3] See section 117, *supra*.

in the register[4] during this period this provision is not as harsh as may first appear and is consonant with the objective that underlies the Act of ensuring the register is as accurate and complete as possible.

Leasehold estates in land[5]

S1.1 1. A leasehold estate in land granted for a term not exceeding seven years from the date of the grant, except for a lease the grant of which falls within section 4(1)(d), (e) or (f).

SC1.1 Paragraph 1: A short lease of less than seven years[6] from the date of grant comprises an overriding interest on first registration and reflects the current position under the Land Registration Act 1925. To this there are three exceptions, namely those leases which fall within section 4(1) (d), (e) or (f). These are:—

(i) the grant of a reversionary lease which takes effect in possession more than three months after the date of grant. The denial of overriding status to this type of lease reflects the fact that such leases can be difficult to identify and thus deserve to be reflected by an entry in the register if they are to bind an individual being registered as proprietor on first registration.

(ii) The grant of a lease in pursuance of Part V of the Housing Act 1985 (the Right to Buy) out of an unregistered legal estate in land. This exception reflects the effect of section 154(7) of that Act.

(iii) The grant of a lease out of an unregistered legal estate in land in circumstances where section 171A of the Housing Act 1985 applies (disposal by a landlord which leads to a person no longer being a secure tenant). This exception reflects in part the effect of section 171G and schedule 9A to the Housing Act 1985.

Overriding interests under section 70(1)(k) of the Land Registration Act 1925 (leases granted for a term not exceeding 21 years)[6a]

---

[4] See section 117(2), *supra*.

[5] For leases that enjoy overriding status pursuant to section 70(1)(k) of the Land Registration Act 1925 (leases granted for a term not exceeding 21 years) which enjoy overriding status prior to the coming into force of the Act: see Sched. 12, para. 12, *infra*.

[6] This period is of course subject to such order as may be made substituting a different period pursuant to section 118.

[6a] See *Ruoff & Roper*, para. 6–25.

Interests of persons in actual occupation

2. An interest belonging to a person in actual occupation, so far as relating to land of which he is in actual occupation, except for an interest under a settlement under the Settled Land Act 1925 (c. 18). **S1.1.1**

Paragraph 2: This reflects the current position under section 70(1)(g). The rights of a person who is in actual occupation are overriding interests upon first registration. However, to this there is an exception, namely interests under a settlement under the Settled Land Act 1925. This exception reflects the position under the Land Registration Act 1925.[7] **SC1.1.1**

None of the matters mentioned in section 87(1) are capable of being overriding interests.[8]

There are two important differences under paragraph 2 when contrasted with section 70(1)(g) of the Land Registration Act 1925. First those "in receipt of the rent and profits [of land]" will no longer enjoy the protection of overriding status. Secondly, the saving to section 70(1)(g) namely that the rights of a person in actual occupation cease to be overriding "where enquiry is made of such person and the rights are not disclosed" finds no role under paragraph 2, with one exception in relation to interests acquired under the Limitation Act 1980. Different considerations apply on the disposition of a registered interest—see paragraph 2 of Schedule 3.[9]

Easements and profits à prendre[10]

3. A legal easement or profit à prendre **S1.1.2**

Paragraph 3: Clearly under the Act, *equitable* easements will not comprise overriding interests.[11] **SC1.1.2**

Customary and public rights[12]

4. A customary right. **S1.1.3**

5. A public right.

---

[7] See *Ruoff & Roper*, para. 31–06 *et seq.*

[8] Section 87(3).

[9] See section 11(4)(c); section 12(4)(d) *supra*.

[10] See *Ruoff & Roper*, para. 6–05.

[11] See generally *Ruoff & Roper*, para. 6–06.

[12] *ibid.*, paras 6–08, 6–09.

SC1.1.3 Paragraph 4: "Customary Rights" are those ancient rights enjoyed by members of a local community or a particular defined class of such persons.

SC1.1.3.1 Paragraph 5: "Public Rights" means those rights which are exercisable by anyone, whether he owns land or not, merely by virtue of the general law. They include such rights as public rights of way, rights to discharge into a public sewer and rights of passage in navigable waters.

Local land charges[13]

S1.1.4 6. A local land charge.

SC1.1.4 Paragraph 6: This provision reflects that contained under the Land Registration Act 1925.[14]

Mines and minerals

S1.1.5 7. An interest in any coal or coal mine, the rights attached to any such interest and the rights of any person under section 38, 49 or 51 of the Coal Industry Act 1994 (c. 21).

8. In the case of land to which title was registered before 1898, rights to mines and minerals (and incidental rights) created before 1898.

9. In the case of land to which title was registered between 1898 and 1925 inclusive, rights to mines and minerals (and incidental rights) created before the date of registration of the title.

SC1.1.5 Paragraph 7: This reflects the current position under section 70(1)(n).[15]

SC1.1.5.1 Paragraphs 8, 9: These reflect the current position under section 70(1)(l).[16]

---

[13] A local land charge which was an overriding interest under the Land Registration Act 1925 (the status of which is preserved by section 19(3) of the Local Land Charges Act 1975 which makes transactional provision following upon an attraction in the definition of "local land charge") retains its overriding status under the schedule: See Sched 12, para. 13.

[14] *Ruoff & Roper*, para. 6–23.

[15] *ibid.*, para. 6–27.

[16] *ibid.*, para. 6–26.

Miscellaneous

10. A franchise. **S1.1.6**

11. A manorial right.

12. A right to rent which was reserved to the Crown on the granting of any freehold estate (whether or not the right is still vested in the Crown).

13. A non-statutory right in respect of an embankment or sea or river wall.

14. A right to payment in lieu of tithe.

15. A right acquired under the Limitation Act 1980 before the coming into force of this Schedule.

Paragraphs 10, 11: These reflect the provisions of section 70(1)(j). "Manorial Rights" consist of rights of fishing and sporting, seigniorial and manorial rights of all descriptions until extinguished. These rights were saved, with the lord's rights to mines and minerals, ancillary rights of winning and working them, privileges in regard to fairs and markets and rights in respect of dykes, sea and river walls which were subsisting on January 1, 1926 from the general enfranchisement that was effected on that date by the Law of Property Act 1922.[17] The Law Commission Report[18] considers that these rights include the lord's sporting rights; the lord's or tenant's rights of mines and minerals; the lord's rights to fairs and markets; the tenant's rights of common and the lord's or tenant's liability for the construction, maintenance and repair of dykes, ditches, canals and other works. **SC1.1.6**

Paragraph 12: This reflects the position under section 70(1)(b).[19] **SC1.1.6.1**

Paragraph 13: This reflects the provisions of section 70(1)(d).[20] **SC1.1.6.2**

Paragraph 14: This saving in regard to payment in lieu of tithe reflects part of section 70(1)(e).[21] **SC1.1.6.3**

---

[17] *ibid.*, para. 6–24.
[18] Law Com No. 271, para. 594, p. 562.
[19] *Ruoff & Roper*, para. 6–10.
[20] *ibid.*, para. 6–12.
[21] *ibid.*, para. 6–13.

SC1.1.6.4 Paragraph 15: Inserted by Sched. 12, para. 7, subject to the limitations specified therein, *i.e.* for the period of three years beginning with the day Schedule 1 comes into force.[22]
PPP leases are overriding interests too.[23]

SCHEDULE 2

Section 27

Registrable Dispositions: Registration Requirements

SC2.0 This Schedule makes provision for the registration requirements of those interests the disposal of which can only be completed by registration.[24] The commentary on this Schedule is dealt with elsewhere.[25]

Part 1

Registered Estates

Introductory

S2.1 1. This Part deals with the registration requirements relating to those dispositions of registered estates which are required to be completed by registration.

Transfer

S2.1.1 2. (1) In the case of a transfer of whole or part, the transferee, or his successor in title, must be entered in the register as the proprietor.
(2) In the case of a transfer of part, such details of the transfer as rules may provide must be entered in the register in relation to the registered estate out of which the transfer is made.

Lease of estate in land

S2.1.2 3. (1) This paragraph applies to a disposition consisting of the grant out of an estate in land of a term of years absolute.

---

[22] See para. S12.1.4, *infra*.

[23] Section 90(5).

[24] See section 27, *supra*.

[25] *ibid.*

(2) In the case of a disposition to which this paragraph applies—

(a) the grantee, or his successor in title, must be entered in the register as the proprietor of the lease, and
(b) a notice in respect of the lease must be entered in the register.

Lease of franchise or manor

4. (1) This paragraph applies to a disposition consisting of the grant out of a franchise or manor of a lease for a term of more than seven years from the date of the grant. **S2.1.3**

(2) In the case of a disposition to which this paragraph applies—

(a) the grantee, or his successor in title, must be entered in the register as the proprietor of the lease, and
(b) a notice in respect of the lease must be entered in the register.

5. (1) This paragraph applies to a disposition consisting of the grant out of a franchise or manor of a lease for a term not exceeding seven years from the date of the grant.

(2) In the case of a disposition to which this paragraph applies, a notice in respect of the lease must be entered in the register.

Creation of independently registrable legal interest

6. (1) This paragraph applies to a disposition consisting of the creation of a legal rentcharge or profit à prendre in gross, other than one created for, or for an interest equivalent to, a term of years absolute not exceeding seven years from the date of creation. **S2.1.4**

(2) In the case of a disposition to which this paragraph applies—

(a) the grantee, or his successor in title, must be entered in the register as the proprietor of the interest created, and

(b) a notice in respect of the interest created must be entered in the register.

(3) In sub-paragraph (1), the reference to a legal rentcharge or profit à prendre in gross is to one falling within section 1(2) of the Law of Property Act 1925 (c. 20).

Creation of other legal interest

S2.1.5 7. (1) This paragraph applies to a disposition which—

(a) consists of the creation of an interest of a kind falling within section 1(2)(a), (b) or (e) of the Law of Property Act 1925, and

(b) is not a disposition to which paragraph 4, 5 or 6 applies.

(2) In the case of a disposition to which this paragraph applies—

(a) a notice in respect of the interest created must be entered in the register, and

(b) if the interest is created for the benefit of a registered estate, the proprietor of the registered estate must be entered in the register as its proprietor.

(3) Rules may provide for sub-paragraph (2) to have effect with modifications in relation to a right of entry over or in respect of a term of years absolute.

Creation of legal charge

S2.1.6 8. In the case of the creation of a charge, the chargee, or his successor in title, must be entered in the register as the proprietor of the charge.

Part 2

Registered Charges

Introductory

S2.1.7 9. This Part deals with the registration requirements relating to those dispositions of registered charges which are required to be completed by registration.

Transfer

10. In the case of a transfer, the transferee, or his successor in title, must be entered in the register as the proprietor. **S2.1.8**

Creation of sub-charge

11. In the case of the creation of a sub-charge, the sub-chargee, or his successor in title, must be entered in the register as the proprietor of the sub-charge. **S2.1.9**

SCHEDULE 3 Sections 29 and 30

UNREGISTERED INTERESTS WHICH OVERRIDE REGISTERED DISPOSITIONS

The matters specified in Schedule 3 comprise overriding dispositions that affect a registered disposition of registered land. As with Schedule 1, it provides for 14 classes of interest which comprise overriding interests upon the registered disposition of registered land and, pursuant to section 90, a fifteenth category is included, namely PPP Leases.[26] Those rights specified in paragraph 10, 11, 12, 13 and 14 will lose their overriding status 10 years after the date upon which the Schedule is brought into force.[27] Schedule 12, paragraph 8 inserts paragraph 2A in this Schedule: see S12.1.4. **SC3.0**

Leasehold estates in land

1. A leasehold estate in land granted for a term not exceeding seven years from the date of the grant, except for— **S3.1**
   (a) a lease the grant of which falls within section 4(1)(d), (e) or (f);
   (b) a lease the grant of which constitutes a registrable disposition.

Paragraph 1: Subject to any orders which may be made pursuant to section 118[28], a short lease for a term not exceeding seven years **SC3.1**

---

[26] Section 90, 90(5) *supra*.

[27] Section *supra*, similar provisions apply in relation to Schedule 1.

[28] See para. A118.1 *et seq.*, *supra*.

comprises an overriding interest save for those which fall within section 4(1)(d), (e) or (f)[29] or one which constitutes a registrable disposition. This last exception covers five instances where a lease granted out of registered land or a registered franchise on manor constitute registrable dispositions that must be completed by registration.[30–32] They are:

(i) the grant of a reversionary lease taking effect in possession more than three months after the date of the grant of the lease.
(ii) a lease under which the right to possession is discontinuous, such as a timeshare lease.
(iii) a lease granted in pursuance of Part V of the Housing Act 1985 (the Right to Buy), thus replicating in part the effect of section 154(7) of that Act.
(iv) in circumstances where section 171A of that Act applies (disposal by a landlord which leads to a person no longer being a secure tenant) thus replicating part of the effect of section 171G and Schedule 9A of that Act.
(v) where the registered estate is a franchise or manor, any grant of a lease deriving therefrom amounts to a disposition which must be completed by registration.

Transitional Provisions: All leases that are prior to the coming into force of the Act retain that status: Sched. 12, paragraph 12.

Interests of persons in actual occupation

S3.1.1 2. An interest belonging at the time of the disposition to a person in actual occupation, so far as relating to land of which he is in actual occupation, except for—

(a) an interest under a settlement under the Settled Land Act 1925 (c. 18);
(b) an interest of a person of whom inquiry was made before the disposition and who failed to disclose the right when he could reasonably have been expected to do so;
(c) an interest—
  (i) which belongs to a person whose occupation would not have been obvious on a reasonably careful inspection of the land at the time of the disposition, and
  (ii) of which the person to whom the disposition is made does not have actual knowledge at that time;

[29] See para. A4.1 *et seq.*, *supra*.
[30–32] Section 27(1); section 27(2)(b)(c).

(d) a leasehold estate in land granted to take effect in possession after the end of the period of three months beginning with the date of the grant and which has not taken effect in possession at the time of the disposition.

2A. *A right under Schedule 12, paragraph 8.*

Paragraph 2: Thus paragraph 1 makes a similar provision to that contained in Schedule 1, paragraph 2, namely an interest belonging to a person in actual occupation[34–35] is an overriding interest upon the registered disposition of the property of which he is in actual occupation. **SC3.1.1**

To this there are four exceptions:—

(i) An interest under a settlement under the Settled Land Act 1925.[36]

(ii) The interests of any person of whom inquiry was made before the disposition and who failed to disclose the right when he could reasonably have been expected to do so. This provision reflects the saving to section 70(1)(g) of the Land Registration Act 1925.

(iii) Paragraph 2(1)(c) strips the overriding status from an individual who is in actual occupation of land in circumstances where:—

   (a) where that person's occupation would not have been obvious on a reasonably careful inspection of the land at the time of disposition and
   (b) the person to whom the disposition is made does not have actual knowledge of it at the time.

   The following points fall to be noted in relation to this exception. First, for it to apply, it is the *occupation* of the individual which needs not to be obvious on a reasonably careful inspection of the land and not that individual's *interest*. Secondly, it requires the occupation not to be obvious on *a reasonably careful inspection* of the land. Thus constructive knowledge of the disponee is irrelevant; the test is whether the occupation would have been *obvious* on a physical inspection at the time of disposition. On the other hand, if the disponee has *actual* knowledge of the person's occupation, the exception will not apply notwithstanding that occupation may not be obvious

[34] See Schedule (2), para. S1.1.1, *supra*.

[36] *Ruoff & Roper*, para. 6–15 *et seq*.

on a reasonably careful inspection at the time of disposition. Such a person's rights will amount to an overriding interest in those circumstances unless inquiry was made of him before the disposition and he has failed to disclose the right when he could reasonably have been expected to do so.

(iv) In the unlikely circumstances that an individual is in occupation of the land and has been granted a leasehold estate therein to take effect in possession after the end of the period of three months beginning with the date of the grant of the lease in question, that interest will not amount to an overriding interest by reason of paragraph 2(1)(d). Since section 4(1)(d) requires such leases to be registered, it is consonant with the policy of the Act that a failure to register would not go without its consequences and thus the overriding nature that may otherwise have been bestowed upon such an interest is denied.

Paragraph 2A: This paragraph[37] preserves the overriding status of the rights of an individual who is in receipt of the rents and and profits from registered land but who is not in actual occupation.

Easements and profits à prendre

S3.1.2 3. (1) A legal easement or profit à prendre, except for an easement, or a profit à prendre which is not registered under the Commons Registration Act 1965 (c. 64), which at the time of the disposition—

(a) is not within the actual knowledge of the person to whom the disposition is made, and

(b) would not have been obvious on a reasonably careful inspection of the land over which the easement or profit is exercisable.

(2) The exception in subparagraph (1) does not apply if the person entitled to the easement or profit proves that it has been exercised in the period of one year ending with the day of the disposition.

---

[37] Inserted by Schedule 12, para. 8, *infra*.

Paragraph 3: A legal easement or *profit à prendre* is an overriding interest.[38] To this there is a qualified exception[39]: **SC3.1.2**

(i) A legal easement or *profit à prendre* which is not registered under the Commons Registration Act 1965 and which at the time of disposition (a) is not within the actual knowledge of the person to whom the disposition is made and (b) would not have been obvious on a reasonably careful inspection of the land over which the easement or profit is exercisable will not amount to an overriding interest.

(ii) To this exception there is a saving. The exception does not apply if the person entitled to the easement or profit proves that it has been exercised for the period of one year ending with the day of the disposition. Thus easements which are not registered under the 1965 Act and of which the disponee does not know and which would not have been obvious on a reasonably careful inspection of the land over which it relates can still amount to an overriding interest where they have been exercised for the period of one year ending with the day of disposition. The importance of this exception relates to "invisible" easements such as rights of drainage or the right to run a water supply over a neighbour's land. These rights may have existed for many years and remain in use but otherwise within sub-paragraphs 3(1)(a) and (b).

It is envisaged this exception will encourage a straightforward system of standard inquiries in relation to easements and profits that will prompt vendors to disclose what they can reasonably be expected to know. In turn, it is envisaged that this will help to ensure that such rights are disclosed to the Registrar by virtue of rules that will be made under section 71. Such rights will then be entered in the register.[40]

Transitional Provisions: Schedule 12, paragraphs 9 and 10 make transitional provision for legal easements and *profits à prendre.*[41]

---

[38] Such easements or profits which are expressly granted or reserved out of registered land after the coming into force of the Act will never amount to an overriding interest since they cannot take effect at law until registered (section 27(1), (2)(d)) and once a notice has been entered in the register in respect of an easement it cannot fall within paragraph 3: section 29(2), 30(2).

[39] For the first three years after Schedule 3 is brought into force, this exception has no application: Schedule 12, para. 10, *infra*.

[40] Law Com No. 271, para. 625, p. 567.

[41] See paras S12.1.4 *et seq.*, *infra*.

SC3.1.2.1 Paragraphs 4–14: The provisions of Schedule 3 are, in relation to these paragraphs, identical to those of Schedule 1.[42]

SC3.1.2.2 Paragraph 15: A right under Schedule 12, para 18(1). See S12.1.7[43] PPP leases are overriding interests too.[44]

Customary and public rights

S3.1.3 4. A customary right.

5. A public right.

Local land charges

S3.1.4 6. A local and charge.

Mines and minerals

S3.1.5 7. An interest in any coal or coal mine, the rights attached to any such interest and the rights of any person under section 38, 49 or 51 of the Coal Industry Act 1994 (c. 21).

8. In the case of land to which title was registered before 1898, rights to mines and minerals (and incidental rights) created before 1898.

9. In the case of land to which title was registered between 1898 and 1925 inclusive, rights to mines and minerals (and incidental rights) created before the date of registration of the title.

Miscellaneous

S3.1.6 10. A franchise.

11. A manorial right.

12. A right to rent which was reserved to the Crown on the granting of any freehold estate (whether or not the right is still vested in the Crown).

---

[42] Accordingly, see S.1.3 *et seq.*, *supra*.

[43] Inserted by Sched. 12, para. 11.

[44] Section 90(5).

13. A non-statutory right in respect of an embankment or sea or river wall.

14. A right to payment in lieu of tithe.

15. *A right under paragraph 18(1) of Schedule 12.*

SCHEDULE 4

Section 65

Alteration of the Register

The provisions of this Schedule are designed to fulfil two objectives. First to make a number of changes to the present law in order to improve its working. Secondly, to recast the legislation so that it reflects the practice of rectification as it is developed under section 82 of the Land Registration Act 1925.[45] **SC4.0**

Introductory

1. In this Schedule, references to rectification, in relation to alteration of the register, are to alteration which— **S4.1**
   (a) involves the correction of a mistake, and
   (b) prejudicially affects the title of a registered proprietor.

Paragraph 1: The Act utilises the concept of *alteration* of the register. An alteration which involves the correction of a mistake *and* prejudicially affects the title of a registered proprietor amounts to rectification. Rectification under the Act involves special considerations. **SC4.1**

Alteration pursuant to a court order

2. (1) The court may make an order for alteration of the register for the purpose of— **S4.1.2**
   (a) correcting a mistake,
   (b) bringing the register up to date, or
   (c) giving effect to any estate, right or interest excepted from the effect of registration.

   (2) An order under this paragraph has effect when served on the registrar to impose a duty on him to give effect to it.

---

[45] Law Com No. 271, para. 628, p. 568.

3. (1) This paragraph applies to the power under paragraph 2, so far as relating to rectification.

(2) If alteration affects the title of the proprietor of a registered estate in land, no order may be made under paragraph 2 without the proprietor's consent in relation to land in his possession unless—

(a) he has by fraud or lack of proper care caused or substantially contributed to the mistake, or
(b) it would for any other reason be unjust for the alteration not to be made.

(3) If in any proceedings the court has power to make an order under paragraph 2, it must do so, unless there are exceptional circumstances which justify its not doing so.

(4) In sub-paragraph (2), the reference to the title of the proprietor of a registered estate in land includes his title to any registered estate which subsists for the benefit of the estate in land.

4. Rules may—

(a) make provision about the circumstances in which there is a duty to exercise the power under paragraph 2, so far as not relating to rectification;
(b) make provision about the form of an order under paragraph 2;
(c) make provision about service of such an order.

SC4.1.2 Paragraph 2: The Court may order the register to be altered for the purposes of:

(a) correcting a mistake (*e.g.* restoring the name of an individual as proprietor where a transfer has been forged)

(b) bringing the register up to date (*e.g.* deleting a leasehold interest in circumstances where the lessor has properly forfeited that interest)

(c) giving effect to any estate, right or interest excepted from the effect of registration.[46] An example would be where land is

[46] See sections 11(6), (7); 12(6), (7) and (8); section 29(2)(a)(iii) and section 30(2)(a)(iii).

registered with a possessory freehold title on the basis of the first registered proprietor's adverse possession. If it subsequently transpires that the estate against which the adversely possessor was not in fact freehold but leasehold, the Court may order that the registered title be altered from freehold to leasehold.[47]

Rules may be made in relation to the circumstances where there is a duty on the Court to exercise its power under paragraph 2, insofar as they do not relate to rectification, and concerning the form of any order and mode of service thereof.[48] It is envisaged that the rules are likely to impose a duty on the Court to make an order for alteration where it has made a determination in proceedings but are unlikely to *require* the Court to make an order where it incidentally discovers in the course of proceedings that some entry on the register is incorrect.[49] No rules have, as yet, been made.

Paragraph 3: Where the Court exercises its power under paragraph 2 where that amounts to rectification as defined in paragraph 1, paragraph 3(2) precludes any alteration that affects the title of a proprietor of a registered estate save where the proprietor consents unless (a) he has by fraud or lack of proper care caused or substantially contributed to the mistake or (b) it would for any other reason be unjust for the alteration not to be made. **SC4.1.2.1**

Paragraph 3(3) imposes a duty on the Court to make an order under paragraph 3(2) if it has power to do so unless there are exceptional circumstances which justifies the contrary. **SC4.1.2.2**

Paragraph 3(4): The title to a registered estate includes the benefit of any registered estate, such as an easement, that subsists for the benefit of that title. **SC4.1.2.3**

Paragraph 4: No rules have, as yet, been made. **SC4.1.2.4**

Alteration otherwise than pursuant to a court order

5. The registrar may alter the register for the purpose of— **S4.1.3**

(a) correcting a mistake,

---

[47] See Law Com No. 271, para. 630, p. 568.
[48] Schedule 4, para. 4.
[49] Law Com No. 271, para. 631, p. 568.

(b) bringing the register up to date,
(c) giving effect to any estate, right or interest excepted from the effect of registration, or
(d) removing a superfluous entry.

SC4.1.3 Paragraph 5: The Registrar's powers bestowed by paragraphs 5 and 6 are the same as those bestowed upon the Court pursuant to paragraphs 2 and 3, save that paragraph 5(d) permits the Registrar to alter the register for the purpose of removing a superfluous entry. If an application is made to the Registrar for the alteration of the register and an individual objects, the matter must be referred to the Adjudicator.[50]

6. (1) This paragraph applies to the power under paragraph 5, so far as relating to rectification.
(2) No alteration affecting the title of the proprietor of a registered estate in land may be made under paragraph 5 without the proprietor's consent in relation to land in his possession unless—
(a) He has by fraud or lack of proper care caused or substantially contributed to the mistake, or
(b) it would for any other reason be unjust for the alteration not to be made.
(3) If on an application for alteration under paragraph 5 the registrar has power to make the alteration, the application must be approved, unless there are exceptional circumstances which justify not making the alteration.
(4) In sub-paragraph (2), the reference to the title of the proprietor of a registered estate in land includes his title to any registered estate which subsists for the benefit of the estate in land.

7. Rules may—
(a) make provision about the circumstances in which there is a duty to exercise the power under paragraph 5, so far as not relating to rectification;
(b) make provision about how the register is to be altered in exercise of that power;
(c) make provision about applications for alteration under that paragraph, including provision requiring the making of such applications;

[50] Sections 73, 108.

(d) make provision about procedure in relation to the exercise of that power, whether on application or otherwise.

Paragraph 7: This paragraph contains similar provisions to that in paragraph 4 concerning alterations pursuant to a Court Order. No rules have, as yet, been made. **SC4.1.3.1**

Rectification and derivative interests

8. The powers under this Schedule to alter the register, so far as relating to rectification, extend to changing for the future the priority of any interest affecting the registered estate or charge concerned. **S4.1.4**

Paragraph 8: The power to rectify the register extends to changing the priority of any interest affecting the registered estate or charge concerned *prospectively*. **SC4.1.4**

Costs in non-rectification cases

9. (1) If the register is altered under this Schedule in a case not involving rectification, the registrar may pay such amount as he thinks fit in respect of any costs or expenses reasonably incurred by a person in connection with the alteration which have been incurred with the consent of the registrar. **S4.1.5**

(2) The registrar may make a payment under sub-paragraph (1) notwithstanding the absence of consent if—

(a) it appears to him—

(i) that the costs or expenses had to be incurred urgently, and

(ii) that it was not reasonably practicable to apply for his consent, or

(b) he has subsequently approved the incurring of the costs or expenses.

Paragraph 9: This paragraph is new; under the Land Registration Act 1925 there is no power for the Registrar to pay a party's costs in relation to an alteration which does not amount to a rectification of the register. It is envisaged that the sort of case in which the power may be exercised is where it appears that there may be a reason to alter the **SC4.1.5** register and an interested party incurs expense in making investigations into the matter.[51]

SCHEDULE 5

Section 92

Land Registry Network

SC5.0 Section 92 enables the Registrar to provide or make arrangements for the provision of an electronic communication network for such purposes as he thinks fit relating to the registration or the carrying out of transactions which involve registration and are capable of being effected electronically.[52]

Schedule 5 makes detailed provision in relation to that network and particularly, makes provision for access to that network by persons other than the Registrar and Land Registry employees. It is by this route that, on the advent of electronic conveyancing, solicitors with the benefit of access to the Land Registry Network will be able to convey a property and register dispositions simultaneously as they are made at the Land Registry.

Access to network

S5.1 1 (1) A person who is not a member of the land registry may only have access to a land registry network under authority conferred by means of an agreement with the registrar.

(2) An agreement for the purposes of sub-paragraph (1) ("network access agreement") may authorise access for—

(a) the communication, posting or retrieval of information,
(b) the making of changes to the register of title or cautions register,
(c) the issue of official search certificates,
(d) the issue of official copies, or
(e) such other conveyancing purposes as the registrar thinks fit.

(3) Rules may regulate the use of network access agreements to confer authority to carry out functions of the registrar.

---

[51] Law Com No. 271, para. 644, p. 570.

[52] See para. A92 *et seq.*, *supra*.

(4) The registrar must, on application, enter into a network access agreement with the applicant if the applicant meets such criteria as rules may provide.

Paragraph 1(1): This paragraph limits access to the Land Registry Network to those who have had authority conferred by means of an agreement with the Registrar. **SC5.1**

Paragraph 1(2): This paragraph sets out the purposes for which a network access agreement may authorise an individual to have access to the Land Registry Network. The matters specified in sub-paragraph (a)-(e) are not cumulative and it thus permits the purposes for which access may be authorised to be varied according to the status of the third party. Thus a solicitor or licensed conveyancer who is authorised to conduct electronic conveyancing may be granted access for all or most of the purposes listed in sub-paragraph 1(2). A mortgagee, on the other hand, may only need to be able to have access for the purposes of sub-paragraphs (a), (b), (c) and, perhaps, (e). Others may have more limited needs of access. **SC5.1.1**

Paragraph 1(3): Since the matters for which sub-paragraph 1(2) authorises a third party to have access are themselves functions of the Registrar, the provisions of paragraph 1(3) merely provide for the making of rules to regulate the use of network access agreements. It is envisaged that they may go further and, for example, allow the removal of spent entries.[53] No rules have, as yet, been made. **SC5.1.2**

Paragraph 1(4): This imposes a mandatory obligation on the Registrar to enter into a network access agreement with such applicants who meet such criteria as rules may provide although regard is to be had to the matters specified. Clearly this provision is aimed to strike a balance between a practitioner's right to practice and convey and the need to maintain standards. An appeal from a decision of the Registrar with respect to entry into or termination of a network access agreement by a person aggrieved as to the Adjudicator.[54] **SC5.1.3**

Terms of access

2\. (1) The terms on which access to a land registry network is authorised shall be such as the registrar thinks fit, subject to sub-paragraphs (3) and (4), and may, in particular, include charges for access. **S5.1.1**

[53] Law Com No. 271, para. 13.39, p. 283.

[54] See Schedule 5, *infra*.

(2) The power under sub-paragraph (1) may be used, not only for the purpose of regulating the use of the network, but also for—

(a) securing that the person granted access uses the network to carry on such qualifying transactions as may be specified in, or under, the agreement,
(b) such other purpose relating to the carrying on of qualifying transactions as rules may provide, or
(c) enabling network transactions to be monitored.

(3) It shall be a condition of a network access agreement which enables the person granted access to use the network to carry on qualifying transactions that he must comply with any rules for the time being in force under paragraph 5.
(4) Rules may regulate the terms on which access to a land registry network is authorised.

SC5.1.1 Paragraph 2(1): This enshrines the principle that access to the Land Registry Network is upon such terms as the Registrar thinks fit, including such charges as may be made for access. However, that right is subject to sub-paragraphs (3) and (4).

SC5.1.1.1 Paragraph 2(2): This paragraph expands on the manner in which the Registrar may authorise use of the Land Registry Network. In particular sub-paragraph 2(2)(a) permits the Registrar to compel those granted access to the Land Registry Network to carry on such "qualifying transactions"[55] via the Land Registry Network and thus electronically. So it may be used to ensure a swift transition from a paper-based system of conveyancing to an electronic based system. It is a power that is likely to be more readily exercised than that under section 93, which is unlikely to be used until electronic conveyancing has become the norm.[56]

SC5.1.1.2 Paragraph 2(2)(c) enables the monitoring of transactions on the network. Regard must also be had to paragraph 9 in relation to the management of network transactions. It is envisaged that in relation to a transaction which is part of a chain, the terms of the network access

---

[55] Defined, para. 12.
[56] Law Com No. 271, para. 13.49, p. 286.

agreement might, for example, require a solicitor or licensed conveyancer to provide the Registrar with information, such as the following, as soon as it became available:—

(i) That his or her client was proposing to enter into a transaction that appeared to be part of a chain;

(ii) That he or she had performed a specified conveyancing step, such as having completed local searches or that his or her client had received a mortgage offer.[57]

Paragraph 2(3) ensures that those with access to the Land Registry Network are obliged to comply with the rules from time to time being in force. **SC5.1.1.3**

Paragraph 2(4): No rules have, as yet, been made. **SC5.1.1.4**

Termination of access

3. (1) The person granted access by a network access agreement may terminate the agreement at any time by notice to the registrar. **S5.1.2**

(2) Rules may make provision about the termination of a network access agreement by the registrar and may, in particular, make provision about—

(a) the grounds of termination,
(b) the procedure to be followed in relation to termination, and
(c) the suspension of termination pending appeal.

(3) Without prejudice to the generality of sub-paragraph (2)(a), rules under that provision may authorise the registrar to terminate a network access agreement if the person granted access—

(a) fails to comply with the terms of the agreement,
(b) ceases to be a person with whom the registrar would be required to enter into a network access agreement conferring the authority which the agreement confers, or

---

[57] Law Com No. 271, para. 655, p. 572. In addition, it is envisaged that the information will include details of overriding interests: *ibid*, para. 13.52, p. 287.

(c) does not meet such conditions as the rules may provide.

SC5.1.2 Paragraph 3(1): The person to whom access has been granted to the Land Registry Network can thus terminate the agreement on notice.

SC5.1.2.1 Paragraph 3(2): Rules thus may provide for the termination of a network access agreement by the Registrar. It is envisaged this would be a matter of last resort.[58] No rules have, as yet, been made.

SC5.1.2.2 Paragraph 3(3) makes further provision as to the matters which the rules may provide for.

Appeals

S5.1.3 4. (1) A person who is aggrieved by a decision of the registrar with respect to entry into, or termination of, a network access agreement may appeal against the decision to the adjudicator.

(2) On determining an appeal under this paragraph, the adjudicator may give such directions as he considers appropriate to give effect to his determination.

(3) Rules may make provision about appeals under this paragraph.

SC5.1.3 Paragraph 4: This paragraph provides for an appeal from any decision of the Registrar with respect to the entry into or termination of a network access agreement by the person aggrieved to the Adjudicator. The appeal will be a full appeal and not merely a review of the decision of the Registrar.[59] The Adjudicator's decision is final although an appeal lies from him to the High Court on a question of law alone.[60]

SC5.1.3.1 Paragraph 4(3): No rules have, as yet, been made.

Network transaction rules

S5.1.4 5. (1) Rules may make provision about how to go about network transactions.

---

[58] Law Com No. 271, para. 13.56, p. 289.

[59] Law Com No. 271, para. 666, p. 574.

[60] Section 111(2).

(2) Rules under sub-paragraph (1) may, in particular, make provision about dealings with the land registry, including provision about—

(a) the procedure to be followed, and
(b) the supply of information (including information about unregistered interests).

Paragraph 5: No rules have, as yet, been made. **SC5.1.4**

Overriding nature of network access obligations

6. To the extent that an obligation not owed under a network access agreement conflicts with an obligation owed under such an agreement by the person granted access, the obligation not owed under the agreement is discharged. **S5.1.5**

Paragraph 6: This provision ensures that the obligations owed by a person under a network access agreement will prevail over any other obligations not owed under that agreement, *i.e.* the terms and obligations imposed by the agreement are paramount. It is envisaged that this provision would cover a situation where, say, a solicitor or licensed conveyancer has entered into a network access agreement and finds himself in a position where he is required to act contrary to the wishes of his client. Paragraph 6 requires him to comply with his obligations under the network access agreement and, by expressly providing for the discharge of those obligations which are not owed under that agreement, it precludes the solicitor from having any liability to the client for acting contrary to his wishes if they conflict with an obligation owed under the network access agreement. **SC5.1.5**

Do-it-yourself conveyancing

7. (1) If there is a land registry network, the registrar has a duty to provide such assistance as he thinks appropriate for the purpose of enabling persons engaged in qualifying transactions who wish to do their own conveyancing to do so by means of the network. **S5.1.6**

(2) The duty under sub-paragraph (1) does not extend to the provision of legal advice.

Paragraph 7: It is envisaged that the Registrar will carry out the necessary transactions in electronic form on the instructions of the **SC5.1.6** person who is undertaking his own conveyancing. That person will be required to pay an appropriate fee for this service.[61] See also paragraph 3.008.

Presumption of authority

S5.1.7 8. Where—

(a) a person who is authorised under a network access agreement to do so uses the network for the making of a disposition or contract, and

(b) the document which purports to effect the disposition or to be the contract—

(i) purports to be authenticated by him as agent, and

(ii) contains a statement to the effect that he is acting under the authority of his principal,

he shall be deemed, in favour of any other party, to be so acting.

SC5.1.7 Paragraph 8: But for the provisions of paragraph 8, a solicitor or licensed conveyancer acting for one party would be entitled to see the written authority from the other party to his solicitor or licensed conveyancer and *vice versa*. This is because a solicitor has no implied authority to sign a contract for the sale or purchase of an interest in land and can only conclude the contract if he has actual authority. The provisions of paragraph 8 obviate the need to exchange authorities before contracts can be concluded electronically. It is intended that under the network transaction rules made under paragraph 5 there will be a standard form of authority which a practitioner will be required to use to obtain his client's agreement where that practitioner is to execute an electronic instrument as an agent for that client.[62]

Management of network transactions

S5.1.8 9. (1) The registrar may use monitoring information for the purpose of managing network transactions and may, in particular, disclose such information to persons authorised to use the network, and authorise the further disclosure of information so disclosed, if he considers it is necessary or desirable to do so.

---

[61] Law Com No. 271, para. 674, p. 575.

[62] *ibid.*, para. 667, p. 575.

(2) The registrar may delegate his functions under sub-paragraph (1), subject to such conditions as he thinks fit.

(3) In sub-paragraph (1), "monitoring information" means information provided in pursuance of provision in a network access agreement included under paragraph 2(2)(c).

Paragraph 9: The management of network transactions is aimed to facilitate and expedite conveyancing and to reduce the risk of any break in a conveyancing chain. The disclosure obligations under paragraph 9 are not limited only to those persons who are authorised to use the Land Registry Network since paragraph 9(1) authorises the further disclosure of information so disclosed in circumstances where the Registrar considers it necessary or desirable. It is envisaged that the sort of information that paragraph 9 will enable the Registrar (or his delegate, "chain manager") to disclose to other parties in that chain is the state of the progress of transactions in that chain. Although the "chain manager" will not have any coercive powers, he will be able to identify the link in the chain that is causing the delay. He will then be able to encourage that party to proceed with due despatch.[63] **SC5.1.8**

Supplementary

10. The registrar may provide, or arrange for the provision of, education and training in relation to the use of a land registry network. **S5.1.9**

11. (1) Power to make rules under paragraph 1, 2 or 3 is exercisable by the Lord Chancellor.

(2) Before making such rules, the Lord Chancellor must consult such persons as he considers appropriate.

(3) In making rules under paragraph 1 or 3(2)(a), the Lord Chancellor must have regard, in particular, to the need to secure—

(a) the confidentiality of private information kept on the network,

(b) competence in relation to the use of the network (in particular for the purpose of making changes), and

(c) the adequate insurance of potential liabilities in connection with use of the network.

---

[63] *ibid.*, para. 680, p. 576.

12. In this Schedule—
"land registry network" means a network provided under section 92(1);
"network access agreement" has the meaning given by paragraph 1(2);
"network transaction" means a transaction carried on by means of a land registry network;
"qualifying transaction" means a transaction which—

(a) involves registration, and

(b) is capable of being effected electronically.

SC5.1.9 Paragraph 10: It is envisaged that the education and training provided with regard to the use of the Land Registry Network will include on-line training and education programmes. Indeed, it is envisaged that continued participation in such programmes is likely to be a condition of the grant and continuation of a network access agreement.[64]

SC5.1.9.1 Paragraph 11: No rules have, as yet, been made.

SCHEDULE 6

Section 97

Registration of Adverse Possessor

SC6.0 Part 9 of the Act[65] disapplies the periods of limitation that would otherwise prevail under section 15 of the Limitation Act 1980 in relation to land or rentcharges, the title to which is registered. Section 97 provides for certain defences to an action for possession of land by the person in occupation of it. It reflects the provisions of Schedule 6. Section 96 simply causes Schedule 6 to have effect. Schedule 6 contains the details pursuant to which an individual may apply to be registered as the proprietor of land if he has been in possession of that for the specified period.

Right to apply for registration

S6.1 1. (1) A person may apply to the registrar to be registered as the proprietor of a registered estate in land if he has been in adverse possession of the estate for the period of ten years ending on the date of the application.

---

[64] *ibid.*, para. 681, p. 576.

[65] Sections 95–97: *supra*.

(2) A person may also apply to the registrar to be registered as the proprietor of a registered estate in land if—

(a) he has in the period of six months ending on the date of the application ceased to be in adverse possession of the estate because of eviction by the registered proprietor, or a person claiming under the registered proprietor,

(b) on the day before his eviction he was entitled to make an application under sub-paragraph (1), and

(c) the eviction was not pursuant to a judgment for possession.

(3) However, a person may not make an application under this paragraph if—

(a) he is a defendant in proceedings which involve asserting a right to possession of the land, or

(b) judgment for possession of the land has been given against him in the last two years.

(4) For the purposes of sub-paragraph (1), the estate need not have been registered throughout the period of adverse possession.

Paragraph 1(1): A person who has been in adverse possession of the land for a period of 10 years ending on the date of the application to the Registrar may be registered as the proprietor of that land subject to paragraph 1(3) below. Paragraph 8 provides for certain restrictions on applications. **SC6.1**

"Adverse possession" is defined in paragraph 11 *et seq*.

Paragraph 1(2): In addition to the 10 year qualification required by paragraph 1(1) a person may also apply to be registered as the proprietor of a registered estate in land if he has been evicted otherwise than pursuant to a court order within the period of six months ending on the date of the application for registration by the registered proprietor or a person claiming under him and would, bar for that eviction, have been entitled to have applied to be registered as the proprietor of the registered estate pursuant to paragraph 1(1). Thus the Act discourages self-help remedies by the registered proprietor to determine an adverse possessor's occupation of the registered land by ensuring that consequent upon such an eviction, an adverse possessor **SC6.1.1** has a period of six months in which to make the application that he would otherwise have been entitled to make under paragraph 1(1).

SC6.1.2 Paragraph 1(3): No application may be made under this paragraph if either sub-paragraph 1(3)(a) or (b) are satisfied.

SC6.1.3 Paragraph 1(4): It is immaterial that the title of the estate which has been adversely possessed is registered or unregistered for part of the 10 year period. For example, voluntary registration after five years' adverse possession would not therefore preclude the period of adverse possession whilst the estate was unregistered from counting towards the 10 year period specified under this paragraph. However, paragraph 5(4)(d) does impose a minimum period of registration prior to the adverse possessor's application.[66]

Notification of application

S6.1.1 2. (1) The registrar must give notice of an application under paragraph 1 to—

(a) the proprietor of the estate to which the application relates,
(b) the proprietor of any registered charge on the estate,
(c) where the estate is leasehold, the proprietor of any superior registered estate,
(d) any person who is registered in accordance with rules as a person to be notified under this paragraph, and
(e) such other persons as rules may provide.

(2) Notice under this paragraph shall include notice of the effect of paragraph 4.

SC6.1.1 Paragraph 2(1): The obligation to notify the categories of individuals specified in paragraph 2(1) is clear. No rules have, as yet, been made. The notice clearly must satisfy the obligation imposed by paragraph 2 (2). Those categories of persons likely to be provided for in the rules under sub-paragraphs (d) and (e) are:—
Sub-paragraph (d) is likely to encompass those persons who can satisfy the Registrar they have some right or interest in land that would be prejudicially affected if the adverse possessor's application was successful: *e.g.* an equitable chargee or someone entitled to the benefit of a rentcharge.

---

[66] See para. 5, S6.1.2 and SC6.1.2.4, *infra* below.

Sub-paragraph (e) individuals: such as the Charity Commission (insofar as the application pertains to land held upon charitable trust) or a bankrupt's trustee in bankruptcy.[67]

Treatment of application

3. (1) A person given notice under paragraph 2 may require that the application to which the notice relates be dealt with under paragraph 5. **S6.1.2**

(2) The right under this paragraph is exercisable by notice to the registrar given before the end of such period as rules may provide.

4. If an application under paragraph 1 is not required to be dealt with under paragraph 5, the applicant is entitled to be entered in the register as the new proprietor of the estate.

5. (1) If an application under paragraph 1 is required to be dealt with under this paragraph, the applicant is only entitled to be registered as the new proprietor of the estate if any of the following conditions is met.

(2) The first condition is that—

(a) it would be unconscionable because of an equity by estoppel for the registered proprietor to seek to dispossess the applicant, and

(b) the circumstances are such that the applicant ought to be registered as the proprietor.

(3) The second condition is that the applicant is for some other reason entitled to be registered as the proprietor of the estate.

(4) The third condition is that—

(a) the land to which the application relates is adjacent to land belonging to the applicant,

(b) the exact line of the boundary between the two has not been determined under rules under section 60,

(c) for at least ten years of the period of adverse possession ending on the date of the application, the applicant (or any predecessor in

---

[67] Law Com No. 271, para. 689, p. 578.

title) reasonably believed that the land to which the application relates belonged to him, and

(d) the estate to which the application relates was registered more than one year prior to the date of the application.

(5) In relation to an application under paragraph 1(2), this paragraph has effect as if the reference in sub-paragraph (4)(c) to the date of the application were to the day before the date of the applicant's eviction.

SC6.1.2 Paragraphs 3 and 4: On receipt of the application, the registered proprietor has an option. He can either require the matter to be dealt with in accordance with paragraph 5 or, failing which, he can by his inactivity consent to the registration of the applicant as the proprietor of the estate in question. No rules have, as yet, been made. It is envisaged that the period in which the registered proprietor can serve the counter-notice on the Registrar and require the application to be dealt with under paragraph 5 will be three months initially but that period may be reviewed once there has been some experience of how the procedure works in practice.[68–69]

SC6.1.2.1 Paragraph 5(1): An applicant for registration as the proprietor of a registered estate can, if the application is required to be dealt with in accordance with paragraph 5, only succeed if one of the three conditions specified in paragraph 5 is met. Unless this is agreed (which will probably be unlikely, otherwise the registered proprietor would not have required disposal pursuant to paragraph 5) the matter will be referred to the Adjudicator for determination.[70] Since the first and second conditions in paragraph 5(2) are not founded upon adverse possession, and the third condition has a number of requirements quite different from those currently prevailing, it can be readily appreciated that the Act substantially alters the law concerning adverse possession and does so in the registered proprietor's favour (always provided he can respond to any notice served upon him).

SC6.1.2.2 Paragraph 5(2): The first condition is a statutory formulation of the equitable principle of proprietary estoppel. Thus in order to satisfy this condition, it will be incumbent on the applicant to show that the registered proprietor has encouraged or allowed him to believe that he

---

[68–69] Law Com No. 271, para. 692, p. 578.

[70] See sections 73(1), (7); 108 (1)(a).

owned the estate or enjoyed the rights in question and that in reliance on that belief he has acted to his detriment to the knowledge of the registered proprietor and, accordingly, that it would be unconscionable for the proprietor to deny him the rights to which he believed he had.[71] When giving effect to a claim of proprietary estoppel, the Court will ascertain the minimum equity necessary in order to satisfy the claimant's claim. This obligation binds the Adjudicator, who must determine how the equity due to the applicant is to be satisfied and, for that purpose, may make any order that the High Court could make in the exercise of its equitable jurisdiction.[72] It would thus be open to the Adjudicator, depending upon the facts of the instant case, to order the registered proprietor to grant the applicant an easement over the registered estate in order to satisfy the equity that has arisen.

It is thus only if the Adjudicator determines that the applicant ought to be registered as the proprietor of the registered estate that the application will succeed; if a lesser remedy would satisfy the equity, the Adjudicator must decline the application and rely upon his powers pursuant to section 110(4).

Paragraph 5(3): The second condition will be satisfied in circumstances where, for example, the applicant has been in occupation of the land for the requisite period and is entitled under the will or intestacy of the deceased registered proprietor to the land in question but no assent has been executed in his favour. Another example is where the applicant has contracted to buy the land and paid the purchase price in circumstances where the legal estate has never been transferred to him.[73] **SC6.1.2.3**

Paragraph 5(4): It is envisaged that this is the most significant of the three cases because it is the only situation in which an adverse possessor may acquire title solely by virtue of his or her adverse possession notwithstanding any objection by the registered proprietor or others upon whom notice is served under paragraph 2.[74] The constituent parts of this condition are as follows:— **SC6.1.2.4**

(a) the land in question is adjacent to land belonging to the applicant;

(b) the boundary in question has not been definitively determined in accordance with section 60[75];

---

[71] See *Ruoff & Roper*, para. 32–06.

[72] Section 110 (4).

[73] Law Com No. 271, para. 698, p. 579.

[74] *ibid.*, para. 699, p. 579.

[75] See paras A60 *et seq.*, *supra*.

(c) for at least 10 years of the period of adverse possession ending on the date of application, the applicant or his predecessor in title reasonably believed that land to which the application relates belonged to him. In circumstances where the physical boundary between two properties is such that suggests that the land in question belongs to the applicant the requirements of this sub-paragraph are likely to be satisfied unless the proprietor of the land against whom the application is made can demonstrate to the contrary. Such circumstances may arise where a fence is erected some distance inside the boundary of the adjacent property and the applicant has treated his neighbour's land on his side of the fence as his own, notwithstanding the legal ownership.

(d) Additionally sub-paragraph (d) must be satisfied. The reason for this requirement is as follows. Title to unregistered land is normally extinguished by 12 years' adverse possession. Under this third condition, title to registered land may be acquired after 10 years' adverse possession. In instances where an adverse possessor has been in possession of unregistered land for a period of more than 10 but less than 12 years and then that land is registered, in the absence of the one year requirement in this sub-paragraph, the requirement of the third condition would otherwise be met and the adverse possessor could apply for registration in circumstances where the registered proprietor had no opportunity to evict the adverse possessor and (since the period was 12 years prior to the land's registration) hitherto no obligation. This sub-paragraph (d) is consistent with the Act's policy of clarifying and simplifying the obtaining of title by adverse possession and making the same more formulaic.

It is envisaged that the third condition will be brought into force one year after the remainder of this Schedule. If this were not so, an adverse possessor might find that he is entitled to be registered as proprietor of the estate under paragraph 5(4) on the day that the legislation is brought into force, even though he had only been in adverse possession for 10 years and, on the day before, the registered proprietor could successfully have initiated possession proceedings. This would clearly be undesirable. The proposed course of action would give a registered proprietor one year to take proceedings against any adverse possessor or to regularise his or her position.[76]

SC6.1.2.5 Paragraph 5(5): This sub-paragraph merely incorporates the provisions of paragraph 1(2) into the third condition. Thus an adverse possessor

[76] Law Com No. 271, para. 702, p. 580.

who is evicted prior to his application in circumstances which satisfy the requirement of that earlier sub-paragraph can still rely upon the third condition.

Right to make further application for registration

6. (1) Where a person's application under paragraph 1 is rejected, he may make a further application to be registered as the proprietor of the estate if he is in adverse possession of the estate from the date of the application until the last day of the period of two years beginning with the date of its rejection. **S6.1.3**

(2) However, a person may not make an application under this paragraph if—

(a) he is a defendant in proceedings which involve asserting a right to possession of the land,

(b) judgment for possession of the land has been given against him in the last two years, or

(c) he has been evicted from the land pursuant to a judgment for possession.

7. If a person makes an application under paragraph 6, he is entitled to be entered in the register as the new proprietor of the estate.

Paragraph 6(1): Subject to paragraph 6(2) if an applicant's application is rejected for whatever reason, he may renew his application to be registered as the proprietor of the estate if he remains in adverse possession of the estate from the date of the application until the last day of the period of two years beginning with the date of its rejection. Thus inactivity by the registered proprietor following upon the dismissal of an application carries with it a grave and inherent risk that if it is dismissed and he does nothing, after the expiry of two years from the date of that application,[77] the adverse possessor will make a further application and obtain his registration as the proprietor of the estate. **SC6.1.3**

Paragraph 6(2): That right is subject to a number of significant exceptions all of which require an element of activity by the registered proprietor. **SC6.1.3.1**

Restriction on applications

8. (1) No one may apply under this Schedule to be registered as the proprietor of an estate in land during, or before the end of twelve months after **S6.1.4**

[77] See para. 7.

the end of, any period in which the existing registered proprietor is for the purposes of the Limitation (Enemies and War Prisoners) Act 1945 (8 & 9 Geo. 6 c. 16)—

(a) an enemy, or
(b) detained in enemy territory.

(2) No-one may apply under this Schedule to be registered as the proprietor of an estate in land during any period in which the existing registered proprietor is—

(a) unable because of mental disability to make decisions about issues of the kind to which such an application would give rise, or
(b) unable to communicate such decisions because of mental disability or physical impairment.

(3) For the purposes of sub-paragraph (2), "mental disability" means a disability or disorder of the mind or brain, whether permanent or temporary, which results in an impairment or disturbance of mental functioning.

(4) Where it appears to the registrar that sub-paragraph (1) or (2) applies in relation to an estate in land, he may include a note to that effect in the register.

SC6.1.4 Paragraph 8 contains two restrictions on an individual's ability to apply to be registered as the proprietor of a registered estate under Schedule 6.

SC6.1.4.1 Paragraph 8(1): First, no application may be made where the existing registered proprietor is for the purposes of the Limitation (Enemies and War Prisoners) Act 1945 an enemy or detained in enemy territory until the expiry of 12 months after the end of the period in which the registered proprietor, is puruant to that Act, either an enemy or so detained.

SC6.1.4.2 Paragraph 8(2): Secondly, no application may be made during any period in which the existing registered proprietor is subject to the mental or physical disabilities or impairments specified in sub-paragraph (a) or (b). "Mental disability" is defined in sub-paragraph 8(3). The Act goes further than the Limitation Act 1980 by extending the protection to those suffering physical impairment in accordance with paragraph 8(2)(b) and further by stipulating that the relevant period for determining the mental disability of physical impairment which gives rise to the applicant's inability to apply is that pertaining at the date of application.[78]

Paragraph 8(4): The Registrar retains a discretion to enter an appropriate note in the register if paragraph 8(1) or (2) applies. The registration of the applicant in circumstances where either of these two situations applied would entitle the individual whose registration was extinguished to apply for rectification under the provisions of Schedule 4. **SC6.1.4.3**

Effect of registration

9. (1) Where a person is registered as the proprietor of an estate in land in pursuance of an application under this Schedule, the title by virtue of adverse possession which he had at the time of the application is extinguished. **S6.1.5**

(2) Subject to sub-paragraph (3), the registration of a person under this Schedule as the proprietor of an estate in land does not affect the priority of any interest affecting the estate.

(3) Subject to sub-paragraph (4), where a person is registered under this Schedule as the proprietor of an estate, the estate is vested in him free of any registered charge affecting the estate immediately before his registration.

(4) Sub-paragraph (3) does not apply where registration as proprietor is in pursuance of an application determined by reference to whether any of the conditions in paragraph 5 applies.

Paragraph 9(1): A successful application will entitle the applicant to be registered with the title of the estate in which he was in adverse possession.[79] This sub-paragraph expressly extinguishes the adverse possessor's right acquired by reason of his adverse possession in order to reflect his registration as proprietor. **SC6.1.5**

Paragraph 9(2): Subject to sub-paragraph (3), this sub-paragraph preserves the priority of any interests affecting the estate. **SC6.1.5.1**

---

[78] Under the Limitation Act, s. 28(1), the relevant point in time is the accrual of the course of action.

[79] See Sched. 6, paras 1(1), 4 and 7.

SC6.1.5.2 Paragraph 9(3): With one exception[80] where a person is registered under Schedule 6 as the proprietor of an estate, the estate is vested in him free of any registered charge affecting the estate immediately before his resignation.

SC6.1.5.3 Paragraph 9(4): The provisions of sub-paragraph (3) do not apply where the applicant is registered as a proprietor in pursuance of an application determined by reference to whether any of the conditions in paragraph 5 applies.

SC6.1.5.4 The reasoning behind this distinction is that in circumstances where no steps are taken by the chargee (upon whom notice of the application must be served),[81] it is appropriate for the applicant to take the registered estate without any charge registered against it binding him. However, in circumstances where the application has been objected to, the adverse possessor will not take free of the charge automatically. The question of whether he takes the estate subject to the charge in question depends upon the priority afforded to his interest and that of the chargee. Sub-paragraph (2) prevents the adverse possessor's registration affecting the priority of any interest affecting the estate and thus the question must be determined in accordance with the rules concerning the effect of dispositions on priority.[82]

Apportionment and discharge of charges

10. (1) Where—

S6.1.6

(a) a registered estate continues to be subject to a charge notwithstanding the registration of a person under this Schedule as the proprietor, and

(b) the charge affects property other than the estate,

the proprietor of the estate may require the chargee to apportion the amount secured by the charge at that time between the estate and the other property on the basis of their respective values.

(2) The person requiring the apportionment is entitled to a discharge of his estate from the charge on payment of—

[80] See para. 9(4), *infra*.

[81] Sched. 6, para. 2(1)(d).

[82] Ss. 28–31, *supra*.

(a) the amount apportioned to the estate, and
(b) the costs incurred by the charge as a result of the apportionment.

(3) On a discharge under this paragraph, the liability of the chargor to the charge is reduced by the amount apportioned to the estate.

(4) Rules may make provision about apportionment under this paragraph, in particular, provision about—

(a) procedure,
(b) valuation,
(c) calculation of costs payable under sub-paragraph (2)(b), and
(d) payment of the costs of the chargor.

Paragraph 10(1): Where the applicant is successful in his application to be registered as proprietor of the estate but takes subject to an existing charge which affects property other than the estate of which he is the newly registered proprietor, he may require the chargee to apportion the amount secured by the charge at that time between the estate and the other property on the basis of their respective values. Thus in circumstances where the registered proprietor achieves registration of part of a charged estate, this sub-paragraph provides a formula by which the proportion of the charge binding the parcel of the registered estate of which the applicant has been registered as proprietor can be calculated. **SC6.1.6**

It is envisaged that rules made pursuant to paragraph 10(4) will enable the chargee to recover the costs of the apportioning exercise from the adverse possessor.[83]

Paragraph 10(2): This sub-paragraph enables the newly registered proprietor to redeem the apportioned charge upon payment of the sum specified in sub-paragraph (a) and (b).[84] **SC6.1.6.1**

Paragraph 10(3): Such provision is unexceptional. **SC6.1.6.2**

Paragraph 10(4): No rules have, as yet, been made. **SC6.1.6.3**

Meaning of "adverse possession"

11. (1) A person is in adverse possession of an estate in land for the purposes of this Schedule if, but for section 96, a period of limitation under section 15 **S6.1.7**

---

[83] Law Com No. 271, para. 716, p. 583.

[84] It thus reverses the current position: see *Caroll v. Manek* (1999) 79 P. & Cr. 173.

of the Limitation Act 1980 (c. 58) would run in his favour in relation to the estate.

(2) A person is also to be regarded for those purposes as having been in adverse possession of an estate in land—

(a) where he is the successor in title to an estate in the land, during any period of adverse possession by a predecessor in title to that estate, or

(b) during any period of adverse possession by another person which comes between, and is continuous with, periods of adverse possession of his own.

(3) In determining whether for the purposes of this paragraph a period of limitation would run under section 15 of the Limitation Act 1980, there are to be disregarded—

(a) the commencement of any legal proceedings, and

(b) paragraph 6 of Schedule 1 to that Act.

SC6.1.7 Paragraph 11(1): "Adverse possession" is given the meaning ascribed to it under section 15 of the Limitation Act 1980.[85] In addition, a person is regarded as being in adverse possession in accordance with paragraph 11(2).

SC6.1.7.1 Paragraph 11(2): Provision is made for a person to be regarded as having been in adverse possession of an estate in land in the circumstances contained in sub-paragraph (a) and (d). Thus where an individual is the successor in title by acquisition of the estate of an earlier adverse possessor and, taken together, the totality of the period of adverse possession is 10 years or more, the later adverse possessor is to be treated as having been in adverse possession of the estate: sub-paragraph 11(2)(a). Moreover, where adverse possessor 1 ("AP1") is dispossessed by adverse possessor 2 ("AP2") and then regains possession, provided the period of possession by AP2 is continuous with the periods of adverse possession by AP1, AP1 can rely upon the time that AP2 was in possession in order to give rise to the requisite period and thus found AP1's basis for an application under Schedule 6. However, in circumstances where AP2 is in adverse possession of the estate on

---

[85] See *Ruoff and Roper*, paras 26–33 *et seq.*; paras 29–04 *et seq.*

the tenth anniversary of AP1's commencement of adverse possession, he will not be able to rely upon the provisions of paragraph 11(2)(a) in order to make his own application for registration as the proprietor of the estate since he is not a successor in title to AP1. AP2 will have to await the expiry of 10 years from the commencement of his adverse possession of the estate prior to making an application unless he can rely on the provisions of paragraph 11(2)(b).

Paragraph 11(3): Sub-paragraph (a) precludes the issue of proceedings from preventing the running of time, which would otherwise be the case under the Limitation Act 1980. The exclusion of paragraph 6 of Schedule 1 to that Act disapplies the technical rules concerning adverse possession and reversionary interests which have no application to the scheme created under Schedule 6. **SC6.1.7.2**

Trusts

12. A person is not to be regarded as being in adverse possession of an estate for the purposes of this Schedule at any time when the estate is subject to a trust, unless the interest of each of the beneficiaries in the estate is an interest in possession. **S6.1.8**

Paragraph 12: Land which is held on trust cannot be adversely possessed in circumstances where the beneficiaries interests under that trust are not all interests in possession. Thus, for example, where land is held upon successive life interests and for the remainderman thereafter, an adverse possessor is not to be regarded as being in adverse possession of the estate during the currency of the life tenants' life interests. Adverse possession can only commence upon the death of the last life tenant and the vesting of the beneficial interest in possession in the remainderman. **SC6.1.8**

Crown foreshore

13. (1) Where— **S6.1.9**

(a) a person is in adverse possession of an estate in land,
(b) the estate belongs to Her Majesty in right of the Crown or the Duchy of Lancaster or to the Duchy of Cornwall, and
(c) the land consists of foreshore,

paragraph 1(1) is to have effect as if the reference to ten years were to sixty years.

(2) For the purposes of sub-paragraph (1), land is to be treated as foreshore if it has been foreshore at any time in the previous ten years.

(3) In this paragraph, "foreshore" means the shore and bed of the sea and of any tidal water, below the line of the medium high tide between the spring and neap tides.

SC6.1.9 Paragraph 13(1): Extends the period for adverse possession of the foreshore from 10 to 60 years in circumstances where the estate belongs to Her Majesty in right of Crown or the Duchy of Lancaster or the Duchy of Cornwall. "Foreshore" means the shore and bed of the sea and of any tidal water below the line of the medium high tide between the spring and neap tides.[86]

SC6.1.9.1 Paragraph 13(2): Where land ceases to be foreshore within the meaning ascribed thereto, it only falls to be treated as foreshore for a period of 10 years after it so ceases. Thus a person who is in adverse possession of land which has ceased to be foreshore may apply to be registered as proprietor if his period of adverse possession is for the shorter of 60 years or 10 years from the time when land ceased to be foreshore.

Rentcharges

S6.1.10 14. Rules must make provision to apply the preceding provisions of this Schedule to registered rentcharges, subject to such modifications and exceptions as the rules may provide.

SC6.1.10 Paragraph 14: No rules have, as yet, been made.

Procedure

S6.1.11 15. Rules may make provision about the procedure to be followed pursuant to an application under this Schedule.

SC6.1.11 Paragraph 15: No rules have, as yet, been made.

---

[86] Para. 13(3).

SCHEDULE 7

Section 99

THE LAND REGISTRY

The contents of this Schedule are considered in relation to section 98.[87] **SC7.0**

Holding of office by Chief Land Registrar

1. (1) The registrar may at any time resign his office by written notice to the Lord Chancellor. **S7.1**
(2) The Lord Chancellor may remove the registrar from office if he is unable or unfit to discharge the functions of office.
(3) Subject to the above, a person appointed to be the registrar is to hold and vacate office in accordance with the terms of his appointment and, on ceasing to hold office, is eligible for reappointment.

Remuneration etc. of Chief Land Registrar

2 (1) The Lord Chancellor shall pay the registrar such remuneration, and such travelling and other allowances, as the Lord Chancellor may determine. **S7.1.1**
(2) The Lord Chancellor shall—

(a) pay such pension, allowances or gratuities as he may determine to or in respect of a person who is or has been the registrar, or
(b) make such payments as he may determine towards provision for the payment of a pension, allowances or gratuities to or in respect of such a person.

(3) If, when a person ceases to be the registrar, the Lord Chancellor determines that there are special circumstances which make it right that the person should receive compensation, the Lord Chancellor may pay to the person by way of compensation a sum of such amount as he may determine.

Staff

3. (1) The registrar may appoint such staff as he thinks fit. **S7.1.2**

---

[87] See paras A98.1 *et seq.*, *supra*.

(2) The terms and conditions of appointments under this paragraph shall be such as the registrar, with the approval of the Minister for the Civil Service, thinks fit.

Indemnity for members

S7.1.3 4. No member of the land registry is to be liable in damages for anything done or omitted in the discharge or purported discharge of any function relating to land registration, unless it is shown that the act or omission was in bad faith.

Seal

S7.1.4 5. The land registry is to continue to have a seal and any document purporting to be sealed with it is to be admissible in evidence without any further or other proof.

Documentary evidence

S7.1.5 6. The Documentary Evidence Act 1868 (c. 37) has effect as if—

(a) the registrar were included in the first column of the Schedule to that Act,
(b) the registrar and any person authorised to act on his behalf were mentioned in the second column of that Schedule, and
(c) the regulations referred to in that Act included any form or direction issued by the registrar or by any such person.

Parliamentary disqualification

S7.1.6 7. In Part 3 of Schedule 1 to the House of Commons Disqualification Act 1975 (c. 24) (other disqualifying offices), there is inserted at the appropriate place—

"Chief Land Registrar.";
and a corresponding amendment is made in Part 3 of Schedule 1 to the Northern Ireland Assembly Disqualification Act 1975 (c. 25).

SCHEDULE 8

Section 103

Indemnities

This Schedule achieves substantially the same effect as section 82 of the Land Registration Act 1925.[88] SC8.0
"Mistake" and "Rectification" are defined in paragraph 11.

Paragraph 1: This paragraph sets out the circumstances in which a person is entitled to be indemnified by the Registrar. SC8.0.1

Paragraph 1(2): This sub-paragraph extends the scope of the persons who are entitled to be indemnified by reason of the rectification of the register in the circumstances specified in sub-paragraphs (a) or (b). Such persons include those who have suffered loss by reason of an upgrade in title under section 62.[89] This latter sub-paragraph covers two situations: first where there is a mistake but the register is not rectified because for example, there is a proprietor in possession[90] and secondly, where the register is rectified but the person whose favour it is rectified still suffers loss as a result of the mistake.[91] SC8.0.2

Paragraph 1(3): No indemnity is payable under sub-paragraph 1(1)(b) until a decision is made to rectify the register. The loss suffered by reason of that mistake is to be determined in the light of that decision. The provision in sub-paragraph 1(1)(b) that the loss is to be determined as if a disposition had not been forged permits the party against whom the rectification is made to recover in appropriate circumstances the full value of the estate which he is denied by rectification.[92] SC8.0.3

Entitlement

1. (1) A person is entitled to be indemnified by the registrar if he suffers loss by reason of— S8.1

(a) rectification of the register,
(b) a mistake whose correction would involve rectification of the register,

---

[88] Substituted by section 2 of the Land Registration Act 1997.

[89] See para. 1(2)(a) and paras A62.1 *et seq.*, *supra*.

[90] See section 83(2) of the Land Registration Act 1925 and *Ruoff & Roper* paras 40–12 *et seq*.

[91] See section 83(1)(b) of the Land Registration Act 1925, *Ruoff & Roper* para. 40–16.

[92] See para. 6.

(c) a mistake in an official search,
(d) a mistake in an official copy,
(e) a mistake in a document kept by the registrar which is not an original and is referred to in the register,
(f) the loss or destruction of a document lodged at the registry for inspection or safe custody,
(g) a mistake in the cautions register, or
(h) failure by the registrar to perform his duty under section 50.

(2) For the purposes of sub-paragraph (1)(a)—

(a) any person who suffers loss by reason of the change of title under section 62 is to be regarded as having suffered loss by reason of rectification of the register, and
(b) the proprietor of a registered estate or charge claiming in good faith under a forged disposition is, where the register is rectified, to be regarded as having suffered loss by reason of such rectification as if the disposition had not been forged.

(3) No indemnity under sub-paragraph (1)(b) is payable until a decision has been made about whether to alter the register for the purpose of correcting the mistake; and the loss suffered by reason of the mistake is to be determined in the light of that decision.

Mines and minerals

S8.1.1 2. No indemnity is payable under this Schedule on account of—

(a) any mines or minerals, or
(b) the existence of any right to work or get mines or minerals,

unless it is noted in the register that the title to the registered estate concerned includes the mines or minerals.

SC8.1.1 Paragraph 2: This reflects the existing law.[93]

---

[93] Land Registration Act 1925, s. 83(5)(b); *Ruoff & Roper* para. 40–24.

Costs

3. (1) In respect of loss consisting of costs or expenses incurred by the claimant in relation to the matter, an indemnity under this Schedule is payable only on account of costs or expenses reasonably incurred by the claimant with the consent of the registrar. **S8.1.2**

(2) The requirement of consent does not apply where—

(a) the costs or expenses must be incurred by the claimant urgently, and

(b) it is not reasonably practicable to apply for the registrar's consent.

(3) If the registrar approves the incurring of costs or expenses after they have been incurred, they shall be treated for the purposes of this paragraph as having been incurred with his consent.

4. (1) If no indemnity is payable to a claimant under this Schedule, the registrar may pay such amount as he thinks fit in respect of any costs or expenses reasonably incurred by the claimant in connection with the claim which have been incurred with the consent of the registrar.

(2) The registrar may make a payment under sub-paragraph (1) notwithstanding the absence of consent if—

(a) it appears to him—

(i) that the costs or expenses had to be incurred urgently, and

(ii) that it was not reasonably practicable to apply for his consent, or

(b) he has subsequently approved the incurring of the costs or expenses.

Paragraph 3: The recovery of costs is not a new feature.[94] Under the Act they are only recoverable (subject to the exception in sub- **SC8.1.2**

[94] See *Ruoff & Roper* para. 40–27 for circumstances where they are recoverable under the existing law.

paragraph 3(2)) in circumstances where they are reasonably incurred by the claimant with the consent of the Registrar. The requirement of consent can be waived in accordance with sub-paragraphs (a) and (b) of paragraph 3(2). The Registrar can retrospectively give his consent: paragraph 3(3). Costs are also recoverable in circumstances set out in paragraph 7.[95]

SC8.1.2.1 Paragraph 4: Similar provisions apply in relation to costs in circumstances where the application for an indemnity has been unsuccessful.

Claimant's fraud or lack of care[96]

S8.1.3 5. (1) No indemnity is payable under this Schedule on account of any loss suffered by a claimant—

(a) wholly or partly as a result of his own fraud, or

(b) wholly as a result of his own lack of proper care.

(2) Where any loss is suffered by a claimant partly as a result of his own lack of proper care, any indemnity payable to him is to be reduced to such extent as is fair having regard to his share in the responsibility for the loss.

(3) For the purposes of this paragraph any fraud or lack of care on the part of a person from whom the claimant derives title (otherwise than under a disposition for valuable consideration which is registered or protected by an entry in the register) is to be treated as if it were fraud or lack of care on the part of the claimant.

SC8.1.3 Paragraph 5: The provisions of this paragraph aim to replicate section 83(5)(a), (6) and (7) of the Land Registration Act 1925.

Valuation of estates etc.

S8.1.4 6. Where an indemnity is payable in respect of the loss of an estate, interest or charge, the value of the estate, interest or charge for the purposes of the indemnity is to be regarded as not exceeding—

---

[95] See para. S8.1.5 *et seq.*, *infra*.

[96] *Ruoff & Roper*, paras 40–17 *et seq.*

(a) in the case of an indemnity under paragraph 1(1)(a), its value immediately before rectification of the register (but as if there were to be no rectification), and
(b) in the case of an indemnity under paragraph 1(1)(b), its value at the time when the mistake which caused the loss was made.

Paragraph 6: This provides for the quantification of the indemnity which is payable in respect of the loss of an estate, interest or charge. The indemnity is not to exceed (in cases of rectification) the value of the estate etc immediately before rectification (on the hypothesis that no rectification were to take place) and, in the case of an indemnity payable by reason of the correction of a mistake in the register which would involve rectification, the value of the estate etc at the time when the mistake which caused the loss was made. **SC8.1.4**

Determination of indemnity by court

7. (1) A person may apply to the court for the determination of any question as to— **S8.1.5**

(a) whether he is entitled to an indemnity under this Schedule, or
(b) the amount of such an indemnity.

(2) Paragraph 3(1) does not apply to the costs of an application to the court under this paragraph or of any legal proceedings arising out of such an application.

Paragraph 7: This replicates the effect of section 2(1) of the Land Registration and Charges Act 1971. The costs and expenses of such a determination may be recovered by the individual who has incurred them notwithstanding the absence of the Registrar's consent: paragraph 7(2). **SC8.1.5**

Time limits

8. For the purposes of the Limitation Act 1980 (c. 58)— **S8.1.6**

(a) a liability to pay an indemnity under this Schedule is a simple contract debt, and
(b) the cause of action arises at the time when the claimant knows, or but for his own default might have known, of the existence of his claim.

SC8.1.6 Paragraph 8: This makes the right to an indemnity analogous to a simple contract debt and specifies the circumstances in which the cause of action for an indemnity shall accrue to the individual concerned.[97]

Interest

S8.1.7 9. Rules may make provision about the payment of interest on an indemnity under this Schedule, including—

(a) the circumstances in which interest is payable, and
(b) the periods for and rates at which it is payable.

SC8.1.7 Paragraph 9: No rules have, as yet, been made. This provision is new although current practice is for interest to be paid on any indemnity from the date of mistake. This practice is based upon section 2(5) of the Land Registration and Land Charges Act 1971, which gives the Registrar the power to settle claims for indemnity by agreement.

Recovery of indemnity by registrar

S8.1.8 10. (1) Where an indemnity under this Schedule is paid to a claimant in respect of any loss, the registrar is entitled (without prejudice to any other rights he may have)—

(a) to recover the amount paid from any person who caused or substantially contributed to the loss by his fraud, or
(b) for the purpose of recovering the amount paid, to enforce the rights of action referred to in sub-paragraph (2).

(2) Those rights of action are—

(a) any right of action (of whatever nature and however arising) which the claimant would have been entitled to enforce had the indemnity not been paid, and
(b) where the register has been rectified, any right of action (of whatever nature and however arising) which the person in whose favour the register has been rectified would have been entitled to enforce had it not been rectified.

---

[97] See *Ruoff & Roper*, para. 40–29.

(3) References in this paragraph to an indemnity include interest paid on an indemnity under rules under paragraph 9.

Paragraph 10: This specifies the circumstances in which the Registrar may recover the amount paid by way of an indemnity.[98] **SC8.1.8**

Interpretation

11. (1) For the purposes of this Schedule, references to a mistake in something include anything mistakenly omitted from it as well as anything mistakenly included in it. **S8.1.9**

(2) In this Schedule, references to rectification of the register are to alteration of the register which—

(a) involves the correction of a mistake, and
(b) prejudicially affects the title of a registered proprietor.

Paragraph 11: Defines "mistake" and "rectification". **SC8.1.9**

SCHEDULE 9

Section 107

The Adjudicator

The contents of this Schedule are considered in relation to section 105. **SC9.0**

Holding of office

1. (1) The adjudicator may at any time resign his office by written notice to the Lord Chancellor. **S9.1**

(2) The Lord Chancellor may remove the adjudicator from office on the ground of incapacity or misbehaviour.

(3) Section 26 of the Judicial Pensions and Retirement Act 1993 (c. 8) (compulsory retirement at 70, subject to the possibility of annual extension up to 75) applies to the adjudicator.

[98] See *Ruoff & Roper*, para. 40–30.

(4) Subject to the above, a person appointed to be the adjudicator is to hold and vacate office in accordance with the terms of his appointment and, on ceasing to hold office, is eligible for reappointment.

Remuneration

S9.1.1 2. (1) The Lord Chancellor shall pay the adjudicator such remuneration, and such other allowances, as the Lord Chancellor may determine.

(2) The Lord Chancellor shall—

(a) pay such pension, allowances or gratuities as he may determine to or in respect of a person who is or has been the adjudicator, or

(b) make such payments as he may determine towards provision for the payment of a pension, allowances or gratuities to or in respect of such a person.

(3) Sub-paragraph (2) does not apply if the office of adjudicator is a qualifying judicial office within the meaning of the Judicial Pensions and Retirement Act 1993.

(4) If, when a person ceases to be the adjudicator, the Lord Chancellor determines that there are special circumstances which make it right that the person should receive compensation, the Lord Chancellor may pay to the person by way of compensation a sum of such amount as he may determine.

Staff

S9.1.2 3. (1) The adjudicator may appoint such staff as he thinks fit.

(2) The terms and conditions of appointments under this paragraph shall be such as the adjudicator, with the approval of the Minister for the Civil Service, thinks fit.

Conduct of business

S9.1.3 4. (1) Subject to sub-paragraph (2), any function of the adjudicator may be carried out by any member of his staff who is authorised by him for the purpose.

(2) In the case of functions which are not of an administrative character, sub-paragraph (1) only applies if the member of staff has a 10 year general qualification (within the meaning of section 71 of the Courts and Legal Services Act 1990 (c. 41)).

5. The Lord Chancellor may by regulations make provision about the carrying out of functions during any vacancy in the office of adjudicator.

Finances

6. The Lord Chancellor shall be liable to reimburse expenditure incurred by the adjudicator in the discharge of his functions. **S9.1.4**

7. The Lord Chancellor may require the registrar to make payments towards expenses of the Lord Chancellor under this Schedule.

Application of Tribunals and Inquiries Act 1992

8. In Schedule 1 to the Tribunal and Inquiries Act 1992 (c. 53) (tribunals under the supervision of the Council on Tribunals), after paragraph 27 there is inserted— **S9.1.5**

"Land Registration	27B. The Adjudicator to Her Majesty's Land Registry."

Parliamentary disqualification

9. In Part 1 of Schedule 1 to the House of Commons Disqualification Act 1975 (c. 24) (judicial offices), there is inserted at the end— **S9.1.6**

"Adjudicator to Her Majesty's Land Registry.";

and a corresponding amendment is made in Part 1 of Schedule 1 to the Northern Ireland Assembly Disqualification Act 1975 (c. 25).

SCHEDULE 10

Section 126

Miscellaneous and General Powers

Part 1

Miscellaneous

Dealings with estates subject to compulsory first registration

S10.1 1. (1) Rules may make provision—

(a) applying this Act to a pre-registration dealing with a registrable legal estate as if the dealing had taken place after the date of first registration of the estate, and
(b) about the date on which registration of the dealing is effective.

(2) For the purposes of sub-paragraph (1)—

(a) a legal estate is registrable if a person is subject to a duty under section 6 to make an application to be registered as the proprietor of it, and
(b) a pre-registration dealing is one which takes place before the making of such an application.

SC10.1 Paragraph 1: This power replicates that contained in Land Registration Act 1925, s.123A (1) (a).[99] No rules have, as yet, been made.

Regulation of title matters between sellers and buyers

S10.1.1 2. (1) Rules may make provision about the obligations with respect to—

(a) proof of title, or
(b) perfection of title,

of the seller under a contract for the transfer, or other disposition, for valuable consideration of a registered estate or charge.

---

[99] See also Land Registration Rules 1925, r. 73.

(2) Rules under this paragraph may be expressed to have effect notwithstanding any stipulation to the contrary.

Paragraph 2: Under the Land Registration Act 1925, s.110, provision was made in detail for the documents that the purchaser can require a vendor to produce.[1] The provisions of that section are considered to be unduly cumbersome in the modern conveyancing environment, particularly given the ease with which the register may be searched. Accordingly, paragraph 2 builds into the Act the facility to make rules concerning proof of and perfection of title.[2] No rules have, as yet, been made. Some of these rules will not be capable of exclusion. **SC10.1.1**

Implied covenants

3. Rules may— **S10.1.2**

(a) make provision about the form of provisions extending or limiting any covenant implied by virtue of Part 1 of the Law of Property (Miscellaneous Provisions) Act 1994 (c. 36) (implied covenants for title) on a registrable disposition;

(b) make provision about the application of section 77 of the Law of Property Act 1925 (c. 20) (implied covenants in conveyance subject to rents) to transfers of registered estates;

(c) make provision about reference in the register to implied covenants, including provision for the state of the register to be conclusive in relation to whether covenants have been implied.

Paragraph 3: Statute provides for the implication of covenants in dispositions of property in order to shorten the instruments of disposition by enabling standard covenants to be entered into without spelling them out in detail. Covenants as to title are, in effect, warranties given by the vendor as to his title and may often provide the only remedy open to the disponee for any defects in title to emerge after completion.[3] Paragraph 3 enables rules to be made concerning the matters set forth in sub-paragraph (a), (b) and (c) as therein specified. Whilst no rules have, as yet, been made, similar matters are addressed under the Land Registration Rules 1925.[4] **SC10.1.2**

---

[1] See *Ruoff & Roper*, para. 17–19.

[2] See also Sched. 11, para. 2.

[3] See *Ruoff & Roper*, paras 16–01 *et seq*.

[4] See, for example, LRR 1925, rr. 76A(5), 77A(3), 76A(4), 109(6).

Land certificates

S10.1.3 4. Rules may make provision about—

(a) when a certificate of registration of title to a legal estate may be issued,
(b) the form and content of such a certificate, and
(c) when such a certificate must be produced or surrendered to the registrar.

SC10.1.3 Paragraph 4: It is envisaged that in future land certificates are unlikely to play any part in the conveyancing process. A land certificate will simply be a document certifying that the registration of a registered estate has taken place and the named person is the registered proprietor; it may not comprise the form or have the content as at present.[5] Nevertheless, it is envisaged that they will continue to perform a useful function. A land certificate might, for example, alert a personal representative that the deceased was the registered proprietor of a property when this would otherwise not have been apparent.[6] No rules have, as yet, been made.

Part 2

General

Notice

S10.1.4 5. (1) Rules may make provision about the form, content and service of notice under this Act.

(2) Rules under this paragraph about the service of notice may, in particular—

(a) make provision requiring the supply of an address for service and about the entry of addresses for service in the register;
(b) make provision about—

(i) the time for service,
(ii) the mode of service, and
(iii) when service is to be regarded as having taken place.

SC10.1.4 Paragraph 5: This provision replicates section 79 of the Land Registration Act 1925. No rules have, as yet, been made.

---

[5] Law Com No. 271, para. 9.91, p. 212.

[6] Law Com No. 271, para. 772, p. 591.

Applications

6. Rules may— S10.1.5

(a) make provision about the form and content of applications under this Act;
(b) make provision requiring applications under this Act to be supported by such evidence as the rules may provide;
(c) make provision about when an application under this Act is to be taken as made;
(d) make provision about the order in which competing applications are to be taken to rank;
(e) make provision for an alteration made by the registrar for the purpose of correcting a mistake in an application or accompanying document to have effect in such circumstances as the rules may provide as if made by the applicant or other interested party or parties.

Paragraph 6: The Act provides many opportunities for application to be made to the Registrar[7] and this paragraph enables rules to be made regulating those applications and the manner in which they are processed. With regard to the sub-paragraphs specified in paragraph 6:— **SC10.1.5**

(a) It is envisaged that all applications in electronic form will be in a prescribed form to ensure the effective working of the system. Prescribed forms for paper applications are also likely to be made.

(c) Such a power will ensure that the registrar is able to determine the order in which competing applications that arrive in the registry can be taken as made.

(d) Similarly, rules under this provision will be made in order to allocate priority to competing applications.

(e) The purpose of this power is to enable the registrar to correct clerical errors without obtaining the consent of the applicant.[8]

Statutory statements

7. Rules may make provision about the form of any statement required under an enactment to be included in an instrument effecting a registrable disposition or a **S10.1.6**

---

[7] See para. C73.1, *supra.*
[8] See Land Registration Rules 1925, r. 13.

disposition which triggers the requirement of registration.

SC10.1.6 Paragraph 7: Examples of such statements are those in the Charities Act 1993, ss. 37, 39 and Settled Land Act 1925, s.5. This provision enables the Registrar to provide standard forms of such statutory statements.

Residual power

S10.1.7 8. Rules may make any other provision which it is expedient to make for the purposes of carrying this Act into effect, whether similar or not to any provision which may be made under the other powers to make land registration rules.

SC10.1.7 Paragraph 8: Whilst the Act makes specific provision throughout for the making of rules in order to augment its contents and achieve the desired purpose, this provision is a "catch-all" similar to that contained in the Land Registration Act 1925, s.144(1)(xxi). It is envisaged that it will not be necessary to employ this residual power as often as has been the case under the 1925 Act.[9]

SCHEDULE 11

Section 133

Minor and Consequential Amendments

SC11.0 This Schedule makes a number of alterations to other statutes in order to make them compliant with and complementary to the provisions of the Act. Some of the more significant are:—

SC11.0.1 Paragraph 2(2): The insertion of section 44(4A) into the Law of Property Act 1925 ensures that where a contract is entered into to grant or assign a lease or to grant a sub-lease out of an unregistered estate, there will be an obligation on the proprietor of that estate to deduce title for the statutory period unless the parties agree to the contrary. Without the insertion of section 44(4A), the position was otherwise. Accordingly, this provision will facilitate the granting of the registration of leases with absolute title.

SC11.0.2 Paragraph 2(4): The disapplication of section 44 of the Law of Property Act 1925 to registered conveyancing reflects the position that the

---

[9] Law Com No. 271, para. 778, p. 593.

requirement to show proof of title for a period of 15 years is of no application to registered land even though that requirement currently applies since registered land is not exempted from provisions of section 44. Under the Act, the register itself is proof of title and any transferee or grantee can inspect the title of the estate that is to be transferred or out of which the grant is to be made.[10]

Paragraph 28: The inclusion of the Adjudicator to Her Majesty's Land Registry in Schedule 5 to the Judicial Pensions and Retirement Act 1993 has the effect of requiring the Adjudicator to retire at the age of 70 even though he may be authorised to continue in office on a yearly basis until the age of 75. **SC11.0.3**

Paragraph 31: The Law of Property (Miscellaneous Provisions) Act 1994 makes provision for the implication of covenants of title into dispositions of property. Section 6 of that Act provides that liability should not attach in relation to some of the covenants in specified circumstances. Within the context of registered land, the current position is that all dispositions take subject to anything that is entered in the register at the time the disposition was executed and any overriding interest of which the person to whom the disposition was made had notice at the time the disposition was registered and which will affect the estate created or disposed of when disposition is registered.[11] Thus there will be no breach of an implied covenant in relation to these matters. **SC11.0.4**

The insertion of section 6(4) into the 1994 Act broadly reflects the existing position. However there is nothing in the new sub-section that corresponds to Land Registration Rules 1925, r.77A(2)(d) in relation to overriding interests since section 6(2) of the 1994 Act makes that unnecessary. Furthermore whilst the new provision only applies to covenants listed in section 6 of the 1994 Act, the existing position is that Land Registration Rules 1925, r.77A(2) currently applies in relation to all of the covenants implied under Part 1 of the 1994 Act. It is envisaged that this change is unlikely to be material and will simplify the present law.[12] **SC11.0.5**

Settled Land Act 1925 (c. 18)

1. Section 119(3) of the Settled Land Act 1925 ceases to have effect. **S11.1**

---

[10] See section 66.

[11] LRR, r. 77A(2).

[12] Law Com No. 271, para. 789, p. 595.

Law of Property Act 1925 (c. 20)

S11.1.1 2. (1) The Law of Property Act 1925 is amended as follows.

(2) In section 44, after subsection (4) there is inserted—

"(4A) Subsections (2) and (4) of this section do not apply to a contract to grant a term of years if the grant will be an event within section 4(1) of the Land Registration Act 2002 (events which trigger compulsory first registration of title)."

(3) In that section, in subsection (5), for "the last three preceding subsections" there is substituted "subsections (2) to (4) of this section".

(4) In that section, at the end there is inserted—

"(12) Nothing in this section applies in relation to registered land or to a term of years to be derived out of registered land."

(5) In section 84(8), the words from ", but" to the end are omitted.

(6) In section 85(3), for the words from the beginning to the second "or" there is substituted "Subsection (2) does not apply to registered land, but, subject to that, this section applies whether or not the land is registered land and whether or not".

(7) In section 86(3), for the words from the beginning to the second "or" there is substituted "Subsection (2) does not apply to registered land, but, subject to that, this section applies whether or not the land is registered land and whether or not".

(8) In section 87, at the end there is inserted—

"(4) Subsection (1) of this section shall not be taken to be affected by section 23(1)(a) of the Land Registration Act 2002 (under which owner's powers in relation to a registered estate do not include power to mortgage by demise or sub-demise)."

(9) In section 94(4), for the words from "registered" to the end there is substituted "on registered land".

(10) In section 97, for "Land Registration Act 1925" there is substituted "Land Registration Act 2002".

(11) In section 115(10), for the words from "charge" to the end there is substituted "registered charge (within the meaning of the Land Registration Act 2002)".

(12) In section 125(2), for the words from "(not being" to "1925)" there is substituted "(not being registered land)".

(13) In section 205(1)(xxii)—

(a) for "Land Registration Act 1925" there is substituted "Land Registration Act 2002", and

(b) the words from ", and" to the end are omitted.

Administration of Estates Act 1925 (c. 23)

3. In section 43(2) of the Administration of Estates Act 1925, for "Land Registration Act 1925" there is substituted "Land Registration Act 2002". **S11.1.2**

Requisitioned Land and War Works Act 1945 (c. 43)

4. (1) Section 37 of the Requisitioned Land and War Works Act 1945 is amended as follows. **S11.1.3**

(2) In subsection (2), for "Land Registration Act 1925" there is substituted "Land Registration Act 2002".

(3) Subsection (3) ceases to have effect.

Law of Property (Joint Tenants) Act 1964 (c. 63)

5. In section 3 of the Law of Property (Joint Tenants) Act 1964, for the words from "any land" to the end there is substituted "registered land". **S11.1.4**

Gas Act 1965 (c. 36)

6. (1) The Gas Act 1965 is amended as follows. **S11.1.5**

(2) In section 12(3), for "Land Registration Act 1925" there is substituted "Land Registration Act 2002".

(3) In sections 12(4) and 13(6), for the words from "be deemed" to the end there is substituted—

"(a) for the purposes of the Land Charges Act 1925, be deemed to be a charge affecting land falling within Class D(iii), and
(b) for the purposes of the Land Registration Act 2002, be deemed to be an equitable easement."

Commons Registration Act 1965 (c. 64)

S11.1.6 7. (1) The Commons Registration Act 1965 is amended as follows.
(2) In sections 1(1), (2) and (3), 4(3) and 8(1), for "under the Land Registration Acts 1925 and 1936" there is substituted "in the register of title".
(3) In section 9, for "the Land Registration Acts 1925 and 1936" there is substituted "in the register of title".
(4) In section 12 (in both places), for "under the Land Registration Acts 1925 and 1936" there is substituted "in the register of title".
(5) In section 22, in subsection (1), there is inserted at the appropriate place—

" "register of title" means the register kept under section 1 of the Land Registration Act 2002;".

(6) In that section, in subsection (2), for "under the Land Registration Acts 1925 and 1936" there is substituted "in the register of title".

Leasehold Reform Act 1967 (c. 88)

S11.1.7 8. (1) The Leasehold Reform Act 1967 is amended as follows.
(2) In section 5(5)—
(a) for "an overriding interest within the meaning of the Land Registration Act 1925" there is substituted "regarded for the purposes of the Land Registration Act 2002 as an interest falling within any of the paragraphs of Schedule 1 or 3 to that Act", and
(b) for "or caution under the Land Registration Act 1925" there is substituted "under the Land Registration Act 2002".
(3) In Schedule 4, in paragraph 1(3)—

(a) for paragraph (a) there is substituted—

"(a) the covenant may be the subject of a notice in the register of title kept under the Land Registration Act 2002, if apart from this subsection it would not be capable of being the subject of such a notice; and", and

(b) in paragraph (b), for "notice of the covenant has been so registered, the covenant" there is substituted "a notice in respect of the covenant has been entered in that register, it".

Law of Property Act 1969 (c. 59)

9. In section 24(1) of the Law of Property Act 1969, for "Land Registration Act 1925" there is substituted "Land Registration Act 2002". **S11.1.8**

Land Charges Act 1972 (c. 61)

10. (1) The Land Charges Act 1972 is amended as follows. **S11.1.9**

(2) In section 14(1), for the words from "Land Registration" to the end there is substituted "Land Registration Act 2002".

(3) In section 14(3)—

(a) for the words from "section 123A" to "register)" there is substituted "section 7 of the Land Registration Act 2002 (effect of failure to comply with requirement of registration)", and

(b) for "that section" there is substituted "section 6 of that Act".

(4) In section 17(1), in the definition of "registered land", for "Land Registration Act 1925" there is substituted "Land Registration Act 2002".

Consumer Credit Act 1974 (c. 39)

11. In section 177(1) and (6) of the Consumer Credit Act 1974, for "Land Registration Act 1925" there is substituted "Land Registration Act 2002". **S11.1.10**

Solicitors Act 1974 (c. 47)

S11.1.11 12. (1) The Solicitors Act 1974 is amended as follows.
(2) In sections 22(1) and 56(1)(f), for "Land Registration Act 1925" there is substituted "Land Registration Act 2002".
(3) Section 75(b) ceases to have effect.

Local Land Charges Act 1975 (c. 76)

S11.1.12 13. In section 10(3)(b)(ii) of the Local Land Charges Act 1975, for "under the Land Registration Act 1925" there is substituted "in the register of title kept under the Land Registration Act 2002".

Rent Act 1977 (c. 42)

S11.1.13 14. In section 136(b) of the Rent Act 1977, for the words from "charge" to the end there is substituted "registered charge (within the meaning of the Land Registration Act 2002)".

Charging Orders Act 1979 (c. 53)

S11.1.14 15. In section 3(2) and (6) of the Charging Orders Act 1979, for "Land Registration Act 1925" there is substituted "Land Registration Act 2002".

Highways Act 1980 (c. 66)

S11.1.15 16. Section 251(5) of the Highways Act 1980 ceases to have effect.

Inheritance Tax Act 1984 (c. 51)

S11.1.16 17. In section 238(3) of the Inheritance Tax Act 1984, for paragraph (a) there is substituted—

"(a) in relation to registered land—
(i) if the disposition is required to be completed by registration, the time of registration, and
(ii) otherwise, the time of completion,".

Housing Act 1985 (c. 68)

S11.1.17 18. (1) The Housing Act 1985 is amended as follows.

(2) In section 37(5), for the words from "and" to the end there is substituted—

"(5A) Where the Chief Land Registrar approves an application for registration of—

(a) a disposition of registered land, or
(b) the disponee's title under a disposition of unregistered land,

and the instrument effecting the disposition contains a covenant of the kind mentioned in subsection (1), he must enter in the register a restriction reflecting the limitation imposed by the covenant".

(3) In section 154(5), for "Land Registration Acts 1925 to 1971" there is substituted "Land Registration Act 2002".

(4) In section 157(7), for the words from "the appropriate" to the end there is substituted "a restriction in the register of title reflecting the limitation".

(5) In section 165(6), for "section 83 of the Land Registration Act 1925" there is substituted "Schedule 8 to the Land Registration Act 2002".

(6) In Schedule 9A, in paragraph 2(2), for the words from the beginning to "the disponor" there is substituted "Where on a qualifying disposal the disponor's title to the dwelling-house is not registered, the disponor".

(7) In that Schedule, for paragraph 4 there is substituted—

"4 (1) This paragraph applies where the Chief Land Registrar approves an application for registration of—

(a) a disposition of registered land, or
(b) the disponee's title under a disposition of unregistered land,

and the instrument effecting the disposition contains the statement required by paragraph 1.

(2) The Chief Land Registrar must enter in the register—

(a) a notice in respect of the rights of qualifying persons under this Part in relation to dwelling-houses comprised in the disposal, and

(b) a restriction reflecting the limitation under section 171D(2) on subsequent disposal."

(8) In that Schedule, for paragraph 5(2) there is substituted—

"(2) If the landlord's title is registered, the landlord shall apply for the entry in the register of—

(a) a notice in respect of the rights of the qualifying person or persons under the provisions of this Part, and

(b) a restriction reflecting the limitation under section 171D(2) on subsequent disposal."

(9) In that Schedule, paragraph 5(3) ceases to have effect.

(10) In that Schedule, in paragraph 6, for sub-paragraph (1) there is substituted—

"(1) The rights of a qualifying person under this Part in relation to the qualifying dwelling house shall not be regarded as falling within Schedule 3 to the Land Registration Act 2002 (and so are liable to be postponed under section 29 of that Act, unless protected by means of a notice in the register)."

(11) In that Schedule, in paragraph 9(2), for "Land Registration Acts 1925 to 1986" there is substituted "Land Registration Act 2002".

(12) In Schedule 17, in paragraph 2(2), for "Land Registration Acts 1925 to 1971" there is substituted "Land Registration Act 2002".

(13) In Schedule 20, in paragraph 17(2), for "Land Registration Acts 1925 to 1986" there is substituted "Land Registration Act 2002".

Building Societies Act 1986 (c. 53)

19. (1) In Schedule 2A to the Building Societies Act 1986, paragraph 1 is amended as follows. **S11.1.18**

(2) In sub-paragraph (2), for "charge or incumbrance registered under the Land Registration Act 1925" there is substituted "registered charge (within the meaning of the Land Registration Act 2002)".

(3) Sub-paragraph (4) ceases to have effect.

(4) In sub-paragraph (5), the definition of "registered land" and the preceding "and" cease to have effect.

Landlord and Tenant Act 1987 (c. 31)

20. In sections 24(8) and (9), 28(5), 30(6) and 34(9) of the Landlord and Tenant Act 1987, for "Land Registration Act 1925" there is substituted "Land Registration Act 2002". **S11.1.19**

Diplomatic and Consular Premises Act 1987 (c. 46)

21. (1) The Diplomatic and Consular Premises Act 1987 is amended as follows. **S11.1.20**

(2) In section 5, after the definition of the expression "diplomatic premises" there is inserted—

" 'land' includes buildings and other structures, land covered with water and any estate, interest, easement, servitude or right in or over land,".

(3) In Schedule 1, in paragraph 1—

(a) before the definition of the expression "the registrar" there is inserted—

" 'registered land' has the same meaning as in the Land Registration Act 2002;", and

(b) the words from "and expressions" to the end are omitted.

Criminal Justice Act 1988 (c. 33)

22. (1) The Criminal Justice Act 1988 is amended as follows. **S11.1.21**

(2) In section 77(12)—

(a) for "Land Registration Act 1925" there is substituted "Land Registration Act 2002", and
(b) in paragraph (a), at the end there is inserted "except that no notice may be entered in the register of title under the Land Registration Act 2002 in respect of such orders".

(3) In section 79(1) and (4), for "Land Registration Act 1925" there is substituted "Land Registration Act 2002".

Housing Act 1988 (c. 50)

S11.1.22 23. (1) The Housing Act 1988 is amended as follows.
(2) In section 81, in subsection (9)(c), for "Land Registration Acts 1925 to 1986" there is substituted "Land Registration Act 2002".
(3) In that section, for subsection (10) there is substituted—

"(10) Where the Chief Land Registrar approves an application for registration of—

(a) a disposition of registered land, or
(b) the approved person's title under a disposition of unregistered land,

and the instrument effecting the disposition contains the statement required by subsection (1) above, he shall enter in the register a restriction reflecting the limitation under this section on subsequent disposal."

(4) In section 90(4), for "Land Registration Act 1925" there is substituted "Land Registration Act 2002".
(5) In section 133, in subsection (8)—

(a) for the words "conveyance, grant or assignment" there is substituted "transfer or grant",
(b) for the words "section 123 of the Land Registration Act 1925" there is substituted

"section 4 of the Land Registration Act 2002", and

(c) in paragraph (c), for "Land Registration Acts 1925 to 1986" there is substituted "Land Registration Act 2002".

(6) In that section, for subsection (9) there is substituted—

"(9) Where the Chief Land Registrar approves an application for registration of—

(a) a disposition of registered land, or

(b) a person's title under a disposition of unregistered land,

and the instrument effecting the original disposal contains the statement required by subsection (3)(d) above, he shall enter in the register a restriction reflecting the limitation under this section on subsequent disposal."

Local Government and Housing Act 1989 (c. 42)

24. (1) Section 173 of the Local Government and Housing Act 1989 is amended as follows. **S11.1.23**

(2) In subsection (8)—

(a) for the words "conveyance, grant or assignment" there is substituted "transfer or grant",

(b) for the words "section 123 of the Land Registration Act 1925" there is substituted "section 4 of the Land Registration Act 2002", and

(c) in paragraph (c), for "Land Registration Acts 1925 to 1986" there is substituted "Land Registration Act 2002".

(3) For subsection (9) there is substituted—

"(9) Where the Chief Land Registrar approves an application for registration of—

(a) a disposition of registered land, or

(b) a person's title under a disposition of unregistered land,

and the instrument effecting the initial transfer contains the statement required by subsection (3) above, he shall enter in the register a restriction reflecting the limitation under this section on subsequent disposal."

Water Resources Act 1991 (c. 57)

S11.1.24 25. (1) Section 158 of the Water Resources Act 1991 is amended as follows.

(2) In subsection (5)—

(a) for paragraphs (a) and (b) there is substituted—

"(a) the agreement may be the subject of a notice in the register of title under the Land Registration Act 2002 as if it were an interest affecting the registered land;

(b) the provisions of sections 28 to 30 of that Act (effect of dispositions of registered land on priority of adverse interests) shall apply as if the agreement were such an interest;", and

(b) in paragraph (c), for "where notice of the agreement has been so registered," there is substituted "subject to the provisions of those sections,".

(3) In subsection (6), for "Land Registration Act 1925" there is substituted "Land Registration Act 2002".

Access to Neighbouring Land Act 1992 (c. 4)

S11.1.25 26. (1) The Access to Neighbouring Land Act 1992 is amended as follows.

(2) In section 4(1), for "Land Registration Act 1925" there is substituted "Land Registration Act 2002".

(3) In section 5, in subsection (4)—

(a) in paragraph (b), for "notice or caution under the Land Registration Act 1925" there is substituted "notice under the Land Registration Act 2002", and

(b) for "entry, notice or caution" there is substituted "entry or notice".

(4) In that section, for subsection (5) there is substituted—

"(5) The rights conferred on a person by or under an access order shall not be capable of falling within paragraph 2 of Schedule 1 or 3 to the Land Registration Act 2002 (overriding status of interest of person in actual occupation)."

(5) In that section, in subsection (6), for "Land Registration Act 1925" there is substituted "Land Registration Act 2002".

Further and Higher Education Act 1992 (c. 13)

27. In Schedule 5 to the Further and Higher Education Act 1992, in paragraph 6(1)— **S11.1.26**

(a) for "Land Registration Acts 1925 to 1986" there is substituted "Land Registration Act 2002", and
(b) for "those Acts" there is substituted "that Act".

Judicial Pensions and Retirement Act 1993 (c. 8)

28. In Schedule 5 to the Judicial Pensions and Retirement Act 1993, there is inserted at the end— **S11.1.27**

"Adjudicator to Her Majesty's Land Registry"

Charities Act 1993 (c. 10)

29. (1) The Charities Act 1993 is amended as follows. **S11.1.28**

(2) In section 37, for subsections (7) and (8) there is substituted—

"(7) Where the disposition to be effected by any such instrument as is mentioned in subsection (1)(b) or (5)(b) above will be—

(a) a registrable disposition, or
(b) a disposition which triggers the requirement of registration,

the statement which, by virtue of subsection (1) or (5) above, is to be contained in the instrument shall be in such form as may be prescribed by land registration rules.

(8) Where the registrar approves an application for registration of—

(a) a disposition of registered land, or

(b) a person's title under a disposition of unregistered land,

and the instrument effecting the disposition contains a statement complying with subsections (5) and (7) above, he shall enter in the register a restriction reflecting the limitation under section 36 above on subsequent disposal."

(3) In that section, in subsection (9)—

(a) for "the restriction to be withdrawn" there is substituted "the removal of the entry", and

(b) for "withdraw the restriction" there is substituted "remove the entry".

(4) In that section, in subsection (11), for "Land Registration Act 1925" there is substituted "Land Registration Act 2002".

(5) In section 39, in subsection (1), at the end there is inserted "by land registration rules".

(6) In that section, for subsections (1A) and (1B) there is substituted—

"(1A) Where any such mortgage will be one to which section 4(1)(g) of the Land Registration Act 2002 applies—

(a) the statement required by subsection (1) above shall be in such form as may be prescribed by land registration rules; and

(b) if the charity is not an exempt charity, the mortgage shall also contain a statement, in such form as may be prescribed by land registration rules, that the restrictions on disposition imposed by section 36 above apply to the land (subject to subsection (9) of that section).

(1B) Where—

(a) the registrar approves an application for registration of a person's title to land in connection with such a mortgage as is mentioned in subsection (1A) above,

(b) the mortgage contains statements complying with subsections (1) and (1A) above, and

(c) the charity is not an exempt charity,

the registrar shall enter in the register a restriction reflecting the limitation under section 36 above on subsequent disposal.

(1C) Section 37(9) above shall apply in relation to any restriction entered under subsection (1B) as it applies in relation to any restriction entered under section 37(8)."

(7) In that section, in subsection (6), for the words from "and subsections" to the end there is substituted "and subsections (1) to (1B) above shall be construed as one with the Land Registration Act 2002".

Leasehold Reform, Housing and Urban Development Act 1993 (c. 28)

30. (1) The Leasehold Reform, Housing and Urban Development Act 1993 is amended as follows. **S11.1.29**

(2) In sections 34(10) and 57(11), for the words from "rules" to the end there is substituted "land registration rules under the Land Registration Act 2002".

(3) In section 97, in subsection (1)—

(a) for "an overriding interest within the meaning of the Land Registration Act 1925" there is substituted "capable of falling within paragraph 2 of Schedule 1 or 3 to the Land Registration Act 2002", and

(b) for "or caution under the Land Registration Act 1925" there is substituted "under the Land Registration Act 2002".

(4) In that section, in subsection (2), for "Land Registration Act 1925" there is substituted "Land Registration Act 2002".

Law of Property (Miscellaneous Provisions) Act 1994 (c. 36)

S11.1.30 31. (1) The Law of Property (Miscellaneous Provisions) Act 1994 is amended as follows.

(2) In section 6 (cases in which there is no liability under covenants implied by virtue of Part 1 of that Act), at the end there is inserted—

"(4) Moreover, where the disposition is of an interest the title to which is registered under the Land Registration Act 2002, that person is not liable under any of those covenants for anything (not falling within subsection (1) or (2) which at the time of the disposition was entered in relation to that interest in the register of title under that Act."

(3) In section 17(3)—

(a) in paragraph (c), for the words from "any" to the end there is substituted "the Adjudicator to Her Majesty's Land Registry", and

(b) for "section 144 of the Land Registration Act 1925" there is substituted "the Land Registration Act 2002".

Drug Trafficking Act 1994 (c. 37)

S11.1.31 32. (1) The Drug Trafficking Act 1994 is amended as follows.

(2) In section 26(12)—

(a) for "Land Registration Act 1925" there is substituted "Land Registration Act 2002", and

(b) in paragraph (a), at the end there is inserted ", except that no notice may be entered in the register of title under the Land Registration Act 2002 in respect of such orders".

(3) In section 28(1) and (4), for "Land Registration Act 1925" there is substituted "Land Registration Act 2002".

Landlord and Tenant (Covenants) Act 1995 (c. 30)

33. (1) The Landlord and Tenant (Covenants) Act 1995 is amended as follows. **S11.1.32**

(2) In sections 3(6) and 15(5)(b), for "Land Registration Act 1925" there is substituted "Land Registration Act 2002".

(3) In section 20, in subsection (2), for the words from "rules" to the end there is substituted "land registration rules under the Land Registration Act 2002".

(4) In that section, in subsection (6)—

(a) for "an overriding interest within the meaning of the Land Registration Act 1925" there is substituted "capable of falling within paragraph 2 of Schedule 1 or 3 to the Land Registration Act 2002", and

(b) for "or caution under the Land Registration Act 1925" there is substituted "under the Land Registration Act 2002".

Family Law Act 1996 (c. 27)

34. (1) The Family Law Act 1996 is amended as follows. **S11.1.33**

(2) In section 31(10)—

(a) for "Land Registration Act 1925" there is substituted "Land Registration Act 2002", and

(b) for paragraph (b) there is substituted—

"(b) a spouse's matrimonial home rights are not to be capable of falling within paragraph 2 of Schedule 1 or 3 to that Act."

(3) In Schedule 4, in paragraph 4(6), for "section 144 of the Land Registration Act 1925" there is substituted "by land registration rules under the Land Registration Act 2002".

Housing Act 1996 (c. 52)

35. In section 13(5) of the Housing Act 1996, for the words from "if" to the end there is substituted "if the first disposal involves registration under the Land **S11.1.34**

Registration Act 2002, the Chief Land Registrar shall enter in the register of title a restriction reflecting the limitation".

Education Act 1996 (c. 56)

S11.1.35 36. In Schedule 7 to the Education Act 1996, in paragraph 11—

(a) in sub-paragraph (a), for "Land Registration Acts 1925 to 1986" there is substituted "Land Registration Act 2002", and
(b) in sub-paragraphs (b) and (c), for "those Acts" there is substituted "that Act".

School Standards and Framework Act 1998 (c. 31)

S11.1.36 37. In Schedule 22 to the School Standards and Framework Act 1998, in paragraph 9(1)—

(a) in paragraph (a), for "Land Registration Acts 1925 to 1986" there is substituted "Land Registration Act 2002", and
(b) in paragraphs (b) and (c), for "those Acts" there is substituted "that Act".

Terrorism Act 2000 (c. 11)

S11.1.37 38. In Schedule 4 to the Terrorism Act 2000, in paragraph 8(1)—

(a) for "Land Registration Act 1925" there is substituted "Land Registration Act 2002", and
(b) in paragraph (a), at the end there is inserted ", except that no notice may be entered in the register of title under the Land Registration Act 2002 in respect of such orders".

Finance Act 2000 (c. 17)

S11.1.38 39. In section 128 of the Finance Act 2000—

(a) in subsection (2), for the words from "rule" to the end there is substituted "land registration rules under the Land Registration Act 2002", and
(b) in subsection (8)(a), for "Land Registration Act 1925" there is substituted "Land Registration Act 2002".

International Criminal Court Act 2001 (c. 17)

40. In Schedule 6 to the International Criminal Court Act 2001, in paragraph 7(1)— **S11.1.39**

(a) for "Land Registration Act 1925" there is substituted "Land Registration Act 2002", and
(b) in paragraph (a), at the end there is inserted ", except that no notice may be entered in the register of title under the Land Registration Act 2002 in respect of such orders".

SCHEDULE 12

Section 134

Transition

Existing entries in the register

1. Nothing in the repeals made by this Act affects the validity of any entry in the register. **S12.1**

2. (1) This Act applies to notices entered under the Land Registration Act 1925 (c. 21) as it applies to notices entered in pursuance of an application under section 34(2)(a). **S12.1.1**
(2) This Act applies to restrictions and inhibitions entered under the Land Registration Act 1925 as it applies to restrictions entered under this Act.
(3) Notwithstanding their repeal by this Act, sections 55 and 56 of the Land Registration Act 1925 shall continue to have effect so far as relating to cautions against dealings lodged under that Act.
(4) Rules may make provision about cautions against dealings entered under the Land Registration Act 1925.
(5) In this paragraph, references to the Land Registration Act 1925 include a reference to any enactment replaced (directly or indirectly) by that Act.

3. An entry in the register which, immediately before the repeal of section 144(1)(xi) of the Land Registration Act 1925, operated by virtue of rule 239 of the Land Registration Rules (S.I. 1925/1093) as a caution under section 54 of that Act shall continue to operate as such a caution.

SC12.1.1 Paragraph 1: All existing entries in the register will, notwithstanding any repeal made by the Act, continue to have effect according to their content and form.

Paragraph 2(1): Notices entered under the Land Registration Act 1925 take effect as if they had been entered under the Act.[13]

Paragraph 2(2): All restrictions and inhibitions entered under the Land Registration Act 1925 are to be dealt with as though they were restrictions entered under the Act.[14]

Paragraph 2(3), (4): The effect of sections 55 and 56 of the Land Registration Act 1925 is preserved in relation to cautions against dealings lodged under that Act. Provision is made for rules to be made concerning those cautions. No rules have, as yet, been made. It is envisaged that such rules will replicate the effect of the existing rules relating to the operation of cautions.[15, 16]

Paragraph 3: Liens protected by notice of deposit or notice of intended deposit before April 3, 1995 take effect as a caution against dealings. Accordingly, the effect of Land Registration Rule 1925, r. 239 is preserved in relation to such instances.

Existing cautions against first registration

S12.1.2 4. Notwithstanding the repeal of section 56(3) of the Land Registration Act 1925, that provision shall continue to have effect in relation to cautions against first registration lodged under that Act, or any enactment replaced (directly or indirectly) by that Act.

SC12.1.2 Paragraph 4: In relation to cautions against first registration,[17] section 56(3) of the Land Registration Act 1925 continues to have effect. That sub-section provides that where a person causes damage to another by entering a caution without reasonable cause he will be liable to that person in damages.

Pending applications

S12.1.3 5. Notwithstanding the repeal of the Land Registration Act 1925, that Act shall continue to have effect in relation to an application for the entry in the register of

---

[13] See sections 32–39, *supra*.

[14] See sections 40–47, *supra*.

[15] Law Com No. 271, para. 794, p. 596; Land Registration Rules 1925, rr. 217–219, 221 and 222.

[16] For cautions against dealings see *Ruoff & Roper*, para. 36–01 *et seq*.

[17] See *Ruoff & Roper*, paras 13–01 *et seq*.

a notice, restriction, inhibition or caution against dealings which is pending immediately before the repeal of the provision under which the application is made.

6. Notwithstanding the repeal of section 53 of the Land Registration Act 1925, subsections (1) and (2) of that section shall continue to have effect in relation to an application to lodge a caution against first registration which is pending immediately before the repeal of those provisions.

Paragraphs 5 and 6: These provisions allow for the application of the Land Registration Act 1925 in relation to applications for the entry in the register of a notice, restriction, inhibition or caution that are pending upon the bringing into effect of the Act. **SC12.1.3**

Former overriding interests

7. For the period of three years beginning with the day on which Schedule 1 comes into force, it has effect with the insertion after paragraph 14 of— **S12.1.4**

"15. A right acquired under the Limitation Act 1980 before the coming into force of this Schedule."

8. Schedule 3 has effect with the insertion after paragraph 2 of—

"2A (1) An interest which, immediately before the coming into force of this Schedule, was an overriding interest under section 70(1)(g) of the Land Registration Act 1925 by virtue of a person's receipt of rents and profits, except for an interest of a person of whom inquiry was made before the disposition and who failed to disclose the right when he could reasonably have been expected to do so.

(2) Sub-paragraph (1) does not apply to an interest if at any time since the coming into force of this Schedule it has been an interest which, had the Land Registration Act 1925 (c. 21) continued in force, would not have been an overriding interest under section 70(1)(g) of that Act by virtue of a person's receipt of rents and profits."

9. (1) This paragraph applies to an easement or profit a prendre which was an overriding interest in relation to a registered estate immediately before the

coming into force of Schedule 3, but which would not fall within paragraph 3 of that Schedule if created after the coming into force of that Schedule.

(2) In relation to an interest to which this paragraph applies, Schedule 3 has effect as if the interest were not excluded from paragraph 3.

10. For the period of three years beginning with the day on which Schedule 3 comes into force, paragraph 3 of the Schedule has effect with the omission of the exception.

11. For the period of three years beginning with the day on which Schedule 3 comes into force, it has effect with the insertion after paragraph 14 of—

"15. A right under paragraph 18(1) of Schedule 12."

12. Paragraph 1 of each of Schedules 1 and 3 shall be taken to include an interest which immediately before the coming into force of the Schedule was an overriding interest under section 70(1)(k) of the Land Registration Act 1925.

13. Paragraph 6 of each of Schedules 1 and 3 shall be taken to include an interest which immediately before the coming into force of the Schedule was an overriding interest under section 70(1)(i) of the Land Registration Act 1925 and whose status as such was preserved by section 19(3) of the Local Land Charges Act 1975 (c. 76) (transitional provision in relation to change in definition of "local land charge").

SC12.1.4 Paragraph 7: This inserts a further category of interest which requires overriding status for a period of three years from the day on which Schedule 1 (unregistered interests which override first registration) comes into force. That category comprises rights *acquired* under the Limitation Act 1980 before the coming into force of that Schedule. Under the Land Registration Act 1925, rights acquired under the Limitation Act amount to an overriding interest under section 70(1)(f).[18] However, that section 70(1)(f) does not require the person who has acquired the right under the Limitation Act 1980 to be in actual occupation. That provision is not reflected under the Act.

---

[18] See *Ruoff & Roper*, para. 6–14.

However, rights that have been acquired on the coming into force of Schedule 1 are protected for the limited period in circumstances where the adverse possessor has obtained those rights and cannot rely upon being in actual occupation under paragraph 2 of Schedule 1. This will provide a reasonable opportunity for any adverse possessor who is no longer in actual occupation of the land which he claims to register his rights.

Paragraph 8: This paragraph inserts paragraph 2A into Schedule 3 and protects the overriding status of an individual who is in receipt of the rents and profits from land. Under the Land Registration Act 1925, s. 70(1)(g), such an individual would have been in actual occupation of the land and thus enjoyed overriding status. That provision is not reflected in the Act. However, those who are in receipt of the rent and profits from land upon the coming into force of Schedule 3 are granted overriding status whilst they continue to be in receipt of those rents and profits. If that receipt ceases, the overriding status will be lost. The recipient of the rents and profits will not enjoy overriding status in circumstances where an enquiry was made of him prior to the disposition and he has failed to disclose the right when he could reasonably have been expected to do so. **SC12.1.4.1**

Paragraph 9: Only legal easements or profits a prendre can comprise overriding interests in relation to registered dispositions under paragraph 3 of Schedule 3. Equitable easements or profits, easements and profits expressly granted or reserved out of registered land[19] and legal easements and profits that fall within one of the exceptions set out in Schedule 3, paragraph 3 will not comprise overriding interests.[20] **SC12.1.4.2**

The transitional provisions in relation to easements which, under the Act could not enjoy overriding status but which, by virtue of the Land Registration Act 1925, enjoy an overriding status when Schedule 3 is brought into force, are simple: they retain their overriding status indefinitely. Those who have the benefit of overriding status are not at risk of losing it.

Paragraph 10: For a period of three years next after Schedule 3 is brought into force, the exception in that paragraph is of no effect and *any* legal easement or profit that is not registered will have an overriding status in relation to a registered disposition. That status is not dependent on when the legal easement or profit arose. However, at the expiry of that three-year period, an unregistered legal easement will only be protected as an overriding interest if it falls within paragraph 3 **SC12.1.4.3**

---

[19] Which can only take effect at law when registered: section 27(1), (2)(d).

[20] See para. SC3.1.2, *supra*.

of Schedule 3 (with the exception operating) or was an overriding interest at the time when the Schedule came into force and continues to be protected by virtue of paragraph 9 above.
Since paragraph 3 of Schedule 3 only applies to *legal easements*, the three years' grace will never apply to equitable easements. Those which are granted after the Act comes into force and which thus cannot take the benefit of overriding status under paragraph 9 above will not be protected under paragraph 10.

SC12.1.4.4 Paragraph 11: This additional category of interest which is capable of subsisting as an overriding interest in relation to registered dispositions is similar to that set out in relation to paragraph 7 above except that it deals with the position where an adverse possessor is entitled to be registered as proprietor of a *registered* estate by virtue of his adverse possession immediately before section 97[21] is brought into force.

SC12.1.4.5 Paragraph 12: This has the effect of preserving the overriding status of leases that are granted prior to the coming into force of the Act for a period of less than 21 years and which, under section 70(1)(k) of the Land Registration Act 1925 amounted to overriding interests. Clearly under the provision of paragraph 1 of Schedules 1 and 3, they would not amount to overriding interest under the Act since they exceed the specified period.

Cautions against first registration

S12.1.5 14. (1) For the period of two years beginning with the day on which section 15 comes into force, it has effect with the following omissions—

(a) in subsection (1), the words "Subject to sub-section (3),", and

(b) subsection (3).

(2) Any caution lodged by virtue of sub-paragraph (1) which is in force immediately before the end of the period mentioned in that sub-paragraph shall cease to have effect at the end of that period, except in relation to applications for registration made before the end of that period.

(3) This paragraph does not apply to section 15 as applied by section 81.

15. (1) As applied by section 81, section 15 has effect for the period of ten years beginning with the day on

[21] See paras A97.1 *et seq., supra*.

which it comes into force, or such longer period as rules may provide, with the omission of subsection (3)(a)(i).

(2) Any caution lodged by virtue of sub-paragraph (1) which is in force immediately before the end of the period mentioned in that sub-paragraph shall cease to have effect at the end of that period, except in relation to applications for registration made before the end of that period.

16. This Act shall apply as if the definition of "caution against first registration" in section 132 included cautions lodged under section 53 of the Land Registration Act 1925 (c. 21).

Paragraph 14: See section above.[22] **SC12.1.5**

Paragraph 15: See section 81.[23] **SC12.1.6**

Paragraph 16: This ensures that cautions against first registration are treated as though cautions entered under section 15 of the Act. **SC12.1.7**

Applications under section 34 or 43 by cautioners

17. Where a caution under section 54 of the Land Registration Act 1925 is lodged in respect of a person's estate, right, interest or claim, he may only make an application under section 34 or 43 above in respect of that estate, right, interest or claim if he also applies to the registrar for the withdrawal of the caution. **S12.1.6**

Paragraph 17: An individual with the benefit of a caution against dealings can only apply for the entry of a notice or restriction pursuant to the Act in circumstances where he also applies to withdraw the caution. **SC12.1.6**

Adverse possession

18. (1) Where a registered estate in land is held in trust for a person by virtue of section 75(1) of the Land Registration Act 1925 immediately before the **S12.1.7**

---

[22] See paras A15.1 *et seq., supra*.

[23] See paras A81.1 *et seq., supra*.

coming into force of section 97, he is entitled to be registered as the proprietor of the estate.

(2) A person has a defence to any action for the possession of land (in addition to any other defence he may have) if he is entitled under this paragraph to be registered as the proprietor of an estate in the land.

(3) Where in an action for possession of land a court determines that a person is entitled to a defence under this paragraph, the court must order the registrar to register him as the proprietor of the estate in relation to which he is entitled under this paragraph to be registered.

(4) Entitlement under this paragraph shall be disregarded for the purposes of section 131(1).

(5) Rules may make transitional provision for cases where a rentcharge is held in trust under section 75(1) of the Land Registration Act 1925 immediately before the coming into force of section 97.

SC12.1.7 Paragraph 18(1): Where, prior to the coming into force of section 97[24] land was held in trust by the registered proprietor for an individual who had obtained title by adverse possession, that individual remains entitled to be registered as proprietor of the estate. If the adverse possessor remains in actual occupation of the property, his rights will continue to be overriding.

SC12.1.7.1 Paragraph 18(2): This stipulates that such a right as referred to in paragraph 18(1) constitutes a defence to any action for possession and, if it succeeds, the Registrar must be ordered by the Court to register that individual as proprietor of the estate in relation to which he is entitled under paragraph 18 to be registered: paragraph 18(3).

SC12.1.7.2 Paragraph 18(5): No rules have, as yet, been made.

Indemnities

S12.1.8 19. (1) Schedule 8 applies in relation to claims made before the commencement of that Schedule which have not been settled by agreement or finally determined by that time (as well as to claims for

---

[24] See para. A97.1 *et seq., supra*.

indemnity made after the commencement of that Schedule).

(2) But paragraph 3(1) of that Schedule does not apply in relation to costs and expenses incurred in respect of proceedings, negotiations or other matters begun before 27 April 1997.

Paragraph 19: This paragraph applies Schedule 8 to all outstanding claims for indemnities at the date upon which Schedule 8 comes into force. Since that Schedule replicates the existing provisions under the Land Registration Act 1925, the change of statutory framework should go unnoticed. **SC12.1.8**

Implied indemnity covenants on transfers of pre-1996 leases

20. (1) On a disposition of a registered leasehold estate by way of transfer, the following covenants are implied in the instrument effecting the disposition, unless the contrary intention is expressed— **S12.1.9**

(a) in the case of a transfer of the whole of the land comprised in the registered lease, the covenant in sub-paragraph (2), and

(b) in the case of a transfer of part of the land comprised in the lease—

(i) the covenant in sub-paragraph (3), and

(ii) where the transferor continues to hold land under the lease, the covenant in sub-paragraph (4).

(2) The transferee covenants with the transferor that during the residue of the term granted by the registered lease the transferee and the persons deriving title under him will—

(a) pay the rent reserved by the lease,

(b) comply with the covenants and conditions contained in the lease, and

(c) keep the transferor and the persons deriving title under him indemnified against all actions, expenses and claims on account of any failure to comply with paragraphs (a) and (b).

(3) The transferee covenants with the transferor that during the residue of the term granted by the

registered lease the transferee and the persons deriving title under him will—

(a) where the rent reserved by the lease is apportioned, pay the rent apportioned to the part transferred,
(b) comply with the covenants and conditions contained in the lease so far as affecting the part transferred, and
(c) keep the transferor and the persons deriving title under him indemnified against all actions, expenses and claims on account of any failure to comply with paragraphs (a) and (b).

(4) The transferor covenants with the transferee that during the residue of the term granted by the registered lease the transferor and the persons deriving title under him will—

(a) where the rent reserved by the lease is apportioned, pay the rent apportioned to the part retained,
(b) comply with the covenants and conditions contained in the lease so far as affecting the part retained, and
(c) keep the transferee and the persons deriving title under him indemnified against all actions, expenses and claims on account of any failure to comply with paragraphs (a) and (b).

(5) This paragraph does not apply to a lease which is a new tenancy for the purposes of section 1 of the Landlord and Tenant (Covenants) Act 1995 (c. 30).

Paragraph 20: This paragraph replicates the effect of the present law in relation to the implied indemnity covenants on transfers of pre-1996 leases.[25]

---

[25] See *Ruoff & Roper, para.* 16–18.

SCHEDULE 13

Section 135

Repeals

S13.1

Short title and chapter	*Extent of repeal*
Land Registry Act 1862 (c. 53).	The whole Act.
Settled Land Act 1925 (c. 18).	Section 119(3).
Law of Property Act 1925 (c. 20)	In section 84(8), the words from ", but" to the end. In section 205(1)(xxii), the words from ", and" to the end.
Land Registration Act 1925 (c. 21).	The whole Act.
Law of Property (Amendment) Act 1926 (c. 11).	Section 5.
Land Registration Act 1936 (c. 26).	The whole Act.
Requisitioned Land and War Works Act 1945 (c. 43).	Section 37(3).
Mental Health Act 1959 (c. 72).	In Schedule 7, the entry relating to the Land Registration Act 1925.
Charities Act 1960 (c. 58).	In Schedule 6, the entry relating to the Land Registration Act 1925.
Civil Evidence Act 1968 (c. 64).	In the Schedule, the entry relating to the Land Registration Act 1925.
Post Office Act 1969 (c. 48).	In Schedule 4, paragraph 27.
Law of Property Act 1969 (c. 59).	Section 28(7).
Land Registration and Land Charges Act 1971 (c. 54).	The whole Act.
Superannuation Act 1972 (c. 11).	In Schedule 6, paragraph 16.
Local Government Act 1972 (c. 70).	In Schedule 29, paragraph 26.

Short title and chapter	*Extent of repeal*
Solicitors Act 1974 (c. 47).	Section 75(b).
Finance Act 1975 (c. 7).	In Schedule 12, paragraph 5.
Local Land Charges Act 1975 (c. 76).	Section 19(3). In Schedule 1, the entry relating to the Land Registration Act 1925.
Endowments and Glebe Measure 1976 (No. 4).	In Schedule 5, paragraph 1.
Administration of Justice Act 1977 (c. 38).	Sections 24 and 26.
Charging Orders Act 1979 (c. 53).	Section 3(3). Section 7(4).
Limitation Act 1980 (c. 58).	In section 17, paragraph (b) and the preceding "and".
Highways Act 1980 (c. 66).	Section 251(5).
Matrimonial Homes and Property Act 1981 (c. 24).	Section 4.
Administration of Justice Act 1982 (c. 53).	Sections 66 and 67 and Schedule 5.
Mental Health Act 1983 (c. 20).	In Schedule 4, paragraph 6.
Capital Transfer Tax Act 1984 (c. 51).	In Schedule 8, paragraph 1.
Administration of Justice Act 1985 (c. 61).	In section 34, in subsection (1), paragraph (b) and the preceding "and" and, in subsection (2), paragraph (b). In Schedule 2, paragraph 37(b).
Insolvency Act 1985 (c. 65).	In Schedule 8, paragraph 5.
Housing Act 1985 (c. 68).	Section 36(3). Section 154(1), (6) and (7). Section 156(3). Section 168(5). In Schedule 9A, paragraphs 2(1), 3 and 5(3).
Land Registration Act 1986 (c. 26).	Sections 1 to 4.

Short title and chapter	*Extent of repeal*
Insolvency Act 1986 (c. 45).	In Schedule 14, the entry relating to the Land Registration Act 1925.
Building Societies Act 1986 (c. 53).	In Schedule 2A, in paragraph 1, sub-paragraph (4) and, in sub-paragraph (5), the definition of "registered land" and the preceding "and". In Schedule 18, paragraph 2. In Schedule 21, paragraph 9(b).
Patronage (Benefices) Measure 1986 (No. 3).	Section 6.
Landlord and Tenant Act 1987 (c. 31).	Section 28(6) In Schedule 4, paragraphs 1 and 2.
Diplomatic and Consular Premises Act 1987 (c. 46).	In Schedule 1, in paragraph 1, the words from "and expressions" to the end.
Land Registration Act 1988 (c. 3).	The whole Act.
Criminal Justice Act 1988 (c. 33).	Section 77(13). In Schedule 15, paragraphs 6 and 7.
Housing Act 1988 (c. 50).	In Schedule 11, paragraph 2(3).
Finance Act 1989 (c. 26).	Sections 178(2)(e) and 179(1)(a)(iv).
Courts and Legal Services Act 1990 (c. 41).	In Schedule 10, paragraph 3. In Schedule 17, paragraph 2.
Access to Neighbouring Land Act 1992 (c. 23).	Section 5(2) and (3).
Leasehold Reform, Housing and Urban Development Act 1993 (c. 28).	Section 97(3). In Schedule 21, paragraph 1.
Coal Industry Act 1994 (c. 21).	In Schedule 9, paragraph 1.
Law of Property (Miscellaneous Provisions) Act 1994 (c. 36).	In Schedule 1, paragraph 2.
Drug Trafficking Act 1994 (c. 37).	Section 26(13). In Schedule 1, paragraph 1.

Short title and chapter	*Extent of repeal*
Family Law Act 1996 (c. 27).	Section 31(11), In Schedule 8, paragraph 45.
Trusts of Land and Appointment of Trustees Act 1996 (c. 47).	In Schedule 3, paragraph 5.
Housing Act 1996 (c. 52).	Section 11(4).
Housing Grants, Construction and Regeneration Act 1996 (c. 53).	Section 138(3).
Land Registration Act 1997 (c. 2).	Sections 1 to 3 and 5(4) and (5). In Schedule 1, paragraphs 1 to 6.
Greater London Authority Act 1999 (c. 29).	Section 219.
Terrorism Act 2000 (c. 11).	In Schedule 4, paragraph 8(2) and (3).
Trustee Act 2000 (c. 29).	In Schedule 2, paragraph 26.
International Criminal Court Act 2001 (c. 17).	In Schedule 6, paragraph 7(2).

Appendix

LAW OF PROPERTY ACT 1925: SECTION 1

1 Legal estates and equitable interests. App.1

(1) The only estates in land which are capable of subsisting or of being conveyed or created at law are:

(a) An estate in fee simple absolute in possession;
(b) A term of years absolute.

(2) The only interests or charges in or over land which are capable of subsisting or of being conveyed or created at law are:

(a) An easement, right, or privilege in or over land for an interest equivalent to an estate in fee simple absolute in possession or a term of years absolute;
(b) A rentcharge in possession issuing out of or charged on land being either perpetual or for a term of years absolute;
(c) A charge by way of legal mortgage;
(d) [. . .][1] and any other similar charge on land which is not created by an instrument;
(e) Rights of entry exercisable over or in respect of a legal term of years absolute, or annexed, for any purpose, to a legal rentcharge.

(3) All other estates, interests, and charges in or over land take effect as equitable interests.

(4) The estates, interests, and charges which under this section are authorised to subsist or to be conveyed or created at law are (when subsisting or conveyed or created at law) in this Act referred to as "legal estates," and have the same incidents as legal estates subsisting at the commencement of this Act;

---

[1] Words repealed by Tithe Act 1936 (c. 43), Sched. 9 and Finance Act 1963 (c. 25), Sched. 14 Pt. VI.

and the owner of a legal estate is referred to as "as an estate owner" and his legal estate is referred to as his estate.

(5) A legal estate may subsist concurrently with or subject to any other legal estate in the same land in like manner as it could have done before the commencement of this Act.

(6) A legal estate is not capable of subsisting or of being created in an undivided share in land or of being held by an infant.

(7) Every power or appointment over, or power to convey or charge land or any interest therein, whether created by a statute or other instrument or implied by law, and whether created before or after the commencement of this Act (not being a power vested in a legal mortgagee or an estate owner in right of his estate and exercisable by him or by another person in his name and on his behalf), operates only in equity.

(8) Estates, interests, and charges in or over land which are not legal estates are in this Act referred to as "equitable interests," and powers which by this Act are to operate in equity only are in this Act referred to as "equitable powers."

(9) The provisions in any statute or other instruments requiring land to be conveyed to uses shall take effect as directions that the land shall (subject to creating or reserving thereout any legal estate authorised by this Act which may be required) be conveyed to a person of full age upon the requisite trusts.

(10) The repeal of the Statute of Uses (as amended) does not effect the operation thereof in regard to dealings taking effect before the commencement of this Act.

Index